A teacher's guide to classroom research

Fifth edition

David Hopkins

Open University Press

Open University Press
McGraw-Hill Education
McGraw-Hill House
Shoppenhangers Road
Maidenhead
Berkshire
England
SL6 2QL

email: enquiries@openup.co.uk
world wide web: www.openup.co.uk

and Two Penn Plaza, New York, NY 10121-2289, USA

First published 1985
Second edition published 1993
Third edition published 2002
Fourth edition published 2008
First published in this fifth edition 2014

A catalogue record of this book is available from the British Library

ISBN-13: 978-0-335-26468-1
ISBN-10: 0-335-26468-9
eISBN: 978-0-335-26469-8

Library of Congress Cataloging-in-Publication Data
CIP data applied for

Typeset by RefineCatch Limited, Bungay, Suffolk

Praise for this book

"The fifth edition of this book is a rarity in educational publishing. It is not full of jargon and abstract theories instead it is accessible and practical and a 'must read' for all those trying to make sense of children's learning and how to research what is happening in their classrooms. There is little surprise that this is the fifth edition as it is the definitive publication in its field. The reader is guided by a clear structure and real world case studies which are a delight to read. I recommend this book most highly."

Brent Davies, Emeritus Professor, University of Hull, UK

"It is a tribute to David Hopkins's place in education that this book now enters its fifth edition. The book has always focused on what can improve the professional practice of teachers and benefit pupils and David Hopkins knows, like few others, how to hold firm to the never changing importance of teaching but constantly adapting it so it is both up to date and relevant. In this edition, David captures the importance of the growing emphasis on research led practice; all teachers, no matter who or what they teach will find something in this book that they will want to see reflected in their practice."

Estelle Morris, former Secretary of State for Education

"The fact that many reform movements around the globe are placing practitioners at the centre of leading change makes this volume even more important and timely than when it was first published almost 20 years ago. The fifth edition of A Teachers Guide to Classroom Research not only signals how ahead of the times Hopkins was in his thinking about connecting research to practice and vice versa, it is also testimony to the rigour, quality of insight and relevance to teachers that can be found within these valuable pages."

Professor Chris Chapman, Director, Robert Owen Centre for
Educational Change, University of Glasgow, Scotland

For Jeroen, Jessica and Dylan with love

In short the outstanding characteristic of the extended professional [teacher] is a capacity for autonomous professional self-development through systematic self-study, through the study of the work of other teachers and through the testing of ideas by classroom research procedures.

Lawrence Stenhouse, *An Introduction to Curriculum Research and Development*

Learning experiences are composed of content, process and social climate. As teachers we create for and with our children opportunities to explore and build important areas of knowledge, develop powerful tools for learning, and live in humanising social conditions.

Bruce Joyce, Emily Calhoun and David Hopkins, *Models of Learning – Tools for Teaching*

Appreciating a phenomenon is a fateful decision, for it eventually entails a commitment – to the phenomenon and to those exemplifying it – to render it with fidelity and without violating its integrity. Entering the world of the phenomenon is a radical and drastic method of appreciation.

David Matza, *Becoming Deviant*

And what is good, Phaedrus,
And what is not good –
Need we ask anyone to tell us these things?

Robert Pirsig, *Zen and the Art of Motorcycle Maintenance*

You cannot stay on the summit forever:
you have to come down again. . . .
So why bother in the first place?
Just this: What is above knows what is below,
But what is below does not know what is above.
One climbs, one sees, one descends, one sees no longer.
But one has seen.
There is an art of conducting oneself in the lower regions by the memory of what one has seen higher up.
When one can no longer see, one can at least still know.

Rene Daumal, *Mount Analogue*

Contents

Contents

Preface to the fifth edition

It is now thirty years since this book was originally published, and the educational landscape in Britain and most other Western countries has changed dramatically since 1985. One of the most dominant changes observed since then is the increase in centralized policy-making; this, however, far from undermining the role of 'teacher-researcher', has, in my opinion, made such a professional ethic all the more necessary. The evidence of research and practice is making increasingly clear that 'top-down' change does not necessarily 'mandate what matters', and that it is the work of teachers that is most influential in determining the achievements of students. If we are serious about enhancing the quality of education in our schools, teachers need to be more, not less, involved in curriculum development, school improvement and pedagogy.

It seems to me that the major difference between now and the mid-1980s is that teacher-researchers have to increasingly take a whole-school and at times systemic perspective. They now have to interpret and adapt policy to their own teaching situation, and link their classroom research work to that of other colleagues and whole-school priorities, as well as to the process of teaching and learning.

It is a great privilege to have the opportunity to update a book at regular intervals, for it allows one to keep pace with what has proven to be a rapidly changing educational scene. In successive editions of *A Teacher's Guide to Classroom Research*, I have tried to take new perspectives into account while retaining the structure and simplicity of the original book.

In the second edition I placed more emphasis on the importance of viewing teacher research within a whole-school context. In particular, I emphasized the crucial role of classroom observation in supporting teacher and school development and added a new chapter on linking classroom research to other whole-school initiatives.

In the third edition I argued that teacher research should not only be a whole-school activity, but also focus unrelentingly on the teaching and learning process. It has become increasingly apparent to me that if teaching and learning are not the centrepoint of our classroom research efforts then the achievement of the young people in our schools will continue to lag behind the aspirations we have for them. And more importantly, we will have failed them during the most crucial learning opportunity of their lives. As we pursue an increasingly ambitious educational reform agenda it is vital that we take the opportunity to create a discourse around teaching and learning in our schools and communities.

In the fourth edition, I extended this perspective to embrace and emphasize the importance of moral purpose, the personalization of learning and the importance of locating teacher research within a systemic context. This reflects my experience at that time as a national policy-maker and international consultant. In addition, I made three significant changes. The first was to expand the original Chapter 9 into two separate chapters to accommodate new experience and knowledge about analysing and then reporting classroom research. The second was to take the opportunity to rewrite the chapter on teaching and learning to expand the discussion on learning *per se* and to accommodate the contemporary emphasis on personalized learning. Third, I combined the discussion in Chapters 11 and 12. This was mainly to make a further argument about the role of teacher research in systemic reform. In so doing I emphasized the importance of creating increasingly powerful learning communities in and between schools, of enhancing the professional judgements of teachers and the contribution classroom research can make to whole-school development.

In preparing this fifth edition, I have revised and updated the text. I have also added a number of additional examples and cameos that reflect the increased focus on teaching and learning and curriculum development. In a few places I have rearranged certain sections in order to accommodate other necessary revisions. In addition, I have rewritten the last two chapters to emphasize the contribution that classroom research can make to enhancing the learning and achievement of students at scale, reflecting again my recent experiences in the UK and elsewhere, notably Victoria, Australia.

In the preface to the second edition, I mentioned that since the initial publication of the book I had become the proud father of Jeroen, Jessica and Dylan. That was and continues to be a great joy, and among other gifts they have given me, they have consistently challenged my own ideas on education and forced me to rethink and rewrite as they have developed their own individual learning histories. By the time this new edition is published they should have all been awarded degrees, be working towards other vocational qualifications and in so doing obtaining a wide variety of experiences. Despite this relative success, what I still wish for Jeroen, Jessica and Dylan as young adults is not only that they continue to meet and if possible surpass existing educational standards, but also that they find learning exciting, compelling and intrinsically worthwhile. I wish them to become increasingly competent and purposeful, and to develop sound, secure and healthy self-concepts to help them face the challenges that await them. It is here that the personal and the professional converge. What I want for my children is, I believe, the same as what most teachers wish for their students. There is a striking quality about fine teachers – they care deeply about the young people in their school. Most teachers came into teaching because they wanted to make a difference. Classroom research by teachers is one way of focusing educational efforts to ensure that this difference is being made.

The book continues to have a modest aim: it is to provide teachers and students with a practical guide to doing research in their own classrooms and to link these research efforts to the extension of their teaching and learning repertoires and to whole-school developments. Despite the proliferation of texts on action research in recent years, I believe that there is still a place for a practical and straightforward introduction to teacher-based classroom research, particularly one that is committed to teacher and school development. In this way, the book complements the existing literature rather than competes with it.

In rereading the book I was struck once more by how far the original text was influenced by the work of Lawrence Stenhouse and how relevant his ideas still are for us today. Given the great educational challenges that we continue to face, more colleagues of his stature and wisdom are needed who have a vision of education and can translate it into a coherent philosophy and a pragmatic course of action. It is also becoming increasingly clear to me that, following his example, we need to reignite the debate on curriculum research and development if our young people are to match global stand-ards of achievement and learning. On my office wall there is still the quotation from Lawrence that is on his memorial plaque in the grounds of the University of East Anglia: 'It is teachers who, in the end, will change the world of the school by understanding it.' I hope that in some small way this book continues to contribute to the realization of that aspiration.

David Hopkins
Argentière Mont-Blanc
30 January 2014

Acknowledgements

I am grateful to the late Mike Bruce, Don Cochrane, Peter Norman, the late Jean Rudduck and Ann Kilcher for the care with which they reviewed the original manuscript; and for conversations that clarified my thinking on this and other matters. Their friendship and professional collaboration have meant a great deal to me. Suzzane de Castell, Gill Harper-Jones, Pat Holborn, my now deceased sister Mary Schofield, Louise Pelletier and the late David Pritchard also provided material and intellectual support at critical and opportune times: my thanks to them too. A number of colleagues and students graciously allowed me to use some of their material as illustrations and examples in the first edition. In this regard, I remain indebted to Stan Auerbach, Judy Byer, Heather Lockhard, Sandra Meister, Marianne Schmidt, Ann Waldo and Harvey Walker. The three anonymous reviewers of the original book proposal made comments that encouraged me to revise and improve that manuscript. I anticipate that at least two of them were satisfied with the outcome.

The original argument of the book was developed from ideas first published in the *CARN Bulletin*, the Department of Education and Science (DES 1989) booklet *Planning for School Development*, the *Empowered School, Managing Schools Today, Phi Delta Kappan, School Organization* and *The Times Educational Supplement*. Finally, I must also acknowledge the Deakin University Press, the Ford Teaching Project and Universitetsforlaget AS for allowing me to reproduce copyright material.

In preparing the second edition of this book, my colleagues at Cambridge were characteristically generous in taking time to review and help me with the manuscript. I am particularly grateful to Mel Ainscow for his thoughtful and creative comments, and more generally for exploring with me the boundaries of professional partnership. Colin Conner, Dave Ebbutt and Julie Howard also reviewed parts of the manuscript and made helpful comments. I am grateful to the Bedfordshire LEA/University of Cambridge Institute of Education 'Developing Successful Learning Project', Howard Bradley and Rob Bollington, Jere Brophy and Tom Good, Walter Doyle, Rex Gibson, David Hargreaves, Pamela Hughes, David Jeffries, Denis Lawton, James McKernan and The Sanders Draper School for letting me use some of their material in that edition. John Skelton, my publisher at Open University Press, was most supportive throughout.

The task of preparing the third edition was greatly eased by the assistance of Julie Temperley and John Beresford. They both made numerous and helpful suggestions for updating the text and through our discussions shared with me their own experience of facilitating teacher research. Once again my colleagues were more than generous in allowing me to include work that we had published elsewhere. In this respect I am grateful to Mel Ainscow, John Beresford, David Fulton Publishers, David H. Hargreaves, Alma Harris, David Jackson, Barbara MacGilchrist, Collette Singleton and Ruth Watts.

Thanks also to Shona Mullen of the Open University Press who is one of the best and most supportively critical editors with whom I have had the pleasure to work.

In the interval between the second and third editions I had the privilege of working with networks of schools in Nottinghamshire, Derbyshire, Bedfordshire, South Wales, Leicester and Walsall on our 'Improving the Quality of Education For All' (IQEA) school improvement project. This work has focused more than ever before on strategies for teaching and learning and the facilitation of action inquiry and classroom-based research. As always, I have learned a great deal from the commitment, enthusiasm and sheer professionalism of colleagues involved in those networks. It is here that the energy for the transformation of our school system lies. My thanks and admiration to them.

In preparing the fourth edition I benefited from the editorial support of Elpida Ahtaridou, and I am most grateful to her for that. I spent most of the period between the publication of the third and fourth editions working in government. Apart from being a remarkably formative period for me personally, it also convinced me of the importance of the teacher research role in the realization of broader system goals. It gave me the valuable experience of working alongside great national institutions such as DEMOS, the National Strategies, the National College for School Leadership, the Innovation Unit and the Specialist Schools and Academies Trust. I am also profoundly grateful to the headteachers I met during this period who so openly shared their enthusiasms and frailties, successes and failures with me and from whom I have learned so much. I also acknowledge the outstanding colleagues and teachers such as Jane Reed, Kathryn Riley, Rebecca Jones and Christine Artington and those whose names I have been unable to locate, and who have allowed me to showcase their work.

In undertaking the preparation of the fifth edition I have been greatly assisted by the editorial support of Susan Blanch and Sinead O'Connor; I am most grateful for the care and attention that they have given to producing the new edition. In the space between the fourth and fifth editions I have enjoyed four additional professional experiences that have deepened and extended my understanding of the practice and impact of classroom research by teachers. The first has been the work with Wayne Craig and colleagues in Melbourne's Northern Metropolitan Region (NMR) that is reported in the new final chapter of the book. The Powerful Learning strategy, which has extended now over a five-year period, has greatly benefited the life chances of many tens of thousands of students in Melbourne and Victoria and provides an exemplary case study of how classroom research by teachers can contribute to sustained school improvement at scale (Hopkins *et al.* 2011). The second was the opportunity to establish with Sir Michael Barber, Simon Day, Nigel Buchanan, Trish Franey and Steve Howe the Adventure Learning Schools (ALS) charity which has as its heart the creation of adventurous and learning experiences for young people inside and outside the classroom that sustain and deepen their learning and achievement. The opportunity to work with all those thoughtful and committed heads and teachers in the ALS network has given me greater insights into the positive impact of classroom research by teachers (Hopkins 2012). The third was the opportunity to work with gifted educators such as Trish Franey and Oli Knight in developing the whole-school design for Bright Tribe schools, which has helped me see that if we are serious about creating school systems that are driven by moral purpose and globally high levels of learning and achievement then classroom research by teachers is an essential ingredient in the mix (Bright Tribe 2014a, 2014b). Finally, I owe a debt of gratitude to Open University Press and ACER Press for encouraging me to complete my school improvement trilogy with the publication of *Exploding the Myths of School Reform* (Hopkins 2013). This gave me the opportunity to reflect more deeply about how to sustain school and system reform and the place of classroom research by teachers within it.

Above all it has been the collaboration with Trish, Wayne and Oli that has provided me with another great series of learning partnerships and helped me understand and get a better grip on the great work of school improvement. My thanks to them for this as well as many other things.

1 A teacher's guide to classroom research

This book is a practical guide for teachers who wish to undertake research in their classrooms and schools for the purpose of improving practice. Classroom research, in the sense that I refer to it here, is an act undertaken by teachers to enhance their own or a colleague's teaching, to test the assumptions of educational theory in practice, or as a means of evaluating and implementing whole-school priorities. So, when I write of classroom research or of the teacher as researcher, I am not envisioning scores of teachers carrying out technical research projects to the exclusion of their teaching. My vision is more of teachers who have extended their role to include systematic reflection upon their craft with the aim of improving it.

Although lip service is often paid to this idea, we live in an educational system that tends to limit individual initiative by encouraging conformity and control. Teachers and pupils (and society too) deserve better than that. Undertaking research in their own and colleagues' classrooms is one way in which teachers can take increased responsibility for their actions and create a more energetic and dynamic environment in which teaching and learning can occur.

The origins of teacher research as a movement can be traced back to the Schools Council's Humanities Curriculum Project (HCP, 1967–72) with its emphasis on an experimental curriculum and the reconceptualization of curriculum development as curriculum research. The HCP, in its attempt to encourage a non-partisan and critically reflective attitude to teaching on the part of teachers, had a radical and controversial influence on teaching in British schools during the 1970s.

Following the HCP, the concept of teacher research was nurtured by John Elliott and Clem Adelman in the Ford Teaching Project (1972–75). This involved 40 primary and secondary school teachers in examining their classroom practice through action research. These teachers developed hypotheses about their teaching which could be shared with other teachers and used to enhance their own teaching.

At about the same time, Lawrence Stenhouse, who directed the HCP, further popularized the concept of 'the teacher as researcher' by utilizing it as the major theme in his influential book, *An Introduction to Curriculum Research and Development* (Stenhouse 1975). Encouraged by the considerable impact that Stenhouse had on the theory and practice of curriculum and teaching, and the popularity and publicity enjoyed by the Ford Teaching Project, the teacher research movement mushroomed. As well as burgeoning teacher research groups in the UK, Australia, the USA and Canada, pockets of teacher-researchers have developed in Scandinavia, France, Chile and many other countries. Although teacher research was not an entirely new concept in the late 1960s, it is from this period that it became an identifiable movement.

Much, however, has changed in the context of education in most Western countries since the concept of the teacher as researcher became popular. The main difference between the 1970s and the second decade of the twenty-first century is that classroom research now has to be seen within a whole-school and increasingly system context. It is no longer sufficient for teachers to do research in their own classrooms, without relating their inquiries to the work of their colleagues and the aims and direction of the school and the system as a whole. We need to strive consciously for a synthesis between teacher research, school development and system reform. That is why this book is not just a primer on classroom research techniques, it also attempts to relate teacher research to teacher education, whole-school development and the wider context of education.

All books emerge out of a specific set of individual circumstances that have influenced the author, and this book is no exception. The journey that preceded this book is still continuing, and so the story remains unfinished. But two influences in particular have been crucial in developing the ideas presented here and provide a context in which to consider the book. The first is the work of Lawrence Stenhouse, whose intellectual and personal example still challenges me. In the HCP and his other work, Stenhouse was primarily concerned with the concept of emancipation. He wrote (1983: 163):

> My theme is an old-fashioned one – emancipation . . . The essence of emancipation as I conceive it is the intellectual, moral and spiritual autonomy which we recognise when we eschew paternalism and the role of authority and hold ourselves obliged to appeal to judgement.

There are four levels at which this concept of emancipation can operate – at the level of the student, the teacher, the school and the system.

At the level of the student, emancipation refers to the ability to stand outside the teacher's authority on forms of knowledge, and to discover and own it for oneself. It was in the HCP that Stenhouse most notoriously signalled his commitment to this theme. In that project he was principally concerned with the emancipation of pupils through a particular teaching strategy. There were three elements to this aspect of the project: the use of discussion; the use of documents as evidence to inform discussion; and the assumption by the teacher of the role of neutral chairperson. By adopting this approach, Stenhouse was moving away from a teacher-dominated classroom to a setting where pupils, unconstrained by the authority of the teacher, could create meaning for themselves on the basis of evidence and discussion.

If the HCP was in part a curriculum designed to emancipate pupils, the phrase 'teacher as researcher' was intended to do the same for teachers. Teachers are too often the servants of heads, advisers, researchers, textbooks, curriculum developers, examination boards or the ministry of education, among others. By adopting a research stance, teachers are liberating themselves from the control and command situation they often find themselves in. Stenhouse encouraged teachers to follow the specification of a curriculum or teaching strategy, but at the same time to assess it critically. Such curriculum proposals and teaching specifications are probably intelligent but are not necessarily correct. Their effectiveness should therefore be monitored by teachers in the classroom. By adopting this critical approach, by taking a research stance, the teacher is engaged not only in a meaningful professional development activity, but also in a process of refining and becoming more autonomous in professional judgement. This applies as much to the National Curriculum and 'personalized learning' as it did to the HCP.

The third level at which emancipation can operate is that of the school. Here it is a question of the school liberating itself from a bureaucratic educational system. The image of the 'ideal' type of emancipated school is represented by the words 'autonomous', 'creative', 'moving' or 'problem-solving'. These successful schools take the opportunity of the recent changes and use them to support developments already under way or planned for in the school. They adapt external change for internal purposes. In the most successful or emancipated schools, there is also a realization that change inevitably involves learning on the part of teachers. This implies that such change strategies involve a seamless web of activities that focus on, are integrated with and enhance the daily work of teachers. This can result in quite profound alterations to the culture of the school and the ways in which teachers, heads and governors work together towards the goal of student achievement. More recently, we have seen the emergence of the system leader, driven by a commitment to the improvement and sustaining of other schools as well as their own. It is here that the genesis of system transformation lies.

The fourth level, of course, is that of the system, and the potential impact of emancipation here is even more pervasive. If we can harness the power of system reform in terms of moral purpose and social justice, then we not only increase the life chances of so many more citizens but also create a learning and work culture premised on curiosity, competence and collaboration. Barber (2009) observed that it was the school effectiveness research in the 1980s that gave us increasingly well-defined portraits of the effective school that led in the 1990s to increasing knowledge of more effective school improvement processes (i.e. how to achieve effectiveness). In the same way, we have in the last decade begun to learn more about the features of an effective educational system, but are only now beginning to understand the dynamics of improvement working at the system level. The impact of international benchmarking studies such as PISA has not only helped develop our understanding of the dynamics of system-level change, but also given us a framework in which to consider emancipation at this level. Early in my time in government and following the publication of the first round of PISA results, Estelle Morris, David Miliband and I were framing our moral purpose for the English system in terms of both 'high excellence and high equity'. What we meant by this is a system where not only standards are high but also the range of variation becomes increasingly small. Studies such as PISA were giving us an increased understanding of how we could achieve such an emancipatory policy framework at the system level (Hopkins 2013).

The second influence on this book is much more personal. During the 1970s I trained as a teacher and taught, worked as an Outward Bound instructor and mountain guide and read for postgraduate degrees in education. Although somewhat different activities, they were all characterized by a desire, often hesitant and naive, to create ways in which people could take more control of their own lives. Irrespective of the context – practice teaching, an O-level history class, counselling a 'delinquent' pupil, assisting in a youth club, on the rock face, out in the wilderness, or discussing ideas in a seminar – there were similarities in overall aim and pedagogic structure.

Later, as a teacher in a Canadian university, I taught courses in curriculum development, analysis of teaching and classroom research, and found in Stenhouse's work a theoretical framework within which I could put my ideas into action. This book emerged from that experience, more specifically from a course I taught in classroom research and some papers I wrote on the topic (Hopkins 1982, 1984a, 1984b). Thus, the book is based on a set of ideas that have the enhancement of teacher judgement and autonomy as a specific goal, and is grounded within the practical realities of teachers and students.

My interest in classroom-based work, although always in my mind linked to school improvement, assumed a broader perspective while teaching at Cambridge (1985–96) and Nottingham universities (1996–2001). Much of my work then was concerned with assisting teachers, schools and local authorities (LAs) to handle and reflect on the change process. I learned an enormous amount from them, as I did from my involvement in the evaluation of the Technical Vocational Education Initiate, the then Department of Education and Science[1] projects on teacher appraisal and school development plans, and in particular our school improvement project 'Improving the Quality of Education for All' (IQEA). I have also been fortunate to have worked over a slightly longer period with the Organisation for Economic Co-operation and Development's Centre for Educational Research and Innovation on a number of school improvement-related projects. This work has helped me to see the teacher's role in the wider context of the school as an organization and workplace. In particular, it has impressed on me the crucial importance of the culture of the school in sustaining teacher development.

Some have said that in the early 2000s, I turned from being a poacher into a game-keeper! At that time, I found myself in a new role as a national policy-maker concerned not just with regional networks of schools and teacher education but with a part responsibility for transforming a whole system. Working with ministers such as Estelle Morris, Charles Clarke and David Miliband, we made a concerted attempt to shift the English education system from one that was dominated by 'informed prescription' to one that was driven by 'informed professionalism' which is at the heart of Stenhouse's notion of emancipation. I think that we can claim some small success in doing that (Hopkins 2007a). Having served a parliamentary term as the chief adviser to three Secretaries of State, I then returned to an international role in educational leadership, where I attempted to use this relatively unique experience to inform practice, policy and

---

[1] The government department responsible for education in England was called the Department for Children, Schools and Families (DCSF), but this was replaced by the Department for Education after the general election of 2010.

research in education. These experiences have convinced me not only that every school should be a great school, but also that this is now a reasonable, realizable and socially just goal for any mature educational system. Inevitably the fourth edition of the book emphasized some of the issues that I wrestled with in government – the importance of moral purpose in system reform, the primacy of personalized learning and the absolute necessity of getting all parts of the system moving in the same direction.

As is now probably becoming clear, I am by background and temperament a school improvement activist. Over the past thirty years or so I have self-consciously located myself at the intersection of practice, research and policy. Although it has not always proven to be the most comfortable place to be situated, it is here that I felt I could best contribute to the process of educational reform and emancipation. Reflecting back over this time, one of the initiatives of which I am most proud is the work we did on the IQEA school improvement programme where we collaborated with hundreds of schools in England and elsewhere in developing a model of sustainable school improvement (Hopkins 2002). As I probably enter the last phase of my own professional life, I find myself being drawn back to these themes. My recent work in Melbourne on the 'Powerful Learning' strategy, the progress of the Adventure Learning Schools (ALS) charity and the whole-school designs we are developing for Bright Tribe schools all build on these initial ideas and reflect the aspirations of emancipation just described. These are some of the evolving themes that characterize the fifth edition of this book.

It is this commitment to a practical philosophy of emancipation and empowerment as well as a particular set of individual circumstances that underpin the argument in this book. After this introduction, a few case studies of teacher-based research are given to provide a context for what follows. In Chapter 3, two arguments are considered for teacher-based research – the need for professionalism in teaching, and the inadequacy of the traditional research approach in helping teachers improve their classroom practice. In Chapter 4, action research, which has become the main vehicle for teacher research, is discussed and critiqued; from that discussion, six criteria for teacher-based research are suggested. Chapter 5 discusses the ways in which teacher research problems are formulated and initiated. Chapters 6 and 7 describe the principles and practice of classroom observation, and in Chapter 8 various other ways of gathering data are described. Chapter 9 outlines a method for analysing these data and Chapter 10 discusses how to report and disseminate them. These six chapters constitute the heart of the teacher research process. There is, in Chapter 11, an explicit focus on teaching and particularly learning, as well as an emphasis on the importance of personalized learning. In arguing that pedagogy should become the heartland of classroom research, I review the research on effective teaching and models of teaching and provide practical examples of three common models of learning and teaching. The discussion in Chapter 12 locates the role of the teacher-researcher in the broader systems context. I use the examples of our recent work on the design and implementation of the Powerful Learning framework mentioned above to illustrate the themes of teacher and school development, in particular the creation of a culture that promotes networks and professional learning communities within and outside the school.

A continuing emphasis throughout the book is the importance of establishing a professional ethic for teaching. Implicit in this idea is the concept of teacher as researcher. The teacher-researcher image is a powerful one. It embodies a number of characteristics that reflect on the individual teacher's capacity to be, in Stenhouse's phrase, 'autonomous in professional judgement'. A major factor in this is the teacher's ability to think systematically and critically about what they are doing and to collaborate with other teachers. Central to this activity is the systematic reflection on one's classroom experience, to understand it and to create meaning out of it.

Interestingly, Michael Fullan, the contemporary 'guru' of educational change makes a similar argument in his recent book, *Change Leader*. He says (Fullan 2011a: 12): 'don't try to figure out someone else's theory, but rather use practice to get at theory, and more directly use practice to discover strategies that work. The source of creative breakthroughs, then, is learning about practice, not theory.'

By becoming self-conscious, collaborative and critical about their teaching, teachers develop more power over their professional lives, extend their teaching repertoires, and are better able to create classrooms and schools that are responsive to the vision they and we have for our children's future. The purpose of this book is to describe a methodology or practice for doing this. We begin by looking in the next chapter at a series of examples of classroom research in action and then move on from there.

Further reading

The key source for any teacher-researcher is still the work of Lawrence Stenhouse and in particular *An Introduction to Curriculum Research and Development* (1975). Although he died before making his own comprehensive statement on classroom research by teachers, Jean Rudduck and I (Rudduck and Hopkins 1985) edited his published and unpublished writing to make such an argument in *Research as a Basis for Teaching*. Elliott and Norris (2012) have recently published a book on the work of Lawrence Stenhouse which looks at the relevance of his work today. Until the mid-1980s most of the work on teacher research was either philosophical discussion (Kemmis 1983, 1988), reports by researchers (Elliot and Adelman 1976) or teachers' own accounts of their research (Nixon 1981). Since that time, however, there has been a dramatic growth in the number of books on the topic. Pride of place must go to John Elliott's (1991) *Action Research for Educational Change*, which traces the development of the teacher research movement, describes its methodology and explores how it can be 'a form of creative resistance' to centralized policy-making. I set out my own approach to linking teacher research to school improvement in my inaugural lecture at the University of Nottingham: 'Powerful learning, powerful teaching and powerful schools' (Hopkins 2000). Other books that attempt in different ways to link teacher research to school development and educational change are Helen Simons's (1987) *Getting to Know Schools in Democracy*, Rob Halsall's (1998) collection *Teacher Research and School Improvement*, our own *The Empowered School* (Hargreaves and Hopkins 1991) and *The New Structure of School Improvement* (Joyce *et al.* 1999). However, more recently an increasing number of books have more directly linked teacher research with school improvement, among them *Improving Schools through Collaborative Enquiry* (Street and Temperley 2005), *Guiding School Improvement with Action Research* (Sagor 2000) and *Teacher-Led School Improvement* (Frost *et al.* 2000). Much else of relevance to the theme of 'classroom research by teachers' has been published recently. Among these are Baumfield *et al.* (2013), Mertler (2009) and Reason and Bradbury (2001). I have referred to more specific sources in the further reading section at the end of the most appropriate chapter. Some of the key texts on action research referred to in earlier editions and that were central to the argument being made in the book are now sadly out of date. I have, however, continued to cite them in this edition as they continue to illustrate many of the key themes in the work and will in any case be available from libraries and other sources.

2 Classroom research in action

To some, the phrase 'classroom research' brings to mind images of white-coated (or grey-suited!) educational researchers undertaking research in a sample of schools or classrooms and using as subjects the teachers and students who live out their educational lives within them. This book, however, is about another kind of research in which teachers look critically at their own classrooms and use research primarily for the purpose of improving their teaching and the quality of education in their schools. But even the phrase 'classroom research by teachers' can sound a little daunting. It might be useful therefore to begin with some examples of teachers who have engaged in systematic enquiry with the purpose of understanding and improving their practice.

Case Studies 2.1–2.3 were written by teachers. The first of these begins as an exploratory case study that through the reading of literature on learning becomes a focused systematic inquiry. Case Study 2.2 is an interesting example of how the process of research can reveal surprising insights that necessitate the rethink of the research focus. Case Study 2.3 is the most systematic one and illustrates the use of quantitative data in some detail.

Subsequent case studies reflect the focus in this fifth edition of the book on teaching and learning and school improvement. Case Study 2.4 demonstrates how learning can be shared between departments in a school. Case Study 2.5 was written by John Beresford, the research officer on the IQEA project, describing how he collaborates with schools in providing data on teaching and learning styles to assist in defining the focus of their improvement strategies. Case Study 2.6 is by David Jackson who, at the time of writing the cameo, was head of a longstanding IQEA school, Sharnbrook Upper School and Community College in Bedfordshire. (David later became Head of Research at the National College for School Leadership.) This example describes how the school improvement focus on teaching and learning is organized at Sharnbrook, and how students are involved in the process. Case Study 2.7 by Trish Franey broadens the school improvement perspective by illustrating a practitioner research strategy across an Education Action Zone network. Case Study 2.8 is different from the others as it illustrates a more sophisticated use of 'quantitative' methods than Case Study 2.3. It was written by Lawrence Stenhouse.

In each of these cases, the teachers are engaging in classroom research for the express purpose of improving the quality of educational life in their classroom. This is no deficit model of improvement. The teachers involved are genuinely interested in understanding the dynamics of their own teaching style. They believe that 'you do not have to be ill to get better'. The motivation for doing research may be varied – a research degree, natural curiosity, a stimulating article or talk – but the process and its implications are essentially the same. Taken together, these cases illustrate the range and benefits of doing research in your own classroom and provide examples of the reflective professional in practice.

Case Study 2.1 is by Rebecca Jones, a school teacher at Llanrhidian Primary School. Her research was initiated because of the school's involvement with the International Network for School Improvement project set up by Swansea LA.[1]

CASE STUDY 2.1

School context

The school serves a large area of North West Gower, comprising the communities of Llanrhidian, Llangennith, Llanmadoc and several small hamlets. The school accommodates children between the ages of 1 and 11 who are taught in split age group classes.

Selecting the focus for the project

As a group of colleagues we began by making a list of what we believed to be the characteristics of a good learner. We then went away to consider these characteristics in relation to our own class and to draw out any of our own conclusions about what makes an effective learner.

In the weeks that followed the meeting, I observed my Y1/Y2 class with these factors in mind. My primary area of interest was the children's communication skills since it was clearly the 'better learners' in the class who were more articulate and better able to express themselves. It was these children who were much more likely to approach me to discuss the aspects of their work they were finding difficult or were enjoying and to question me about it. Many children in the class, however, seemed to expect me to second-guess the difficulties they were having instead of attempting to formulate an appropriate question.

Reading about children's learning, I became increasingly interested in children's questioning, and a lot of what I read strikes a chord with my own personal experiences. For example, the fact that very young children are enthusiastic communicators and seem to have an innate ability to ask questions.

We have all been driven to distraction by the young child who asks question after question in their insatiable quest for knowledge about the world around them. So I had to ask myself why it was that in my infant class of 5–7-year-olds this instinctive ability to ask questions was not apparent.

---

[1] The then International School Effectiveness Centre, now the International Network for School Improvement and part of the London Centre for Leadership in Learning, (in 2005) was invited by Swansea LA to work with a group of schools to study the effectiveness of the learning and curriculum in their schools through classroom inquiry. This case study was one of those produced by teachers during the project. It has been edited and published with the permission of Rebecca Jones and Jane Reed, head of the International Network for School Improvement.

The audit process

We began with the question: 'How can we get children to ask the types of questions that will further their learning?' This was then broken down into five focused questions, which could form the basis of our research project. I used the Y1s as my target group from my mixed Y1/Y2 class:

1   What are children's current attitudes towards question-asking?
2   Which children in the class ask the most/least questions?
3   What types of question are currently being asked by the children?
4   Does curriculum area affect the frequency and type of question being asked?
5   Does current planning facilitate the asking of questions across the curriculum?

Question 1

I began by conducting a class discussion to find out what were the children's current attitudes towards question-asking. I prepared a set of questions to form the basis of the discussion. I divided the children into two groups to interview separately, to allow the less confident children to be interviewed together, thus preventing the more forthcoming children from dominating the discussion. I taped the discussions so that I could analyse the data later.

The children participated enthusiastically in the discussions and I was amazed that they held such well-developed views on the subject.

Although both groups were adamant that they were not frightened to ask me a question, several children expressed a concern that their questions might be regarded as 'silly' or 'not good'. Some children felt concerned that their questions may be deemed irrelevant.

My second main finding was even more disconcerting. The children were not at all sure about when it would be an appropriate time to ask me a question. In general, they seemed to believe that it was OK to ask me a question if it's *not* in lesson time. Dinnertime, playtimes and the end of the day were all suggested as good times.

It seems that the children strongly believe that their questions are not of importance and that maybe only teacher questions have a place in the classroom. The children seem to view their questions as interruptions.

Question 2

I carried out a survey over the course of one normal school day to record the frequency of each child's questions. I planned a typical day's lessons and deliberately did not open the class up for questions at any point to see how many spontaneous questions were asked.

The results highlighted the fact that on the whole the children asked very few questions. Only eight questions were asked in total, and most arose from the children requesting help with their work.

The second part of the survey gave the children more scope for asking questions since I carried out two focused lessons, one in history and one in science, that were conducive to children's questioning. I planned appropriate breaks in the lessons to invite the children's questions.

To answer my question about who was asking the most questions, it was one of the students who asked 5 in history and 8 in science. Another student asked 5 questions in science but only 1 in history. Three children asked no questions at all.

Questions 3 and 4

Classroom observations lead me to the conclusion that the types of questions asked by the children tend to be functional – such as 'should I underline the heading?' – or they relate to lack of understanding of tasks – 'what am I supposed to do on question 5?' Such questions are unlikely to lead them to significant further learning and rarely arise from a real curiosity in a subject. However, when I made room for children's questions by planning opportunities into the lesson, the children asked questions which demonstrated that they were able to reflect on what had been learnt and were genuinely curious to find out more. In such lessons I found that listening to the children's questions enabled me to assess how much of the lesson had been understood and to plan subsequent steps.

To assess the impact of the curriculum area on children's questioning I carried out a survey over one normal school day, but this time recorded the children's questions according to subject. The results highlighted again that the children are asking very few questions, regardless of curriculum area. No questions were asked in the maths lesson and the most asked was three in a drama session – most questions related to the children's need for further explanation of tasks.

I wanted to analyse the frequency and type of questions asked by the children given the optimum conditions, i.e. lessons with planned opportunity for question asking, so I used the tape-recording of the history and science lesson described earlier to analyse the questions asked.

The science lesson produced the most questions from the children. Twenty-six were asked in total, whereas the history lesson of the same length produced only 14.

I then categorized the questions according to five groups. Nine of the science questions were found to be unanswerable. It seemed that some children had difficulty formulating a good question and also maybe that some children were asking any old question for the sake of it. In history, 14 out of 14 questions were researchable.

My conclusions from this piece of research are that in science the children need to ask more observable questions and perhaps more testable questions that would lead to investigation. In history there is a need for more subjective questions that focus on the thoughts and feelings of people from the past.

Questions 5

I scrutinized my Y1/Y2 planning across the whole two-year cycle and noted down where activities had been planned which would promote the asking of questions. I found planned opportunities in language, science, history, Welsh, geography and RE, but less specific questioning activities in maths, IT, art, music and technology. This has obvious implications for my future planning.

Summary of main findings

The main findings from the audit phase could be grouped into four main areas:

- *Attitudes*. Children often see their questions as irrelevant. Some children equate question-asking with interrupting.

- *Time for questions*. Children did not know when question-asking was allowed. Lesson-time was clearly identified as being an inappropriate time for children's questions.
- *Question type*. In a normal day, questions tend to be functional but when lessons were planned appropriately, good-quality questions were raised. Most questions asked in science were researchable or unanswerable, and in history all were researchable.
- *Who asks the questions?* Some children are naturally better at asking questions than others. Some children have difficulty formulating an appropriate question.

Targets and success criteria

In the light of these findings we formulated a success criteria list outlining what we hoped to achieve by the end of the project:

1   *Children's attitudes*

- Improved attitudes to the asking of questions
- Children to recognize the value of their questions as well as teacher questions in the classroom
- Children to gain an understanding into why question-asking is desirable.

2   *Question type*

- Children to ask 'good' questions at appropriate times, which clarify or further their learning (learning skill)
- The children need to ask more testable questions in science, which might lead to investigation (attainment/achievement skill)
- There is a need for more subjective questions in history (attainment/achievement skill).

3   *Time for questions*

- More planned opportunities for children to ask questions during lesson-time and across the school day (Teaching skill).

4   *More children asking questions*

- Some lessons need to be planned deliberately to improve children's questioning techniques (Teaching skill).

Implementation and strategies

A second class interview was held which focused on two main points: first, why children should ask questions in class; and second, when would be an appropriate time to ask questions. The children obviously could not be given free reign to bombard the teacher with questions at any time; certain boundaries needed to be set. The discussion highlighted a problem, that there may be times when a child has a burning question, which cannot be asked due to inappropriate timing. To overcome this problem Y1/Y2 children are now encouraged to jot such questions down on a sticky note. If related to the current lesson the question can then be asked at a more suitable point, i.e. when the teacher has finished speaking.

To encourage the children to ask their questions which deal with issues not being covered in current class work, they are now asked to stick their question sticky note to the whiteboard. Time is set aside each week to discuss selected questions from the board. After such sessions the children are often motivated into researching their questions themselves, and interestingly a more constructive use of the school library has been noted. Sometimes research is continued at home, and it is now a common occurrence for children to come to school armed with encyclopaedias with pages earmarked for my attention.

To encourage more testable questions in science a question board has been added to the class interactive science display on which children are invited to attach their topic-related questions. The electricity topic evoked a wealth of questions. Some of the questions needed to be answered through research, but many naturally led the children into scientific investigation. Examples include 'Will two bulbs light in a circuit?' and 'How do you make a buzzer buzz?' With the equipment at hand the children were able to answer their own questions through immediate experimentation.

The last two terms have begun by introducing the new topic to the children and inviting them to pose any questions they would like to see answered through their class activities. The ensuing 'brainstorm' then provides a framework for some of the term's work. This approach has given the children a greater deal of motivation towards their classwork by offering them an ownership of their learning. The brainstorm is referred to weekly to see whose question is being answered.

The children also use questions now to help each other edit their creative writing. The children take turns to sit on the 'author's chair' to read their compositions aloud. The audience is allowed to ask any helpful questions that may enhance the author's work, e.g. 'what was the setting?', 'why did the main character leave home at the beginning?' Questions such as these often highlight parts of the story where important details have been omitted and any ambiguities in the storyline.

Evaluating and monitoring the strategies

During the winter term 2001, while continuing with the development work, I also began to turn my attention to monitoring and evaluating the success of the project. First, I carried out a final questionnaire with the target group of children who had just moved into Y3 and so were no longer in my class. I asked their opinion of the strategies that had been in place during their time with me. The children's comments showed a surprising awareness of the benefits of the activities to their learning. Here is a selection of some of the most revealing comments:

- *Sticky note boards*: 'If children asked a question it meant they didn't know it and so they could learn more things'; 'If the teacher is busy you can stick it on the board instead'
- *Topic planning charts*: 'We get to know things we want to learn about'; 'Other children might need to know the same sort of things as we do so it helps them learn too'
- *Children should ask questions because . . .*: 'The teacher will know what we need to learn'; 'It's easier for the teacher to know what we don't know'.

I also carried out a selection of focused lesson observations while the children were engaged in some of the activities described above. On the advice of Jane Reed, the head of the School Effectiveness and Improvement Centre, I devised a recording sheet that allowed commentary of the lesson on three different levels. The first section of the sheet required a description of the activity taking place. Secondly, I would make a reflective/analytical statement about the significance of the activity in terms of the project's aims and objectives. The third section allowed a speculative comment about the activity, i.e. what were the implications of the activity for future project work. Lastly, I would note any unintended benefits or impacts.

Findings

Through the wide range of activities carried out during the last few terms the children have demonstrated that they certainly are eager to ask questions, and when given appropriate opportunities they do ask them. Children need to be given time to articulate their questions, and this must be planned into lessons and not left to chance.

I found some curriculum areas easier to plan with a questioning approach than others, so decided to concentrate on improving the children's questioning skills in English, science and history.

I found that getting children to raise questions about texts gave them a much more sophisticated understanding of plots and characters. During 'hot-seating' activities the children seemed naturally to ask the character about their motives and relationships with others. The child on the hot-seat had to reply in character and refer back to events in the story to substantiate their answers. In this way the children were able to move beyond a literal understanding of text as they began to make inferences and deductions.

Encouraging children to ask the kinds of question that will lead to investigation is at the very heart of successful primary science. The term's science topic always produced more children's questions than any other curriculum area. I found that the questions dealt with more complex aspects of the topic as the term progressed and the children's understanding and knowledge developed. During the topic on electricity Jennifer (age 6) asked 'How do we light the bulb?' and a few weeks later asked 'Do two bulbs light in a circuit?' Her second question shows that she now has the answer to the first question and is ready to move to a further level of understanding. Also the second question demonstrates that she can use subject-specific terminology (i.e. circuit).

History also seemed to naturally lend itself to a question-asking approach. The children asked the most pertinent questions and those they genuinely wanted answers to when they had an identified audience. The children prepared questions for our class trip to Cefn Coed Colliery Museum to ask the guide. Having done a good deal of work already on the topic of mining, the children had plenty of questions already in their minds which they were now able to ask our expert. The questions revealed a strong interest in the lives of the children and horses who worked in the mines which we were able to follow up back in class. Of course in light of the trip there were more questions which arose back in class, the answers to some of which began to take us beyond the realms of the children's understanding. In this way question-asking, like the learning process, is never complete. Questions generate more questions and the teacher needs to be aware of the appropriate point to stop the questions and to consolidate existing knowledge and understanding.

From interviewing the children at the end of the project it is evident that the children gained great enjoyment and satisfaction in investigating and researching questions raised by themselves. They demonstrated greater motivation towards class activities knowing that they had had an input in the planning stage.

Outcomes from the project

Children are more likely to ask good-quality questions when the learning activities are well structured with a tight focus. It was observed that children asked better-quality questions when they had prior knowledge of the study area and had already participated in classroom activities relating to it. When children were invited to ask questions about a brand new topic there was evidence of children offering questions because they felt they had to. In these cases there were more instances of unanswerable questions. This was particularly the case when the new topic had a very broad focus, e.g. 'Houses and Homes'. Topics such as 'Mould' and 'Electricity' produced the best-quality questions.

Evidence gathered from talking to the pupils demonstrates they understand question-asking as a tool to help them learn. During the final interviews with the target group I asked the children to complete the sentence 'Children should ask questions because . . .'. Eight out of 11 children made a direct reference to the benefit of question-asking to their learning.

Evidence from lesson observations shows that children ask good-quality questions when they are given first-hand experiences. When the children were engaged in practical tasks such as observing mouldy food, making electrical circuits or seeing which materials are attracted to a magnet, their questions arose spontaneously and from genuine perplexity or interest.

Good-quality questions are raised when the children have opportunities to talk to each other. An unintended outcome from the project has been the improved group work among the children. Many of the activities introduced in the development phase required the children to work as a pair or a group. As a result the children have much better skills of co-operation and collaboration and have become quite mature in their ability to turn-take and delegate responsibility. The talk observed within the groups was often purposeful and sustained. Children were observed discussing their questions and refining them when necessary. One question from one child would often trigger another child's question.

Case Study 2.2 was produced by an infant school teacher concerned with the behaviour of black boys in her school. It shows how she quickly discovered that the introduction of anti-racist teaching was a bigger priority.[2]

CASE STUDY 2.2

Anti-racist teaching in a multicultural school

Background

The research was triggered by an assumption: that an increase in extreme behaviour in the school could be linked to an increase in the number of children from ethnic minority groups, especially boys with a black African background. The original aim was to investigate ways to support this group of children to prevent them becoming disaffected at such a young age. What the research actually uncovered was something shocking: that I was racist.

[2] This report was published by the General Teaching Council for England, now Crown Copyright.

I discovered that I was clearly influenced by the stereotypes of certain groups of people, and because of this made assumptions about their behaviour and the reasons for it. The fact is that those demonstrating 'out of control' behaviour were not part of any one ethnic group. The focus of the research therefore moved on to look at developing anti-racist practices within the school.

The school setting

This research took place in a larger than average infant school serving a community in the thirty-sixth most deprived local authority in England. The educational background of parents is generally very low. Attainment on entry is well below average, particularly in terms of children's development in communication, language and literacy. The school population is predominantly white, but with a growing number of families from a range of ethnic minority groups.

Research method

The research used an ethnographic approach, which consisted of finding out people's opinions and experiences including my own. I shared my concerns and aims with the participants, regularly discussing my findings with them. The purpose of the exercise was to deepen our understanding of how we were responding to the changing ethnic profile in the school.

I kept a journal of events as they happened and documented questions I could not answer that arose from them. I would then revisit these events over time and evaluate them in light of my reading and discussions with participants. This proved to be a powerful tool to use in honestly examining my own thinking and practice.

I interviewed a range of parents and teachers to find out what they thought about their own education, their own ethnicity, and their experiences of racism. I asked what they thought about existing provision in the school to promote anti-racism and any suggestions they had for improvements.

Findings

Teachers on the whole felt that not enough was being done to promote anti-racism. They were concerned that, although the multicultural approach of learning about other faiths, food and traditions was valuable, it was not enough to ensure equality of provision. However, they were unsure what else they could do. They felt that often they did not deal with issues through fear of saying the wrong thing.

Parents were largely pleased that their children learned about other cultures. Those from minority ethnic groups felt that racism was something they had to put up with, as it was never going to go away. They advised their children to grow a thick skin and ignore racist remarks. Many felt their job opportunities were fewer because of the colour of their skin, and they all felt they had to work harder than white people to gain recognition for the things they did. One parent felt it was good that protective legislation was available, but pointed out that though this did offer some protection it did not change attitudes and had the effect of silencing racist views and sending them 'underground'.

Pupils were initially surprised as teachers became more confident about initiating discussion related to ethnicity. However, they very quickly began to join in and initiate discussions themselves.

The impact of the research

The major impact of this research is a change in the attitudes of teachers, pupils and parents alike.

Teachers are now more confident in being proactive in teaching in an anti-racist manner, both through the curriculum and by recognizing and dealing with racist incidents. Opportunities to highlight and discuss differences are actively sought within the curriculum.

Pupils are comfortable to bring up issues of 'race' and ethnicity, allowing dialogue that promotes equal opportunities and enables misconceptions to be dealt with. Teachers and pupils are more confident to discuss issues of ethnicity as part of class groups. PSHE has become a major vehicle in promoting these discussions, although history, art, religious education and dance are other areas that are developing an anti-racist approach.

Parents who were involved with the research have said they feel listened to and valued, and there has been a marked improvement in relationships. Work with parents is in its infancy, though, and still needs development.

Case Study 2.3 was written by Christine Arthington, a design and technology team leader from High Tunstall School, and was commissioned by the National Teacher Research Panel for the Teacher Research Conference 2004.[3]

CASE STUDY 2.3

Using data to ensure gifted and talented students achieve their full potential in design and technology

Aims of project

The research set out to look into the provision for gifted and talented (GAT) pupils within design and technology at Key Stage 3 in a Hartlepool school, which was currently using a standardized ability test known as Middle Years Information System (MidYIS). Two questions were considered:

- Are test results from MidYIS a reliable indicator for technology GAT pupils?
- Does a more creative delivery encourage GAT pupils to produce higher-level ideas and to be more satisfied with their projects?

---

[3] This research report was published by the Department for Children, Schools and Families.

Context

The project looked at the effectiveness of identification data across one year group of 230 students in an 11–16 comprehensive school. The study then continued through action research involving two groups of approximately 22 mixed-ability students, one acting as a control group and one as the test group.

Summary of main findings

In identifying gifted and talented pupils in design and technology (D&T), evidence suggests that:

- the MidYIS testing was a useful general tool for initial identification of GAT pupils;
- individual components of the overall grade needed to be considered – particularly non-verbal, maths and skills – for identification within D&T;
- analysis of the MidYIS data was very useful when considering underachievement;
- clear guidelines were essential to help identify GAT subject specific talents; and
- reference to professional judgements helped to ensure that special talents were not missed in the identification process.

Implications for delivery of the curriculum were that:

- an emphasis on creativity and individual choice could help to stimulate the interest and motivation of GAT pupils;
- strategies to teach and develop creativity were of benefit to GAT pupils;
- ability grouping appeared to help in creating a climate conducive to stimulating the imagination as part of the design process; and
- pupils needed a 'safe' environment in which they can be encouraged to demonstrate innovative ideas in D&T without fear of ridicule and failure.

Background

High Tunstall School is an 11–16 comprehensive with 1150 students on roll. It is part of Hartlepool Excellence in Cities action zone but does not have a high proportion of disadvantaged families. Prior to the research, identification of GAT pupils in school was carried out by teacher nomination. Within the D&T department, staff used professional judgement, based on pupils' class work, when identifying individuals as GAT, with little reference to performance data. This led to a large number of pupils being nominated with little coherence of standards across the department.

To address such discrepancies the school introduced the Middle Years Information System – a standardized ability test carried out within four areas: vocabulary, maths, non-verbal and skills – for the 2001 Year 7 cohort. Through analysis of these results, pupils could be sorted by rank order and a quantitative measure applied to identify the relevant GAT pupils. The author was keen to discover whether these general tests accurately reflected D&T ability and talent.

In addition, OFSTED has long reported that 'making is better than designing' in D&T, with pupils being taught practical techniques rather than being encouraged to have innovative ideas. One common factor, firmly established in the many checklists for GAT, is an ability to demonstrate creativity. Hence the author also decided to investigate the effects of a more creative delivery method.

Teaching processes and strategies

The author made a simple modification to the delivery of the next textile project by introducing a group design exercise in the first session, prior to any specific material knowledge being taught. She was keen to explore whether this produced more creative designs than the previous technique of designing at a later stage. This exercise was intended to create a non-threatening environment in which pupils felt comfortable to take risks and not to be too concerned with the practicalities of construction. The opinions of the test group were then compared with a control group who had had a 'teacher-led' delivery (traditional emphasis on making) to examine if the more creative delivery (stressing experimentation and discovery) encouraged GAT pupils to produce higher-level ideas and to be more satisfied with their projects.

Findings

Results of Identification by current staff nomination system

Different teachers have identified almost half the cohort as GAT over the course of the year (see Table 2.1); clearly there was a problem with the current system. The author reflects that this could be due to:

- the lack of agreed detailed criteria or baseline assessments;
- pupil's individual preferences for different themes;
- staff personality differences; or
- undue influence of attractive presentation, which may also have influenced nominations, as it does not necessarily reflect ability.

Other factors could be pressure of work on staff leading to lack of quality time for assessment of potential, lack of differentiation or challenge in the curriculum, emphasis on 'making' rather than creativity, and national assessment criteria not being sufficiently rigorously applied.

Identification according to MidYIS test results

If the GAT were identified as the top 20% of pupils ranked by overall MidYIS score, then 44 pupils become the cohort. However, if the GAT were identified using only one individual category such as non-verbal score, a different cohort would be the top 20% as can be seen by the figures in Table 2.2.

Comparison of staff nomination and MidYIS testing

Despite 107 pupils of the cohort being nominated as GAT under the current system, 22 of the most able, according to MidYIS, were never mentioned. Many factors may have

Table 2.1   Staff nominations of GAT pupils after each project

	Autumn	Spring	Summer	Consistent nominations in same category	Total of different pupils nominated
Top 5%	16 total	17 total	13 total	5	
	12 girls	13 girls	9 girls		
	4 boys	4 boys	4 boys		
Top 10%	22 total	24 total	19 total	1	
	20 girls	23 girls	9 girls		
	2 boys	1 boy	10 boys		
Top 20%	16 total	20 total	34 total	2	
	14 girls	13 girls	23 girls		
	2 boys	7 boys	11 boys		
Total (cohort 219 pupils)	54 (23.4%)	61 (26.5%)	66 (28.6%)	8	107 (48.8%)
	46 girls	49 girls	41 girls		70 girls
	8 boys	12 boys	25 boys		37 boys

Table 2.2   Summary of ranked MidYIS test results

	Total size	20%	Top 50 pupils ranked by MidYIS overall score	Number of pupils not in overall top 50 MidYIS group but in top 50 of individual test areas			
				Vocabulary	Maths	Non-verbal	Skills
Year 7	219 total	44 total	50 total	15 (30%)	10 (20%)	15 (30%)	19 (38%)
2001	105 girls	21 girls	25 girls	4 girls	6 girls	8 girls	11 girls
cohort	114 boys	23 boys	25 boys	11 boys	4 boys	7 boys	8 boys

Table 2.3   Staff nomination of pupils compared to MidYIS testing

Top 50 pupils in each area	MidYIS	Vocabulary	Maths	Non-verbal	Skills
Number of pupils missed by staff nominations	22 total	24 total	20 total	20 total	22 total
	4 girls	6 girls	2 girls	5 girls	5 girls
	18 boys	18 boys	18 boys	15 boys	17 boys

contributed to this, including underachievement, attendance, behaviour problems and gender differences. The quiet pupil who does not demand attention and the 'academically able' pupil who may not necessarily be talented in D&T could also have affected nominations. Some pupils may have under- or overperformed in the Table 2.2 tests, and some may argue that 'pencil and paper' tests do not accurately reflect D&T ability. Nevertheless, on consideration of these various factors, it was decided to identify GAT pupils within the sample groups as those with an overall MidYIS A grade.

Outcomes following a change of curriculum placing more emphasis on creativity

Textiles is a totally new experience for the Year 7 D&T groups. The original, teacher-led, control group were provided with experience of materials and equipment prior to producing ideas for a storage hanging (traditional emphasis on making). With the test group, an ability-based group design exercise employing a strong emphasis on 'safe risk taking' was used. Pupils were encouraged throughout the project to investigate and try out the skills necessary to implement their original ideas and discover for themselves which restrictions had to be placed on the construction phase.

The results show the range of ideas produced (see Figures 2.1 and 2.2); when asked, all pupils agreed or strongly agreed that the exercise had been useful. Group 1 (most able) made use of a good range of different ideas and utilized annotation effectively to produce designs that were creative and functional. Group 6 (least able) demonstrated the 'developmental' rather than 'new' aspect of designing. No annotation is present and many of the ideas are reworked versions of another. This group found the exercise particularly difficult, as they had to think quickly, one minute per idea.

Questionnaire results

A questionnaire, developed from an Australian study, was administered to both groups under exam conditions. It was emphasized that there were no 'wrong' answers, and pupils were encouraged to be as truthful as possible. Three factors were identified that significantly defined the D&T learning experience (satisfaction, ease and independence) and the results were considered in relation to these.

When looking at satisfaction in Figures 2.3 and 2.4, the GAT pupils in the test group were more positive than those in the control group, indicating a better learning experience for these pupils. However, the non-GAT pupils in the test group were less satisfied than those in the control – perhaps because they were required to do more 'thinking' and make more individual decisions.

With regard to 'ease' in Figures 2.5 and 2.6, the majority of normal pupils in the control group felt that they had finished the project easily and none were disappointed. However, in the test group, 50% experienced difficulty in completing the work and 10% were disappointed. The author concluded that this was due to the more demanding approach delivered to this group producing a better-differentiated experience for the pupils.

Figure 2.1   Group 1's ideas (most able).

Pupils in the test group felt more independence than pupils in the control group, according to Figure 2.7. This demonstrates the individuality of the more creative approach and allows pupils to take more ownership of their work.

Final outcomes

The final wall hangings that were produced demonstrated the better creativity of the test group. For example, the shape of the backgrounds and number/type of suspension methods were more varied than those of the control group. On comparing the overall outcomes of both groups, it is clear that the test group demonstrated more creativity than the control group but that the standard of construction was similar.

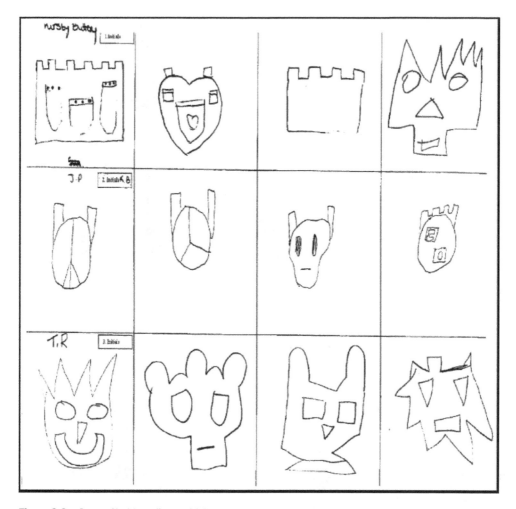

Figure 2.2 Group 6's ideas (least able).

These results lead to the conclusion that, by arranging pupils within groups by ability and introducing a simple creative design exercise at the start of the project, GAT pupils were more satisfied with their work and produced higher-level initial ideas.

Research methods

Students take the MidYIS test on entry to the school, and data from these results were analysed to identify prospective GAT individuals. Design and technology staff were also asked to identify GAT students in their teaching groups, under the current system of using professional judgements, at the end of each project session, resulting in three sets of identification data for examination. These two sets of identification data were then compared in

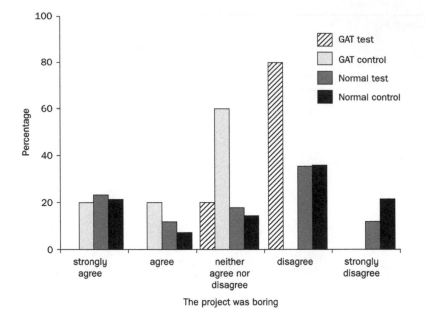

Figure 2.3 Disagreement on 'The project was boring'.

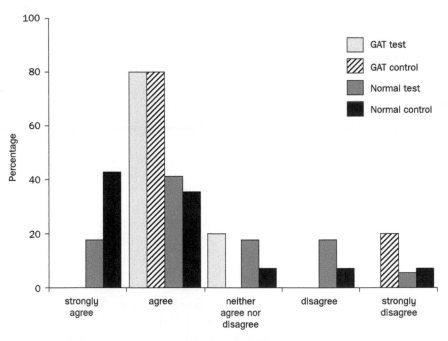

Figure 2.4 Agreement on 'It was worth all the work'.

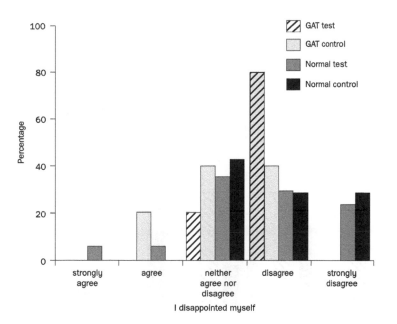

Figure 2.5   Ease: disagreement with 'I disappointed myself'.

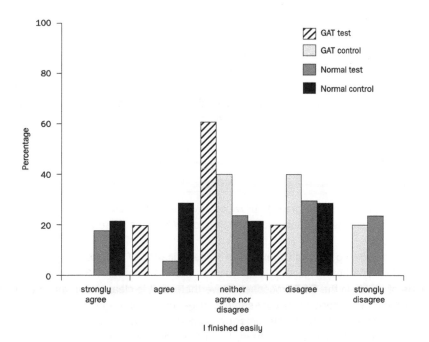

Figure 2.6   Ease: agreement with 'I finished easily'.

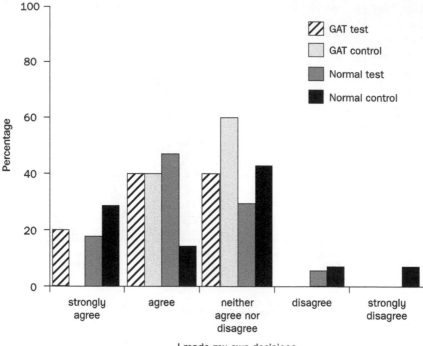

Figure 2.7 Independence: agreement with 'I made my own decisions'.

terms of which students made up the top 20% of the year group, and hence were classed as GAT, to explore if the same students were identified by each method. A questionnaire was then designed that compared the views of winners of D&T awards with 'ordinary' pupils. The objective of the questionnaire was to explore the affective responses of students to the different delivery styles used in the test projects.

Conclusion

Identification

This small-scale research project provides evidence to demonstrate inconsistencies resulting from systems of teacher identification of GAT where there are no clear guidelines to work from.

When considering alternative methods of identification of GAT pupils, colleagues may wish to reflect on whether generic tests such as the in-school MidYIS provide an accurate diagnosis of ability in the D&T processes. Nevertheless, it is clear that in this study MidYIS testing did give an independent assessment of general ability against which D&T talents could be assessed and underachievement considered. Through the limited examination of the different test area scores done here, I feel that non-verbal, maths and skills scores of pupils should be taken into account when producing initial ability lists for consideration. I would suggest that the overall top 50 plus 'extras' from these areas form an initial short list from which the top 20% can be selected by specialist D&T staff.

Focus on creativity

The results demonstrated that pupils found the emphasis on creativity to be more challenging and motivating than the traditional style of delivery. The GAT pupils in the test group were more satisfied with their projects than the GAT in the control group. The variety of ideas produced initially by the group exercise showed a good range of imagination, although many of these were later simplified to accommodate production issues. Overall this proved to be a good method of enriching the curriculum for all and in particular for the GAT pupils. With further improvement and development of strategies/resources to extend this focus, the level of differentiation within the group could be additionally enhanced.

However, for this approach to be most successful, it seems to be important that pupils of similar ability work together at the designing stage in order to stimulate more creative ideas. Once the focus of the project has been established, pupils can work effectively in friendship groups, with GAT pupils offering support to the less able during construction. This, in turn, helps them to consolidate their own skills.

Case Study 2.4 was part of the NCSL-CfBT Research Lesson Study project supported by the Teaching and Learning Research Programme and the Economic and Social Research Council in England. The project aimed to provide network and school leaders with the appropriate tools to conduct research.[4]

CASE STUDY 2.4

Boosting achievement in science using modern foreign language techniques

KS3 subjects: science, modern foreign language (MFL), English as an additional language (EAL)
Pedagogy: literature across the curriculum
Research lesson question: How can we use MFL techniques to boost pupil achievement in science?

Four research lessons studies, three research partner teachers

An analysis of pupil data revealed a group of Year 9 pupils who were predicted to achieve Level 4 in science in Key Stage 3 tests. Their class teacher felt they knew the science and were held back in test scores by their early developmental stage in English, which was causing them to fail to articulate the science he felt they knew.

He worked with colleagues from the MFL department. They used a research lesson to establish the degree to which his hypothesis may be correct – using non-verbal assessment

---

[4] The examples in Case Study 2.4 were published by Networked Learning Communities/CfBT (2005) *Network Leadership in Action: Networked Research Lesson Study in Practice. Booklet 2*, Nottingham: NCSL, p. 6. Crown Copyright.

methods to ascertain the pupils' levels of scientific understanding. They then brainstormed approaches using language learning techniques which may help develop the pupils' abilities to structure, sequence and express their scientific understanding in written answers to questions. The science lessons began to incorporate activities such as cut up instructions to sequence, structured cloze test and DARTs activities which pupils did in pairs and groups. The research lessons were used to establish ways of making these more effective by close observation of focus pupils.

Findings and outcomes

Pupil attainment expressing science orally and in writing soared. All but one of the pupils predicted to attain Level 4 in fact attained Level 5.

Improving science teaching and learning using teachniques from music

KS3 subjects: science, music, EAL.
Pedagogy: peer tutoring
Research lesson question: How does peer tutoring in music work – and how can the science department learn from the technique in order to improve science teaching and learning?

Three research lessons studies, four research partner teachers plus seven ITT students

An advanced skills teacher in science wanted to find out how a successful science department, in a multilingual school, could learn from an exceptionally successful music department. What techniques could be replicated or adapted? Research lessons were used to identify how peer tutoring was used and how pupils utilized and benefited from the techniques. Only this level of study would enable understanding of the process in sufficient depth to begin to design similar approaches in science.

A sequence of lessons was observed and captured on video. The research partners made more and more targeted use of the video to enable subsequent studies of the developments and behaviours of the focus pupils.

Findings and outcomes

The study enabled the research team to be very explicit about the component parts of the peer tutoring which was in use so successfully and to analyse how these worked. They produced artefacts to illustrate these, see www.nationalcollege.org.uk. They also produced evidence of the enhancement of pupil learning of music, English acquisition, self-esteem and confidence to learn. The next quest is to use research lesson study to implement what was learned in science.

Analysis

These two examples both show careful studies, which have enabled learning to travel between departments in the same school. The research teachers took care not to make assumptions about what 'peer music tutoring' or 'writing about science' might involve.

They used the research lessons to ensure that the understandings were deep and shared across the subject boundaries, before attempting to solve the issues. But both also show how the learning about how to teach, which the teachers gained, impacted upon pupil learning and achievement – in the first of the two cases, dramatically improving upon predicted Key Stage 3 and GCSE grades (their validation test). All these colleagues had taught together for some years, but it has been research lessons study which has opened the doors, or glass walls, between departments and subject areas.

In Case Study 2.5, John Beresford, the research officer on the IQEA project, describes how he collaborates with schools in providing data on styles teaching and learning to assist in defining the focus of their improvement strategies.

CASE STUDY 2.5

There is already an extensive literature on the component parts of effective teaching [see, for example, Chapter 11 of the present volume] but less on the process of matching teaching strategies to students' learning styles. Much of the matching of teaching and learning styles has been extremely speculative, based upon the premise that if a sufficient variety of strategies are employed, then a catch-all effect will apply.

The need for some form of dialogue between teachers and students about teaching and learning methods in the classroom has increasingly been recognized by a number of the schools in the IQEA project. These schools have shown themselves willing to discuss with students their views about what constitutes effective teaching. It is also clear that they regard some acknowledgement of student learning preferences, in the teaching which takes place within their classrooms, as an element of effective teaching in its own right. They have also called for an easy-to-administer research instrument that can both help them match what goes on in classrooms more closely to the preferences of their students and provide clues about where to develop the teaching repertoire of their teachers and the learning repertoire of their students.

In order to undertake an audit of the teaching strategies used in its classrooms, and a survey of students' views on those strategies, we developed instruments based on the work of David Kolb. Kolb's (1984) seminal work, *Experiential Learning*, effectively reconceptualizes Piaget's work on developmental learning into four distinct and authentic learning styles, with no implicit hierarchical structure. These four learning styles can be represented as quadrants in a grid where the two dimensions of perceiving and processing information have been juxtaposed, and Kolb also gives useful descriptors of each learning style.

Our colleagues have further identified a range of classroom activities and strategies associated with each of the four learning styles (see Fielding 1994) and from this have produced an observation schedule which can be used to record the incidence of these various activities in a lesson (Beresford 1998). Each activity is coded according to the learning style for which it caters. As each activity occurs in the lesson, its incidence is noted. No assessment is attempted regarding the effectiveness of the various strategies within the context of the lesson. At the end of the period of observation the different number of strategies and learning activities employed by the teacher is totted up and recorded, in the boxes provided, against the appropriate learning style. Hence the lesson can be said to have a particular profile corresponding to the combination of numbers in the boxes. These can be converted into percentages of the total number of strategies and activities used.

In order to assess students' preferences for these characteristic teaching activities, we drew up a similar schedule on which students were asked to indicate which of the activities they preferred. The schedule consists of a list of classroom activities directly related to the teaching strategies listed in the observation schedule. By scoring 'don't like' responses as 0, 'don't mind' as 1 and 'like' as 2 and adding the total for each of the learning style categories, a profile similar to that derived from lesson observations can be derived for each student. By adding the totals of all students in a particular group, a group profile can be obtained. These profiles indicate individual and group learning style preferences (see Beresford 1998, 1999).

The schedule is versatile in as much as it can be used to gauge individual's learning preferences as well as group ones. Students' preferences in individual subjects can be assessed as well as their general learning preferences. Some schools have used the schedules to find out which strategies the students feel are most effective in the teaching of an individual subject, but most have felt that their students lack the necessary analytical skills to arrive at such a judgement. The schedule can also be used to assess any gender differences or differences between year groups.

In Case Study 2.6, David Jackson, who, at the time of writing the cameo, was head of Sharnbrook Upper School and Community College in Bedfordshire, describes how the school improvement focus on teaching and learning is organized at Sharnbrook, and how students are involved in the process.

CASE STUDY 2.6

Sharnbrook Upper School and Community College was established as a 13–19 upper school in 1975 to provide comprehensive education for 32 villages situated in rural mid-England. Sharnbrook's school improvement model is now a continuous, whole-school initiative deeply embedded into our work. At its heart is a fluid group (cadre) of staff committed to working in partnerships and together around areas of mutually agreed enquiry. During the eight years of involvement with IQEA we have had almost as many different modes of operation for the school improvement group, but certain characteristics remain consistent. Some of these are that:

- The school improvement group is led by two staff operating in a co-leadership model.
- The school improvement group breaks down into trios of staff, each engaged in a separate enquiry designed to generate knowledge and understanding about the school's work and to indicate directions for improvement.
- Each of these partnerships undertakes a sustained process of enquiry within the school, drawing also from the knowledge-base within the field and from good practice

elsewhere, and, as an outcome of this data-gathering, suggests improvement to the school's practice, supports the implementation of improvements and then enquires further into their effect upon student learning or the wider school community.

- Each partnership tries to ensure that all those who contribute towards their research are involved, too, in the process of making meaning from the data and, where feasible, in the implementation of outcomes.
- Each partnership also commits to connect with the wider constituency of staff, students, parents and governors in order that all who need to do so can share the emergent journey.
- The school facilitates opportunities for each partnership to lock into consultation and decision-making structures, as appropriate, so that findings from the enquiry will be implemented.
- The entire school improvement group commits to monitoring the value of their own work and to critique each other's practice.

It goes without saying that staff at all levels of the school are involved, including newly qualified teachers, support staff and, more recently, students. Each partnership is entirely free of status positions within the more formal organizational structure of the school and offers leadership opportunities to a variety of staff. Some partnerships might be involved with significant whole-school issues (for example, assessment strategies to improve student achievement) while others may be engaged in focused classroom research activity (questioning technique, or cooperative groupwork). The scale of the intended impact is less significant than the quality of the knowledge deriving from the enquiry. A piece of classroom research, for example, can have equally powerful whole-school impact if the knowledge (about seating arrangements, starts and finishes of lessons – or whatever) is sufficiently significant and widely owned.

By 1997 we had incorporated into the model a group of students who were empowered to operate their own 'school improvement group', complementing and mirroring the style of the wider group. As the student voice dimension of our work evolved, we wanted more authentic and active involvement than 'passive voice'. Between a third and half the staff were, at this stage, involved any one year, focusing exclusively on enquiry and improvement issues.

The 1999/2000 model retains the concept of trios, but reverts to a focus specifically upon teaching and learning. Following a workshop with the whole staff, six areas of classroom practice were identified, and each of the trios has adopted one of these areas mandated by the whole staff. The first 'enquiry' task for each of the partnerships is to develop a powerful theoretical understanding of their particular teaching and learning focus – by researching the knowledge-base, observing classrooms, visiting other schools, or whatever. The trio will then practise and develop their skills in the classroom, providing in-house coaching for one another. The next phase will be to engage in action research with students to seek to validate the impact of this approach upon learning. Throughout this process the remainder of the staff (all staff not involved in one of the partnerships) will choose one of the areas, creating associate groups of about 15 staff for each partnership, who will follow the course of events, engage in workshops and generally become immersed and prepared. When (or if) the action research process validates the impact of the model, the associate staff will be asked to adopt the approach in their own classrooms and to be coached by the trio engaged in the original work.

This is a huge over-simplification of the model, but even described at this level it gives indications of the infrastructural and cultural changes that have evolved through the work of the various models. These would include:

- the opening up of classrooms and classroom practice and the legitimization of inclass coaching;
- the creation of a language to talk about teaching and school improvement;
- the integration of enquiry and professional development approaches;
- the value and authenticity of the student voice and the significance given to their perceptions as learners;
- the willingness of all staff to embrace the value of the development work emanating from the school improvement group;
- the ownership by the whole staff of the school improvement approach;
- the power of a sustained school improvement journey to win over those initially sceptical or even cynical;
- the expansion of leadership capacity.

Case Study 2.7 is a summary of a full report – *Working Smarter Together* – by Trish Franey, the Action Zone leader, which describes a challenge – how to embed action learning through practitioner enquiry across a network of schools formally recognized as a small Excellence in Cities Action Zone. The context for this report is a small action zone's effort to exemplify how theory can impact upon practice through the development of practitioner enquiry teams.

CASE STUDY 2.7

The action zone profile

Within the action zone schools wanted to build:

- a perspective which understands leadership expertise as extending beyond individual leaders;
- an infrastructure of shared resources, collaborative learning and support for leadership opportunities;
- multiple contexts for pupils and teachers to assume leadership roles;
- 'capacity' for future learning, school improvement and managing change.

The zone included one infant, one junior, one secondary and nine primary schools. Within the LEA three of the schools were seen as 'high performing', two were in 'special measures' as a result of OFSTED inspections and the remainder were underachieving by national standards. Prior to the formation of the zone there were no significant school-to-school relationships. Most of the headteachers and senior staff were recruited relatively recently. One outcome of meetings between the headteachers and the zone team was an aspiration towards 'working smarter together'. A strong element of this would be empowering' leading links' (nominated teachers) to focus upon an area for school-based inquiry which would lead to improvement and impact across schools.

The development period

Over the development period of 3 months, key priority areas for improving pupils' learning were agreed with the headteachers. A feature of the action planning was a focus on clear pupil outcomes, and a commitment to building leadership capacity within and across schools. A product of the zone's developmental stage was the commitment to an 'innovation strand', that is, new approaches to entrenched issues. The 'leading links' would support the development and, with the zone team, ensure the dissemination and further development of outcomes.

Recruitment, induction and professional development

It was possible to identify substantive themes and strands in the applications of the leading link teachers. This served as a valuable resource for the zone team in clarifying their understanding of the teachers' perceptions of teamwork and guiding the process of induction and professional development in relation to working as an inter-school team.

The main challenge was how to organize and facilitate the bonding of 12 leading link teachers, and how to build upon and develop their current knowledge and skills so that they would feel confident to pursue school-based inquiry. Integral to our planning was a partnership with a local university and an educational consultancy.

A framework for development was agreed at our meetings with the teachers and a planned model of adult learning promoted by the zone team. The model incorporated what Munro (1999) advocates as a necessary set of conditions for change in teachers:

- learning through meaningful and active processes;
- valuing tacit knowledge about learning;
- framing challenges for learning;
- engaging in collegiate, collaborative activities;
- engaging in self-direction and systematic reflection of practice;
- exploring and demonstrating new teaching approaches.

The framework for professional development identified four areas of learning:

- a coaching model;
- classroom observation for improvement;
- action learning for team development;
- dissemination strategies.

These components, delivered by a local university, a consultancy and the zone team, provided the structure to enable effective practitioner inquiry for school improvement.

The inquiry project

The collective inquiry project focused on improving an aspect of teaching and learning in relation to their own classrooms. In discussion with the zone team it had emerged that all leading link teachers expressed concerns about the limited opportunities for collaborative learning amongst pupils. They agreed that an inquiry project would be used to identify how interactive whiteboards might enhance collaborative learning amongst pupils. The interactive whiteboards were a means to an end – not an end in themselves.

- The zone team would provide ongoing support by demonstrating the use of the whiteboards, giving feedback to teachers on their use of the equipment, and supportively challenging the project's progress.
- Leading links teachers would identify the area of inquiry from school/class data and compile a learning log of the progress of improving professional practice in their classroom/school.
- The inquiry would be reflective and self-evaluative, with judgements based upon evidence, and open to peer scrutiny.
- There would be a collective onus to utilize the project's findings in order to promote greater understanding of the work through active dissemination of the outcomes.

Lessons learned

- Over a relatively short period of time (two terms) teachers can develop as action learners. They need to start with a defined, limited project.
- Professional development is meaningful when it develops the individual, relates to school improvement and impacts within the classroom.
- Professional empowerment stems from collaborative work with peers, the distribution of responsibility, accountability and available resources.
- Reflective practice practitioner research and coaching through teachers working together help to enhance the craft skills of teaching and encourage innovation.
- An inquiry team across schools encourages a wider scope for solutions and action related to generic challenges and support for specific contextual issues.
- Effective support is best provided at different levels – within schools, from peers and externally from trusted outsiders.
- Improving the classrooms observation skills of teachers encourages peer observation and coaching for improvement.
- School development is best served through an alignment between personal, interpersonal and organizational learning.
- Teachers can be motivated and energized through an approach that provides a supportive framework for collaborative learning.
- Inquiry teams cutting across traditional school boundaries have the potential for work that is exciting, challenging and important. The team of leading links worked well together for the greater good of the zone (network) while individuals remained focused on inquiry for improvement at a school level.

- Working together with the zone team created a collective confidence amongst headteachers and teachers for developing ideas, creating leadership opportunities and building a platform for innovation.

The major learning from the project has been that it is possible in a relatively short period of time to establish an inquiry team across a network of schools. This generated work processes and relationships which have met personal and professional needs. It allowed teachers the opportunity to grow professionally and become powerful learners, and to feel empowered in turning ideas into working practices contributing to whole-school improvement.

Case Study 2.8 is taken from a paper by Lawrence Stenhouse (1979: 71–7; reprinted by permission of Universitetsforlaget AS). He describes, in the first person singular, the fictionalized predicament of a teacher who turns to the research literature for advice on which teaching strategy to use.

CASE STUDY 2.8

I teach social studies in the form of a human issues programme covering such topics as the family, poverty, people and work, law and order, war and society, relations between the sexes. I wonder whether I should include race relations. A complicating factor is my style of teaching controversial issues to adolescent students. I set up discussions and use evidence such as newspapers, stories, pamphlets, photographs and films. I act as neutral chairman in those discussions, in order to encourage critical attitudes without taking sides. In short, I have been influenced by and am in the tradition of the English Humanities Curriculum Project (Stenhouse 1970).

I am very concerned that my teaching should contribute positively to race relations in my multiracial society, if that is possible. I wonder whether I should teach about race relations at all. If so, I wonder whether it is appropriate in this case to take the role of neutral chairman, even though this is a teaching convention and not a position professing personal neutrality. So I turn to a research report on 'Problems and Effects of Teaching about Race Relations' for enlightenment (Stenhouse et al. 1982, cited in Rudduck and Hopkins 1985).

Here I find that the project has monitored on a pre-test, post-test basis two different strategies of teaching about race relations, one in which the teacher is neutral (called strategy A), the other in which the teacher feels free to express, whenever he feels it appropriate, his committed stance against racism (called strategy B). Strategy A was conducted in 14 schools and strategy B in 16 schools. The samples are not true random samples because of problems of accessibility of schools and students, but I know something about this from my study of education at college (Campbell and Stanley 1963). Control groups have been gathered in the same schools as the experimental groups whenever this was possible, though this was not possible in all cases. I came across this table (see Table 2.4) of results on a scale purporting to measure general racism.

This seems to help me a good deal at first sight. My neutral strategy is strategy A. Attitudes in the strategy A group seem to improve and, though the improvement does not

Table 2.4   Scores on the General Racism Scale of the Bagley–Verma test[a]

Teaching style	Experimental sample			Control sample			
	Pre-test mean (S.D.)	Post-test mean (S.D.)	Direction of shift and t-value difference of means	Pre-test mean (S.D.)	Post-test mean (S.D.)	Direction of shift and t-value difference of means	t-value for difference between the experimental and control groups
Strategy A							
Experimental (n = 258)	17.24	16.51	1.71	16.06	17.61	2.11*	2.83**
Control (n = 124)	(10.05)	(10.25)		(9.66)	(10.49)		
Strategy B							
Experimental (n = 359)	17.25	16.17	2.27	17.42	17.87	0.72	1.91
Control (n = 180)	(9.61)	(9.78)		(9.93)	(10.58)		

[a] A decrease in score represents a decrease in racism.
*P < 0.05; **P < 0.01.

quite reach even the 0.05 level of significance, the control groups, left to general influences, deteriorate in attitude significantly and the comparison of experimental and control shows at least by one criterion a 0.01 level discrimination in favour of teaching about race relations by strategy A. Strategy B does not look markedly superior to strategy A, so I don't seem to need to change my teaching style. So it seems that research has helped me by enabling me to decide the right style in which to teach about race relations.

But, oh dear, here's a problem. On a later page the same data are presented in a different form to show the situation in individual schools and this seems to complicate the issue as shown in Table 2.5. Now, looking at this table, I personally feel that, given comment codes A, B or C, I certainly ought to proceed, given comment codes D and possibly E, I should proceed with great care, and given codes F and G, I might be better to give a lot more thought to the matter. In seven out of 12 schools, the result seems encouraging, in four schools results seem doubtful and in one of the 12 rather alarming. How do I know what category my school will fall into? This is really rather disturbing for my decision. Perhaps I should shift to strategy B. Let's look at the strategy B table (see Table 2.6).

Oh dear! This is no better. Here eight out of 15 schools are reassuring, three are doubtful and three are alarming. Strategy B seems no refuge.

Can it be that statistically significant discriminations between two treatments when presented through means and standard deviations can mask such a range of within-sample variance as this? It can indeed. In the psycho-statistical research paradigm, the effects are

Table 2.5 Differences between pre- and post-test school means for the experimental and control groups on the General Racism (GR), Anti-Asian (AA) and Anti-Black (AB) Scales of the Bagley–Verma test: Strategy A

1	2	3	4	5	6	7	8
School code	Experimental GR	Experimental AA	Experimental AB	Control GR	Control AA	Control AB	Comment code
03	−1.83	−0.35	−1.22	–	–	–	C
07**	1.58	0.54	0.31	−0.86	0.21	−0.71	G
09	−0.22	0.55	−0.90	2.11	1.45	1.09	A
10*	−0.63	−0.18	−1.54	–	–	–	C
13	−0.85	0.37	−1.29	−0.89	−0.56	−0.67	D
17	−2.50	−1.17	−1.78	–	–	–	C
18	1.70	2.40	0.90	6.63	4.38	3.75	B
19	0.37	−0.04	0.62	–	–	–	D
29	−3.42	−1.75	−1.67	2.0	0.87	−0.25	A
31**	−0.12	0.77	0.65	0.34	0.50	−1.16	D
32**	−1.61	−0.70	−0.83	−0.07	−0.77	−0.38	A
39*	1.20	−0.50	1.05	–	–	–	D
Mean of strategy A controls (individuals)				(1.30)	(0.83)	(0.49)	

*5–25% non-white; **over 25% non-white.

Table 2.6 Differences between pre- and post-test school means for the experimental and control groups on the General Racism (GR), Anti-Asian (AA) and Anti-Black (AB) Scales of the Bagley–Verma test: Strategy B

1	2	3	4	5	6	7	8
School code	Experimental GR	Experimental AA	Experimental AB	Control GR	Control AA	Control AB	Comment code
01	−3.51	−1.60	−2.57	−1.75	1.43	−1.34	A
02	0.00	−0.67	−0.10	2.43	1.22	1.43	A
04*	1.04	0.10	0.24	–	–	–	E
05	−2.27	−0.34	−0.97	–	–	–	C
06*	−2.00	1.29	−1.30	0.55	0.34	−0.52	D
08	1.09	0.30	0.07	−5.40	−1.20	−2.33	G
09	−2.89	−0.22	−1.97	2.11	1.45	1.09	A
11	−1.58	−0.48	−0.53	–	–	–	C
14**	−0.33	0.39	0.91	–	–	–	D
15	−2.25	0.17	−1.42	–	–	–	C
20	−0.39	0.05	−0.22	−1.15	0.86	−1.43	F
21	−1.77	−1.32	−1.19	1.59	1.04	0.59	A
24*	0.19	0.37	0.60	4.93	1.07	1.65	B
30*	3.79	1.27	2.16	–	–	–	E
33	1.00	0.43	0.38	−0.83	0.83	−0.08	G
Mean of strategy B controls (individuals)				0.90	0.71	0.30	

*5–25% non-white; **over 25% non-white.

not 'other things being equal'; they are 'by and large' or 'for the most part'. So doing one thing is only sometimes better than doing the other! This, apparently, depends on your school context or school environment or perhaps yourself or your pupils.

What I have to find out now is whether teaching about race relations by strategy A is good for my pupils in my school. However, that reminds me that I haven't looked at pupils as individuals, only as means and standard deviations. Suppose I took these data and looked at them in a way that depicted the fate of individuals. How about a histogram of change scores? There are, of course, problems with such scores but, bearing them in mind, I'll give it a go (see Figures 2.8 and 2.9).

My goodness, it looks as if the same teaching style and the same subject matter make some people worse as they make other people better. One man's meat is another man's poison. If I teach about race relations, some people get worse. But if I refuse to teach about race relations, even more people get worse. I suppose I should have thought of that anyway. I know that when I teach literature some people come not to like it, but I believe that even fewer would enjoy literature if I didn't introduce them to it all.

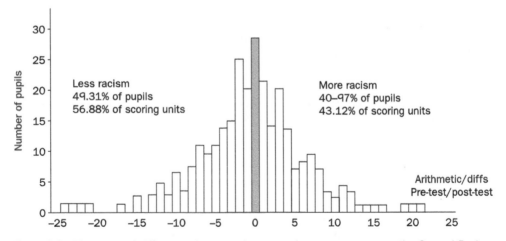

Figure 2.8   Histogram of differences between the pre- and post-test scores on the General Racism Scale of the Bagley–Verma test: strategy A experimental (*n* = 288).

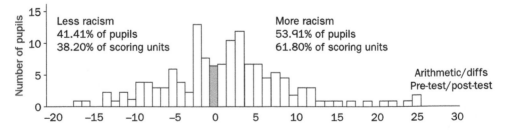

Figure 2.9   Histogram of differences between the pre- and post-test scores on the General Racism Scale of the Bagley–Verma test: strategy A control (*n* = 128).

I need to steady myself. After all, engineers don't always build exactly the same bridge. Nor do chess players always play the same game. There must be ways of fitting action to situation and perhaps even to individuals in that situation.

I've clearly got to think things out for myself. Does this mean that research cannot help me? What was that piece in the paper by Cronbach they gave us in Ed. Psych.? Here are my notes. And here it is:

> When we give proper weight to local conditions, any generalization is a working hypothesis, not a conclusion.
>
> (Cronbach 1975: 125)

That seems to mean that the results of research need testing in local conditions. What research gives me is most often not findings about all teaching but hypotheses about my teaching.

This is a bit of a shock, but it makes reasonable enough sense. And the hypotheses I've got are already of some use. I must test whether strategy A works well for me in my class-room, whether I can sustain its logic in practice and whether it is giving good results in attitudes. At the same time, I know that even in a good result some individuals may be deteriorating in attitude.

What I am going to do is this. I'm getting a student to come in and pre- and post-test my pupils and a control group in my school. But I'm also going to tape our sessions on race relations on a portable cassette-recorder. To do this, I have to tape other lessons too, so that I don't seem to be concentrating on race. I've started this. I'm explaining to the students that I'm doing a study of my own teaching and that this should help me to teach better. And I'm beginning to get them talking about how well my teaching and their learning goes.

Of course, there's a problem about how to handle the tapes. I played some at home and tried a Flanders interaction analysis (Flanders 1970) on them. It did tell me that I talked too much, but not a lot more. Then I tried the Humanities Curriculum Project analysis, which worked quite well because I was involved in discussion teaching. But I want to look at pupil behaviour as well as teacher behaviour. I'm beginning to ask myself whether I can develop a theory of individuals who cause me concern in class. I don't even need paper to do that. I can play cassettes in my car as I drive to and from work.

The more I come to study my own classroom, and my own school as well, the more I come to understand why the research provides case studies of classrooms. Comparing other people's experiences with my own throws up all sorts of illuminating possibilities – hypotheses, I mean.

At the end of this session, I'm going to try to set up a club in the district for teacher-researchers. They have clubs for people who tinker with motorcycles to get more perform-ance from them, so why not the same for teachers who are tinkering with their teaching?

I'd like to set about testing Piaget. Most of his experiments are a kind of teaching. And I have a feeling that if I work with a small sample, like he did, I'll find out quite a lot for myself. I've got a better laboratory than he had: it's a real classroom!

I'm not sure if I'm doing research. I am testing hypotheses by experiment as systemati-cally as a busy job allows.

The *Shorter Oxford English Dictionary* says that research is: 'Investigation, inquiry into things. Also, habitude of carrying out such investigation.' Well, it is beginning to become a habit.

Further reading

There are a number of sources for further examples of classroom research by teachers. In *A Teacher's Guide to Action Research*, Jon Nixon (1981) presents a series of descriptive accounts by teachers of a variety of classroom research projects. Extended illustrations of teacher research are given by Michael Armstrong (1980) in *Closely Observed Children*. Classic examples of classroom research in this tradition, although involving the participation of an external researcher, are found in Smith and Geoffrey's (1968) *The Complexities of an Urban Classroom* and Stephen Rowland's (2012) *The Enquiring Classroom*. Jean Rudduck and her colleagues (Hull *et al.* 1985; May and Rudduck 1983; Rudduck 1981) have produced collections of teacher research accounts as a result of their funded research projects. During the 1980s, the Classroom Action Research Network (CARN), the Ford Teaching Project, and the Teacher–Pupil Interaction and the Quality of Learning (TIQL) project (Ebbutt and Elliott 1985; Elliott and Ebbutt 1985a, 1985b) all published accounts of their classroom research activities that were available from the Centre for Applied Research in Education, University of East Anglia. More recent collections of teacher research case studies are found in *Action Research in Classrooms and Schools* (Hustler *et al.* 1986), which mainly focuses on secondary schools, and Rosemary Webb's (1990) *Practitioner Research in the Primary School*. Four other books that contain detailed examples of classroom research as well as descriptions of method and philosophical discussions are Oja and Smulyan's (1989) *Collaborative Action Research*, Richard Winter's (1989) *Learning from Experience*, Atweh *et al.*'s (1998) *Action Research in Practice: Partnership for Social Justice in Education*, and Burnaford *et al.*'s (2001) *Teachers Doing Research: The Power of Action Through Inquiry*. Further examples of teacher research are found in Baumfield *et al.*'s (2013) *Action Research in Education* and Koshy's (2010) *Action Research for Improving Educational Practice*.

3 Why classroom research by teachers?

In asking the question 'Why classroom research by teachers?', one is raising a whole series of issues around the topics of professionalism, classroom practice, the social control of teachers and the usefulness of educational research. Each of these issues provides a rationale for teacher research. For example, classroom research by teachers can be justified by references to professionalism because systematic self-study, particularly the relationship between diagnosis and treatment or action, is a hallmark of those occupations that enjoy the label 'professional'. Unfortunately, the teacher's claim to professionalism sometimes falters at this definition. In this chapter, however, I will focus on three other themes that justify and, indeed, make imperative a concept of classroom research by teachers. The first is the link between classroom research by teachers and the establishing and refining of professional judgement. The second is making the focus of classroom research, curriculum and improvements in teaching and learning. The third is the inappropriateness of the traditional academic or research paradigm for helping teachers improve their teaching. I conclude the chapter with a reflection on the nature of classroom research itself.

'Autonomous in professional judgement'

Lawrence Stenhouse (1984: 69) described the ideal role of the teacher as follows:

> Good teachers are necessarily autonomous in professional judgement. They do not need to be told what to do. They are not professionally the dependants of researchers or superintendents, of innovators or supervisors. This does not mean that they do not welcome access to ideas created by other people at other places or in other times. Nor do they reject advice, consultancy or support. But they do know that ideas and people are not of much real use until they are digested to the point where they are subject to the teacher's own judgement. In short, it is the task of all educationalists outside the classroom to serve the teachers; for only teachers are in the position to create good teaching.

This is a very different image from the contemporary approach to schooling that is based on the assumption that instructions issued from the top – from the minister, an inspection agency such as OFSTED, the director of education or equivalent and, at times, even the headteacher – are put into practice at the appropriate level lower down the organization. This approach to education tends to equate schools to factories that operate on a rational input–output basis, with pupils as raw material, teachers as mechanics, the curriculum as the productive process and the school leaders as factory managers.

This image of schooling stands in direct contrast to the aspirations of the teacher research movement. John Elliott (in Nixon 1981: 1) has observed that 'the teacher as researcher movement emanated from the work and ideas of Lawrence Stenhouse'. Crucial to an understanding of Stenhouse's intellectual position is, as we saw in Chapter 1, the notion of emancipation (see Stenhouse 1983). In this context, emancipation refers to the process involved in liberating teachers from a system of education that denies individual dignity by returning to them some degree of self-worth through the exercise of professional judgement.

In terms of curriculum and teaching, the path to emancipation involves reconceptualizing curriculum development as curriculum research, and the linking of research to the art of teaching (Rudduck and Hopkins 1985). When viewed through this particular lens, centrally imposed curricula are in danger of becoming prescriptive blueprints that tend to inhibit autonomy in teaching and learning. On the other hand, the process model of curriculum, as described by Stenhouse (1975), is liberating or emancipatory because it encourages independence of thought and argument on the part of the pupil, and experimentation and the use of judgement on the part of the teacher. As Stenhouse (1975: 142) said (see quote in full on page 45):

> The crucial point is that the proposal is not to be regarded as an unqualified recommendation but rather as a provisional specification claiming no more than to be worth putting to the test of practice. Such proposals claim to be intelligent rather than correct.

The major consequence of doing this is that teachers take more control of their professional lives. Teachers who engage in their own research are developing their professional judgement and are moving towards emancipation and autonomy as a consequence of adopting the practices and approaches described in this book. Such an approach is not inimical at all to the idea of a National Curriculum or other curriculum guidelines, or indeed well-specified programmes such as the National Literacy or Numeracy strategies were in the last decade. In such circumstances, teachers adopt educational propositions, cast in the form of a curriculum proposal, and test them out and refine and improve them within their own classroom settings.

The concept of professional judgement is so central to the notion of the teacher as researcher that it is important to define it in practical as well as conceptual terms. In *The Empowered School* David Hargreaves and I argued any successful school improvement requires teachers to use their professional judgement in a systematic way (Hargreaves and Hopkins 1991: Chapter 9). It is not the mechanistic completion of tasks that is important, but rather it is the enhancing of the teachers' professional judgement that is the crucial aspect of embedding an ethos of inquiry and reflection within a school. This process provides the interface between development planning, classroom research and school improvement. We articulated a number of different levels at which a teacher's professional judgement could and should operate.

Teachers already, as part of their everyday activities, monitor and evaluate their own actions as well as the behaviour and work of pupils. If teachers did not rely on their *intuitive professional judgement*, they would not be able to cope with the complexities of their work. There are occasions, however, when it cannot be wholly relied on as a basis for making a decision. Such occasions are when teachers are not entirely confident about their intuitive judgement, or the issue is of considerable importance or significance. In these circumstances, teachers make a *considered professional judgement*, which requires some action to check the intuitive judgement. A considered professional judgement is reached through reflection and further investigation. Using intuitive and considered professional judgements is a routine part of being a teacher. Both are a natural and inherent part not only of assessing progress and impact but also more generally of the school improvement process.

The introduction of new practices often creates altered working circumstances with which the teacher is less familiar. Since teachers usually want any innovation to succeed, there may be a bias towards noticing the most favourable evidence. Professional judgement may therefore be less trustworthy than usual. In these cases a *refined professional judgement* is required. This is an opportunity for enhancing professional judgement, and is achieved:

- through discussion with colleagues about the extent of progress or success in school improvement work;
- by establishing agreement on standards used to make judgements;
- through mutual observation in the classroom;
- through the use of informed opinion; and
- by the analysis of pupil, class and whole-school data.

When they are well structured, school improvement activities provide ample opportunities for teachers to talk with others, to seek agreement on standards, to observe one another and to read relevant documentation: all are means of refining the professional judgements which are so essential for positive impact on student learning. Extending teachers' professional judgements in these ways links the professional development of the individual teacher to the development of the school as a whole as well as improving the quality of teaching and learning.

There are circumstances when teachers need to *complement* even a refined professional judgement with additional evidence. Such occasions are when others need to be persuaded of the validity of teachers' judgements, or when there are benefits to all if teachers' judgements are backed by independent evidence. Collecting complementary evidence is usually more time-consuming than making professional judgements, so careful thought needs to be given to questions such as: what kind of complementary evidence is appropriate to documenting success? How can it be collected as quickly and easily as possible without adding substantially to existing workloads? There are different types and sources of complementary evidence, and it is these that reflect what is often regarded as more formal approaches to evaluation:

- observations (e.g. mutual observation as part of professional development or performance management);
- views and opinions (e.g. short questionnaire to colleagues, students or parents);
- written materials (e.g. a 'book look' of students' work);
- statistical information (e.g. trends in student rates of progress);
- more formal research (e.g. by a colleague on a master's degree course).

To summarize, the notion of being autonomous in professional judgement is not only an attractive theoretical construct but also an intensely practical and productive one. Used in the ways just described, the exercise of professional judgement provides the essential practical link between professional development, school improvement and enhanced levels of student learning and achievement.

Curriculum and teaching as the focus of classroom research

Successful implementation of any centralized innovation requires adaptation by teachers at the school level. It is not an either/or situation or a straight choice between 'top-down' or 'bottom-up' – it is a combination of both. As Denis Lawton (1989: 85) argues in his book *Education, Culture and the National Curriculum*, we need:

> more curriculum development which is at least partly school-based. This is not to suggest that the centre–periphery or 'top-down' models of curriculum development are completely outmoded: it is a question of balance. It would be unreasonable to expect every school to develop its own curriculum from first principles, but it would be equally foolish to attempt to impose a detailed, uniform curriculum on every school, leaving no room for school-based development geared to specific local needs.

This balance is maintained through the professionalism of teachers. As Lawton (1989: 89) further comments:

> The increasing desire of teachers to be treated as professionals rather than as state functionaries, has encouraged a tendency to look for ways in which teachers could solve their own professional problems at a local level rather than react to more remote initiatives. Hence the emphasis on the school as the obvious location for curriculum renewal, the in service education of teachers, the evaluation of teaching and learning, and even educational research.

The crucial point that Lawton is making is that the claim of teaching to be a profession lies in the ability and opportunity for teachers to exercise their judgement over the critical tasks involved in their role, namely curriculum and teaching. Most centralized school systems prescribe what is to be taught to pupils, but require the teacher to put the curriculum into practice. At a very basic level, this involves the teacher in some form of 'translation' of the curriculum policy into schemes of work or lesson plans. More emphasis on research-based teaching would, I believe, result in better 'translations' of centralized curriculum into practice and in teachers who are more confident, flexible and autonomous.

Over a quarter of a century ago, Stenhouse made essentially the same point by suggesting that classroom research be used as a means of testing curriculum ideas. The context of that proposal is worth reproducing in full (Stenhouse 1975: 142–3):

> I have argued that educational ideas expressed in books are not easily taken into possession by teachers, whereas the expression of ideas as curricular specifications exposes them to testing by teachers and hence establishes an equality of discourse between the proposer and those who assess the proposal. There is, of course, no implication as to the origins of the proposal or hypotheses being tested. The originator may be a classroom teacher, a policy-maker or an educational research worker. The crucial point is that the proposal is not to be regarded as an unqualified recommendation but rather as a provisional specification claiming no more than to be worth putting to the test of practice. Such proposals claim to be intelligent rather than correct.
>
> I have identified a curriculum as a particular form of specification about the practice of teaching and not as a package of materials of a syllabus of ground to be covered. It is a way of translating any educational idea into a hypothesis testable in practice. It invites critical testing rather than acceptance.
>
> I have reached towards a research design based upon these ideas, implying that a curriculum is a means of studying the problems and effects of implementing any defined line of teaching.
>
> The uniqueness of each classroom setting implies that any proposal – even at school level – needs to be tested and verified and adapted by each teacher in his own classroom. The ideal is that the curricular specification should feed a teacher's personal research and development programme through which he is progressively increasing his understanding of his own work and hence bettering his teaching.
>
> To summarise the implications of this position, all well-founded curriculum research and development, whether the work of an individual teacher, of a school, or of a group working in a teachers' centre or of a group working within the co-ordinating framework of a national project, is based on the study of classrooms. It thus rests on the work of teachers.

Here Stenhouse is linking classroom research by teachers firmly to the curriculum and teaching. This is an important point that may become lost in all the talk about the gathering and analysis of data. Teacher research is not an end in itself, but is inextricably linked to curriculum change and the adoption of new teaching strategies. It is also at this point that teaching becomes a profession.

Outstanding (or expert) teaching is not just about pedagogy – the strategies and techniques that the teacher uses. It is about what is being taught – the curriculum the school and department has chosen to follow. Over the past 10 years, there has been a move away from academic subjects towards genericism and competence-based frameworks in schools. This has proceeded hand in hand with the mistaken view that teaching academic subjects is merely about providing information, rather than about developing forms of disciplinary *thinking*. It is fashionable now to ask 'if we have Google why do we need subjects? Pupils just need the *skills* to find the information.' The argument here is to emphasize that teachers have to engage with the process of knowledge creation and understand the underlying structures of academic subjects.

In the words of Counsell (2011):

> The view that disciplines can neither engage nor serve most pupils often betrays two misapprehensions: first, an assumption that a subject equates to information, as opposed to knowledge; second, a lack of awareness that a school subject such as history has long involved the active and engaging exploration of the structure and form of that knowledge, using concepts and attendant processes.

The 'thinking skills' argument ignores the distinctive purposes of academic disciplines. Disciplines are not sets of 'skills' so much as distinctive ways of building knowledge, weighing evidence and finding truth. The particular disciplinary context of a subject is central to that particular way of thinking, of researching, of judging evidence and of building knowledge about the world. Academic subjects in schools, therefore, provide disciplined forms of criticality; disciplined ways of reading, writing and speaking; a disciplined understanding of how different types of knowledge are constructed. The best subject teachers are those who combine a flair for delivery and lesson design with a deep understanding of the foundational rules and principles of their subjects.

Therefore, the curriculum is central in that it 'forces' the teacher to engage with the foundational rules of a subject and thus 'professionalize' their practice in that through this reflection they begin to connect action and analysis of impact in terms of the types of thinking they are engendering in their students. This thinking should model the thinking of experts in that particular discipline/field. Therefore, a successful curriculum enables students to think like a historian, to talk like a physicist and to approach and solve problems as an engineer in the field would. In the primary context this could relate to the development through oracy of a particular language associated with a subject, for example mathematical language developed through mathematical activities and the modelling of language by the teacher which promotes dialogue or questions to further mathematical understanding.

Problems in traditional approaches

Perhaps the most unfortunate aspect of traditional educational research is that it is extremely difficult to apply its findings to classroom practice. Case Study 2.8 in Chapter

2 is a good illustration of this. In a quandary about which teaching strategy to use, the fictionalized teacher went to the research literature for guidance. His subsequent experience was as frustrating as it was predictable, because the literature contains few unequivocal signposts for action. This dilemma is widespread: teachers quite rightly (in most cases) regard educational research as something irrelevant to their lives and see little interaction between the world of the educational researcher and the world of the teacher. This tension has in my opinion exacerbated during the thirty years since the publication of the first edition of this book. Having spent a significant amount of that time working in universities, I have experienced at first hand some of the perverse effects of quality assurance initiatives such as the Research Assessment Exercise (RAE) and Research Excellence Framework (REF). Despite well-meaning criteria designed to embrace the user perspective and to measure impact, much published academic research has (with some notable exceptions noted below) little to contribute to daily work of teachers in improving their practice to the advantage of their students.

Some time ago Arthur Bolster (1983: 295) asked 'Why has research on teaching had so little influence on practice?', and his response to the question is still worth quoting:

> The major reason, in my opinion, is that most such research, especially that emanating from top-ranked schools of education, construes teaching from a theoretical perspective that is incompatible with the perspective teachers must employ in thinking about their work. In other words, researchers and school teachers adopt radically different sets of assumptions about how to conceptualize the teaching process. As a result, the conclusions of much formal research on teaching appear irrelevant to classroom teachers – not necessarily wrong, just not very sensible or useful. If researchers are to generate knowledge that is likely to affect classroom practice, they must construe their inquiries in ways that are much more compatible with teachers' perspectives. Collaboration between researchers and teachers generates a reciprocal benefit and closes the gap between theory and practice.

Most researchers, when they enter classrooms, bring with them perspectives derived from academic disciplines. Their view of how knowledge evolves and how it is determined is firmly established by their formal training. The world view that guides researchers' actions is consequently at odds with that of teachers. Teachers derive their knowledge of teaching from continual participation in situational decision-making and the classroom culture in which they and their pupils live out their daily lives. So one reason why traditional educational research is of little use to teachers is the differing conceptions of teaching held by teachers and researchers. But there are other problems.

Research in education is usually carried out within the psycho-statistical research paradigm. This implies tightly controlled experimentation and the testing of hypotheses by assessing the effectiveness of a treatment across randomly selected groups through the use of statistical analysis. This approach is based on the agricultural research designs of R.A. Fisher (1966) in the 1930s. At that time, educationalists, desiring to link research to action, began to utilize Fisher's very successful 'agricultural botany' designs in educational settings. This has continued (and increased) down to the present day, as can be seen by the myriad of postgraduate theses that use this research design. The basic idea underlying Fisher's designs is that experiments are conducted on samples, usually divided into a control and an experimental group, with the results generalized to the target population. The point is that samples are randomly drawn and are consequently representative of that target population.

Stenhouse (1979) describes Fisher's approach as follows:

> The strength of Fisher's paradigm is the recognition of random sampling, in which a sample is drawn such that each member of the target population has an equal chance of being included in the sample because it is a device of chance . . .
>
> In Fisher's agricultural setting, the hypotheses were not derived from scientific theory . . . They were hypotheses regarding the relative effectiveness of alternative procedures, and the criteria of effectiveness was gross crop yield.
>
> The result of an experiment of this kind is an estimate of the probability that – other things being equal – a particular seed strain or fertilizer or amount of watering will result in a higher gross yield than an alternative against which it has been tested . . . It is in applying experimental methods to teaching and curriculum evaluation in the schools that researchers have used the Fisherian model. The assumption is that one teaching procedure or curriculum can be tested against alternatives as a seed strain or fertilizer can in agriculture, i.e. procedures can be tested against yield without a real theoretical framework.

This approach to educational research is problematic, particularly if its results are to be applied to classrooms. First, it is extraordinarily difficult to draw random samples in educational settings (e.g. a random sample of schools, pupils and teachers would have to be drawn separately). Second, there are a myriad of contextual variables operating on schools and classrooms (e.g. community culture, teacher personality, school ethos, socio-economic background) that would affect the results. Third, it is difficult to establish criteria for effective classroom or school performance. Even if one could resolve these difficulties, there are, as Stenhouse (1979) points out, two deeper problems that relate to the nature of educational activity.

First, the 'agricultural botany' paradigm is based on measures of gross yield (i.e. how much produce can be gathered in total from a section of land). That is an inappropriate measure for education. As teachers, we are concerned with the individual progress of students rather than with aggregated scores from the class or the school. Our emphasis is on varying teaching methods to suit individual pupils in order to help them achieve to the limit of their potential. Stenhouse (1979: 79) puts the paradox like this: 'The teacher is like a gardener who treats different plants differently, and not like a large scale farmer who administers standardised treatments to as near as possible standardised plants.'

The second deeper problem relates to meaningful action. The teacher–pupil or pupil–pupil interactions that result in effective learning are not so much the consequence of a standardized teaching method but the result of both teachers and pupils engaging in meaningful action. And meaningful action cannot be standardized by control or sample. This is a similar argument to the one commonly used against those who overrate the utility of behavioural objectives. Behavioural objectives provide an excellent means for the teaching of skills or evaluating rote learning, but they tend to be counter-productive with more complex and sophisticated content areas. In the instance of rote learning, one can accept the parallel with standardized treatments, but not so easily with poetry appreciation. Here pupil response is the result of individual negotiation with the subject, mediated through and by the teacher – namely, a form of meaningful action. In this case, education as induction into knowledge is, as Stenhouse (1975: 82) memorably points out, 'successful to the extent that it makes the behavioural outcomes of pupils unpredictable' and, therefore, not generalizable. The implications of this line of thinking for teacher-researchers is to encourage them to look outside the psycho-statistical paradigm for their research procedures.

To summarize, I have made two points in arguing that the traditional approach to educational research is not of much use to teachers. The first point is that teachers and researchers do not conceptualize teaching in the same way. They live in different intellectual worlds and so their meanings rarely connect. Second, the usual form of educational research, the psycho-statistical or agricultural botany paradigm, has severe limitations as a method of construing and making sense of classroom reality. For these two reasons, teachers and those concerned with understanding classroom life have increasingly adopted different approaches to classroom research.

Having said all this, it is important to ensure that in critiquing traditional approaches to educational research we do not throw the baby out with the bathwater. The critique outlined above was particularly relevant in the final decades of the last century when it was important to argue against a dogmatism and myopia in educational research that distorted the reality of classroom life. More recently, however, new approaches to experimental research in education have given teacher-researchers more precise tools with which to do and to make sense of their work. The contributions of Robert Slavin and John Hattie are of particular importance here.

Both Slavin (e.g. 1986) and Hattie (2009) have in their different ways contributed to the increasing popularity of assessing the impact of teaching and learning through using the statistical technique of 'effect size'. 'Effect size' describes the magnitude of the gains in student learning to be expected from a change in teacher behaviour – by measuring the impact that the practice has on the curve of normal distribution, moving it, as seen below, more to the right. Effect size provides a means of gauging the effect of a particular change in teaching method or classroom organization on learning and achievement. By the same token, it can also be used to predict what can be accomplished by using that practice. The computation of effect size involves the meta-analysis of a large number of empirical studies that measure the impact of a specific teacher behaviour on student learning. First developed as a statistical technique by Gene Glass and colleagues, it was subsequently adopted by Bruce Joyce to measure the impact of models of teaching on learning and by ourselves as described in Chapter 12 (Glass *et al.* 1981; Joyce *et al.* 2009; Northern Metropolitan Region 2011).

Figure 3.1 illustrates the effect size of using higher-order questions. In this case it is 0.73 standard deviations that is the metric utilized by effect size analyses. This means that the average student in the 'experimental group' – where the teacher used higher-order questions – would be performing at the about the 65th percentile level, compared with the 50th percentile level in the 'control group' where the teacher was using closed questions.

This approach has been widely disseminated by John Hattie (2009) in his book *Visible Learning* where he has computed the effect size for over 800 influences on student learning. Hattie has developed his own 'barometer of influence' that provides a heuristic way of expressing the concept. Although both developmental and teacher effects are important, we should always aim to be adopting practices that are in the zone of desired effects. As Hattie (2009: 19) comments:

> The development of this barometer began not by asking whether this or that innovation was working, but whether this teaching worked better than possible alternatives; not by asking whether this innovation was having positive effects compared to not having the innovation, but whether the effects from this innovation were better for students than what they would achieve if they had received alternative innovations.
>
> For each of the many attributes investigated in [*Visible Learning*], the average of each influence is indexed by an arrow through one of the zones on the barometer. All influences above the [0.40] point are labeled in the 'Zone of desired effects' as these are the influences that have the greatest impact on student achievement outcomes.

An example of Hattie's barometer is seen in Figure 3.2. It relates to one of the teacher theories of action described in Chapter 12 that is well within Hattie's zone of desired effects.

The increasingly widespread use of effect size provides an understandable, accessible and reliable methodology for linking together the art and science of teaching in the pursuit of ever higher levels of student learning. The challenge for all teacher researchers and school improvers is to develop increasingly powerful specifications and strategies for teaching that will push the normal curve of distribution way to the right.

Two of Robert Slavin's many significant contributions to educational research are relevant to this discussion. First, over the past 25 years he has argued strenuously for the use of 'best evidence syntheses' as a means of codifying and presenting relevant research knowledge that has a practical and demonstrable impact on practice. Slavin (1986: 5) maintains that a 'best-evidence synthesis'

> combines the quantification of effect sizes and systematic study selection procedures of quantitative syntheses with the attention to individual studies and methodological and substantive issues typical of the best narrative reviews. Best-evidence syntheses focus on the 'best evidence' in a field, the studies highest in internal and external validity, using well specified and defended a priori inclusion criteria, and use effect size data as an adjunct to a full discussion of the literature being reviewed.

Each of our theories of action draws on a strong evidence base.

As we researched our ten theories of action, we found there was strong empirical evidence for their effectiveness. There are findings in the educational research that back up what we found together through our own observations and experiences during instructional rounds.

The concept of 'effect size' is helpful for describing the magnitude of the gains in student learning to be expected from applying each theory of action. 'Effect size' refers to the impact that the 'practice' has on the curve of normal distribution.

Take the effect size for higher order questions, which is the subject of one of our theories of action for teachers, when we employ higher order questions, the effect on student learning is positive.

As the graph below shows, when higher order questions are employed by teachers, the performance curve for their students (shown by the dotted line) moves to the right.

In his book, Visible Learning, John Hattie analyses the evidence about how different practices influence student learning. He assesses the results from more than 500,000 studies involving more than that 236 million students and teachers. He then presents the findings using the concept of 'effect size'.

The effect size is represented on a barometer like the one at the right. Hattie compares the influence on learning of each practice. The barometer shows the effect size of different practices on learning.

The Effect Size barometer

A barometer like this accompanies each theory of action on the following pages.

Some strategies fall in the zone below 0 Standard Deviation (SD). They impede learning.

Some learning is attributed to developmental effects – as children and young people grow, they develop new learning capabilities. Hattie tells us that learning occurring in the zone between 0 and 0.15 SD is learning that would probably occur even if there were no schooling.

The zone between 0.15 SD and 0.4 SD includes teaching strategies leading to learning outcomes that would occur in a typical year of schooling.

As teachers and school leaders, our task is to apply strategies that fall in the 0.15 SD and above 0.4 SD zones. They are high value strategies. Compared to other strategies, they have the largest effect size – that is, they make the biggest difference for our students' learning.

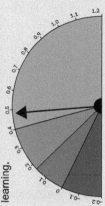

Effect Size for Higher Order Questions

ES = 75
— Control group
- - - Experimental group

	2 %	14 %	34 %	34 %	14 %	2 %	
Standard dimentions	-3rd	-2nd	-1st	0	1st	2nd	3rd
Cumulative percentages		2	16	50	54	95	99.9

Figure 3.1 Effect size for higher-order questions.

(text and diagrams reproduced from Northern Metropolitan Region 2011: 4).

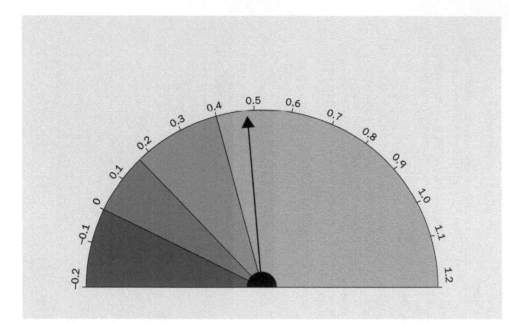

Figure 3.2   Hattie's barometer of success.

The second of Slavin's influences is his advocacy of randomized controlled trials in education (see for example, Coalition for Evidence-Based Policy, 2007). Well-designed randomized controlled trials, Slavin would argue, are recognized as the gold standard for evaluating the effectiveness of an intervention (i.e. programme or practice) in many diverse fields, such as medicine, welfare and employment, and psychology, but are relatively rare in education. This is because they are seen to be both too expensive and burdensome on schools to be practical. From his UK base at the University of York's Institute for Effective Education, Slavin has argued otherwise. He and colleagues have also produced a number of examples of randomized controlled trials, mainly in the USA, including a series on his own 'Success for All' literacy programme (Borman *et al.* 2007; Slavin and Madden 2009).

Hence, although still holding to the original critique of 'traditional approaches', it is important to recognize that more recent approaches to statistical research in education can offer important insights and tools for the teacher-researcher wishing to enhance their practice and the learning and achievement of their students.

The nature of classroom research

So far in this chapter I have been arguing for classroom research by teachers on three grounds: the first being its role in refining professional judgement; the second being its focus on the key professional activities of teachers; and the third being the inadequacy of existing research paradigms for teacher researchers. There is, however, a further issue on which to reflect when discussing the importance of classroom research: the nature of the research activity itself. This is an issue that has vexed teacher-researchers and those that comment on it for some time.

As a precursor to the discussion, let me quote from Ebbutt (1985: 157):

> If action research is to be considered legitimately as research, the participants in it must, it seems to me, be prepared to produce written reports of their activities.
>
> Moreover these reports ought to be available to some form of public critique. I would go as far as to say that if this condition is not satisfied by participants then no matter how personally and professionally valuable the exercise is in which they are engaged, it is not action research.

While I would agree with Ebbutt's call for written reports and critique, particularly by other teacher-researchers, I disagree with the implication that unless the research is published it is not research. It seems to me that many current commentators on classroom research have a misplaced conception of what research actually is. Michael Armstrong (1982) exemplified this position well:

> I have grown impatient with the concept of 'research'. In the context of a study of education it has acquired too narrow a connotation especially in regard to criteria for rigour, evidence and validity. I prefer the word 'enquiry' . . . The form of enquiry which I have in mind is grounded in the experience of teaching and in particular in that practice of sustained observation which is inseparable from good teaching.

Armstrong seems to be saying 'let's call it enquiry and let's keep it in the classroom and then we won't need to tangle with such questions as what counts as research'. Hull *et al.* (1985) complicate this position even further. They appear to say 'let's call what Armstrong does self-monitoring "an investigation of one's own practice in private" but let's recognize that there is also teacher research'. Hull *et al.* (1985) argue that teacher research

> must feed a tradition – from which individual researchers can derive support. In this way it is quite different from the activity which has been called 'self-monitoring' where a teacher uses some of the data-gathering techniques developed by researchers to record instances of their own practice as a basis for reflection. The self-monitoring teacher makes no claims to be methodologically reflexive. He or she does not undertake responsibility either to introduce 'system' into the investigations or make accounts of the studies available to other teachers. Self-monitoring is essentially a privatised encounter between a practitioner and practice. As such it has immense value. We conceive teacher research however, as potentially the root of a tradition of enquiry into educational processes which might stand alongside the academic tradition as an alternative body of knowledge rooted firmly in practice.

These claims are to me both confused and pedantic. The dichotomy that Armstrong and Hull and their co-workers point to is just not there. Armstrong's *Closely Observed Children* (1980) is one of the best teacher research studies. It is sensitive, insightful and profound; it is research at a high level of sophistication, imagination and rigour. Armstrong is doing teacher research in general, and himself in particular, a grave disservice to claim otherwise. One can readily appreciate Armstrong's 'impatience with the concept of research', but to call it something else is not to change anything. What he is impatient of is narrowly defined psycho-statistical research that has little to say to teachers, not research *per se*.

Research, inquiry and self-monitoring are all aspects of a similar activity because they all require systematic, self-conscious and rigorous reflection to be of any value. The problem is that psychological research, with its emphasis on statistical manipulation, has captured the educational imagination to such an extent that most people cannot think of research in any other terms. But criteria, such as validity or internal consistency, are necessary if teacher-researchers are to escape the sentimental anecdote that often replaces statistical research designs in education, and gives teacher research such a bad name. Inquiry, self-monitoring and teacher research need to establish standards and criteria that are applicable to their area of activity, rather than assume (and then reject) criteria designed for different procedures.

Teacher research, like inquiry and self-monitoring, is a form of research. These forms may be presented to different audiences and formulated in different ways, but all are attempts to create meaning out of complex situations. And the meaning is only valid when it is subject to certain methodological standards. It is naive to argue that just because we call what we do inquiry or self-monitoring instead of research we can escape the demand for valid judgement. Again, that is throwing the baby out with the bathwater. It is equally incorrect to assume that just because we engage in research, we have to follow the criteria of the psycho-statistical research paradigm. If these criteria are inappropriate then other more suitable methods, such as those discussed in subsequent chapters, have to be sought.

There are two important points to be drawn from this discussion. The first is that classroom research by teachers is a valid form of research because it results in hypotheses generated through a rigorous process of inquiry and grounded in the data to which they apply. This meets contemporary criteria for research. In the article to which I have already referred, Ebbutt (1985: 157) cites:

> Shulman's conception of what counts as research, that it is 'a family of methods which share the characteristics of disciplined inquiry' . . .
>
> 1   arguments and evidence can be examined
> 2   not dependent solely on eloquence or surface plausibility
> 3   avoids sources of error when possible and discusses margin for possible errors in conclusion
> 4   can be speculative, freewheeling and inventive.

This, it seems to me, is an accurate description of classroom research as it is being described in this book.

The second point is that it is important for teacher-researchers to open up their work to critique and, if possible, to publish it. The importance of public critique in classroom research is that it encourages a discourse among teachers, that is research-oriented and committed to action and the improvement of practice. It is the sharing of our experiences and the social and intellectual benefits that emanate from it, not the meeting of some abstract academic criteria, that provide the logic for publication and critique in classroom research. But the important point is that the mere fact of publication cannot be a judgement on the nature of the process that led (or did not lead) to publication. .

Further inquiry conducted in this way is informative and influential in planning actions for whole-school development. In addition, schools networking together which establish a learning focus for teacher inquiry drawn from school-level data or contextual evidence present new ways of studying and learning from what is happening in different schools and ways of improving learning opportunities for pupils. As the National College for School Leadership (2004) commented:

> We know that when teachers are engaged in actively researching and enquiring about existing practice, processes and outcomes with teachers from other schools they are more likely to improve their own analytical thinking and . . . to generate network-wide knowledge that can have a direct impact on the children in classrooms across all schools.

In this section, I have argued strenuously against those who claim that teacher research is not really research. Their position is untenable because: it is a capitulation in the face of the norms of traditional research; it devalues the quality of teacher research efforts; and it avoids the necessity of establishing a rigorous methodology for classroom research. For these reasons I am calling the form of research in which teachers do research in their own classrooms for the purpose of improving practice 'teacher research'. The phrase 'teacher research' has the advantage of being simple and identifies the major actor and the process involved. It is in this sense and with this aspiration that the terms 'classroom research by teachers', 'teacher-based research' and the 'teacher-researcher' are used in this book. It is the description of such an approach to classroom research that provides the substance of the following chapter.

Further reading

The notion of professionalism used in this chapter comprises a major theme in two of Lawrence Stenhouse's books: *An Introduction to Curriculum Research and Development* (1975) and *Authority, Education and Emancipation* (1983). An important discussion of the historical background to the nature of teacher professionalism is included in Dan Lortie's (2002) *School Teacher*. An excellent wide-ranging discussion of the practical implications of professionalism is found in Donald Schön's (1991) *The Reflective Practitioner* and (1996) *Educating the Reflective Practitioner: Toward a New Design for Teaching and Learning in the Professions*. A more contemporary discussion of reflective professionalism in teaching is found in the contributions to *Quality in Teaching*, edited by Wilf Carr (1989). Zeichner and Noffke's (2001) discussion on classroom research and its direct link to the teacher profession and Sachs's (2003) *The Activist Teaching Profession* (part of the *Professional Learning* series) plea for teachers to participate and contribute to a more democratic society are also of interest. For a more detailed exposition of Stenhouse's critique of the traditional approach to educational research, see *Research as a Basis for Teaching* (Rudduck and Hopkins 1985). An entertaining and comprehensive review of the arguments against traditional educational research as well as an alternative approach is found in *Beyond the Numbers Game* (Hamilton *et al.* 1977). These arguments are also well rehearsed in Winter's (1989) *Learning from Experience*, Carr and Kemmis's (1986) *Becoming Critical*, Elliott's (1991) *Action Research for Educational Change* and Carr's (1995) *For Education*. A broader perspective on this 'alternative approach' to educational research is found in texts such as Lincoln and Guba's (1985) *Naturalistic Inquiry* and in their chapter in Denzin and Lincoln's (2005) third edition of the *Sage Handbook of Qualitative Studies* entitled 'Paradigmatic Controversies, Contradictions and Emerging Confluences', Sara Delamont's (1992) witty and perceptive *Fieldwork in Educational Settings* and Colin Robson's (2011) comprehensive and wise *Real World Research*. A contemporary approach to curriculum development that embodies the perspectives of this chapter is found in Knight and Benson's (2013) *Creating Outstanding Classrooms*.

4 Action research and classroom research by teachers

In the previous chapter, I outlined a series of problems associated with the traditional approach to educational research that limits its usefulness for teachers who wish to improve their practice. There are, however, at least three other research traditions to which teachers can turn. One tradition is associated with the work of sociologists and anthropologists. Social anthropological, ethnographic, phenomenological, naturalistic and illuminative research are examples of these research approaches. These are long words that describe essentially the same approach – one that attempts to understand a social situation and to derive hypotheses from that effort of appreciation. The procedures that such social scientists have developed for analysing fieldwork data are used in this book as a guide for making sense of classroom data. They are described in some detail in Chapter 9.

The second approach is the research on teaching that has in recent years added another dimension to the work of the teacher-researcher. By developing specifications of teaching practices that have a proven impact on student learning, teachers now have a toolbox they can use to create ever more powerful learning experiences for their students. These are the specifications, guidelines or protocols that in Stenhouse's phrase are 'intelligent . . . worth putting to the test of practice'. They give increasing precision to teacher behaviours in the classroom, backed up by research evidence often using effect size analyses. We have already noted the work on *Visible Learning* by John Hattie (2009, 2012), and later, particularly in Chapters 11 and 12, will review *Looking in Classrooms* by Good and Brophy (2007) and the seminal work on *Models of Teaching* by Bruce Joyce and his colleagues (e.g. Joyce *et al.* 2009).

The third research tradition that is most closely associated with the themes of this book and has a strong link with contemporary social science research is the method known as action research. In recent years, teacher-researchers have adopted the label 'action research' to describe their particular approach to classroom research. In this chapter, I describe and critique this application of action research, and from the discussion propose six criteria for classroom research by teachers. To conclude the chapter, I look at the ethics for classroom research which should be a consideration for anyone carrying out such research.

Action research

Action research combines a substantive act with a research procedure; it is action disciplined by inquiry, a personal attempt at understanding while engaged in a process of improvement and reform.

Here are five definitions of action research. The first is by Robert Rapoport (1970), who says that action research

> aims to contribute both to the practical concerns of people in an immediate problematic situation and to the goals of social science by joint collaboration within a mutually acceptable ethical framework.

The second is by Stephen Kemmis (1983), who writes:

> Action research is a form of self-reflective enquiry undertaken by participants in social (including educational) situations in order to improve the rationality and justice of (a) their own social or educational practices, (b) their understanding of these practices, and (c) the situations in which the practices are carried out. It is most rationally empowering when undertaken by participants collaboratively, though it is often undertaken by individuals, and sometimes in cooperation with 'outsiders'. In education, action research has been employed in school-based curriculum development, professional development, school improvement programs, and systems planning and policy development.

The third is taken from a paper by Dave Ebbutt (1985), who not only gives a definition of his own, but also quotes from Kemmis. He writes that action research

> is about the systematic study of attempts to improve educational practice by groups of participants by means of their own practical actions and by means of their own reflection upon the effects of those actions.
>
> Put simply action research is the way groups of people can organise the conditions under which they can learn from their own experience. (Kemmis)
>
> Action research is trying out an idea in practice with a view to improving or changing something, trying to have a real effect on the situation. (Kemmis)

The fourth is from John Elliott (1991: 69; emphasis in original):

> Action-research might be defined as *the study of a social situation with a view to improving the quality of action within it*. It aims to feed practical judgement in concrete situations, and the validity of the 'theories' or hypotheses it generates depends not so much on 'scientific' tests of truth, as on their usefulness in helping people to act more intelligently and skillfully. In action-research 'theories' are not validated independently and then applied to practice. They are validated through practice.

The fifth and last is from Mills (2009)

> Action research is any systematic inquiry conducted by teacher researchers to gather information about the ways that their particular school operates, how they teach, and how well their students learn. The information is gathered with the goals of gaining insight, developing reflective practice, effecting positive changes in the school environment and on educational practices in general, and improving student outcomes.

The development of the idea of action research is generally attributed to Kurt Lewin, who in the immediate post-war period used it as a methodology for intervening in and researching the major social problems of the day. Lewin maintained that through action research advances in theory and needed social changes might simultaneously be achieved. Action research, according to Lewin, 'consisted in analysis, fact-finding, conceptualisation, planning execution, more fact-finding or evaluation; and then a repetition of this whole circle of activities; indeed a spiral of such circles' (quoted in Kemmis 1988: 13).

Lewin's ideas on action research were almost immediately applied to education, as well as to social science more generally. It was the work of Stephen Corey at Teacher's College, Columbia University, however – in particular, his book *Action Research to Improve School Practice* (1953) – that spread the word about action research into 'mainstream' American education.

More recently, action research has been seen as a methodology through which the aspirations of critical theory, which itself is regarded as an increasingly important trend in the philosophy of social science and the study of education, might be realized. Critical theory builds on the work of Marx, Freud and the traditions of the Frankfurt School of philosophy, in particular the writings of Jürgen Habermas. In line with the educational philosophy of Lawrence Stenhouse, the central purpose of critical theory is emancipation – enabling people to take control and direction over their own lives. An early commentator on critical theory and its educational implications was my colleague at Cambridge, the late Rex Gibson. Gibson (1986: 5–6) describes the central characteristic of critical theory as follows:

> Critical theory acknowledges the sense of frustration and powerlessness that many feel as they see their personal destinies out of their control, and in the hands of (often unknown) others ... Critical theory attempts to reveal those factors which prevent groups and individuals taking control of, or even influencing, those decisions which crucially affect their lives ... In the exploration of the nature and limits of power, authority and freedom, critical theory claims to afford insight into how greater degrees of autonomy could be available.
>
> This characteristic marks out critical theory's true distinctiveness: its claim to be *emancipatory*. Not only does it provide enlightenment (deeper awareness of your true interests); more than that (indeed, because of that), it can set you free. Unlike scientific theory, it claims to provide guidance as to what to do.

More recently, theorists have extended their interpretation of critical theory to include, among others, the work of Pierre Bourdieu and Antonio Gramsci. What connects the work of all these philosophers are concerns about the way power operates within social action and the ways various institutions and interests deploy power. When viewed through a more productive lens, critical theory can be regarded as a means of improving the human condition through the process of emancipation. In methodological terms the approach adopted has been described by Denzin and Lincoln (2011) as both 'dialogical (being a conversation with the reader) and dialectic (being an attempt to resolve the contradictions and conflicts that emerge in the production of power)'. In Joe Kincheloe's (2004: 83) emergent 'resistant version of critical theory' there is a recognition in action that 'human identities are shaped by their entanglement in the webs power weaves'.

In the even more recent past, Kevin Flint and his colleagues (e.g. Flint and Peim 2012) have begun to explore a practice-based approach derived from critical theory using 'deconstruction' as the key analytic tool. In doing this, Flint has been heavily influenced by the work of Martin Heidegger. Heidegger sees deconstruction as a process of exploring and critiquing the concepts and realities that our cultural history has generated, in order to understand them and as a consequence to be potentially liberated from them. To Jacques Derrida this approach is necessary but not sufficient, as he argued that deconstruction should also involve the creation of new concepts. This is the process of emancipation, and action research can also be regarded as a methodology for achieving this. Flint's practice-based approach provides a range of examples including a focus on school improvement, research and the understanding of 'place' in education (Flint 2014).

Obviously, neither critical theory nor action research are panaceas and they should not be regarded as such. We shall continue to see in this book, however, that their practical applications do provide a rationale and method for teachers who wish to take more control of their professional (and personal) lives. From even this brief description, it can be seen how the method of action research with its twin emphasis on committed action and reflection is particularly suited to putting into practice such an emancipatory philosophy. There is also a pleasing symmetry between this more abstract discussion and the practical educational philosophy of Lawrence Stenhouse, and those who have followed his lead, as we see in the following section.

Models of action research

The combination of the action and the research components has a powerful appeal for teachers. In the UK, Lawrence Stenhouse was quick to point to the connection between action research and his concept of the teacher as researcher. Later, John Elliott popularized action research as a method for teachers doing research in their own classrooms through the Ford Teaching Project, and established the Classroom Action Research Network.

Subsequently, Stephen Kemmis refined and formalized the concept of action research and how it applies to education. His articles on action research (Kemmis 1983,

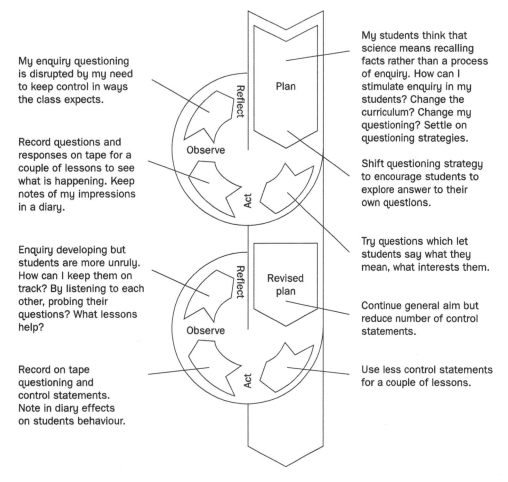

My enquiry questioning is disrupted by my need to keep control in ways the class expects.

Record questions and responses on tape for a couple of lessons to see what is happening. Keep notes of my impressions in a diary.

Enquiry developing but students are more unruly. How can I keep them on track? By listening to each other, probing their questions? What lessons help?

Record on tape questioning and control statements. Note in diary effects on students behaviour.

Reflect

Plan

Observe

Act

Reflect

Revised plan

Observe

Act

My students think that science means recalling facts rather than a process of enquiry. How can I stimulate enquiry in my students? Change the curriculum? Change my questioning? Settle on questioning strategies.

Shift questioning strategy to encourage students to explore answer to their own questions.

Try questions which let students say what they mean, what interests them.

Continue general aim but reduce number of control statements.

Use less control statements for a couple of lessons.

Figure 4.1   The 'action research spiral'.

(based on Kemmis and McTaggart 1988: 14).

1988) are a useful review of how educational action research has developed from the work of Lewin and established its own character. Of more interest to us here is his 'action research planner' (Kemmis and McTaggart 1988), where a sequential programme for teachers intending to engage in action research is outlined in some detail. He summarizes his approach to action research in the model shown in Figure 4.1.

John Elliott was quick to take up Kemmis's schema of the action research spiral and he, too, produced a similar but more elaborate model, as seen in Figure 4.2. Elliott (1991: 70) summarizes Kemmis's approach and then outlines his elaborations as follows:

> Although I think Lewin's model is an excellent basis for starting to think about what action research involves, it can allow those who use it to assume that 'the

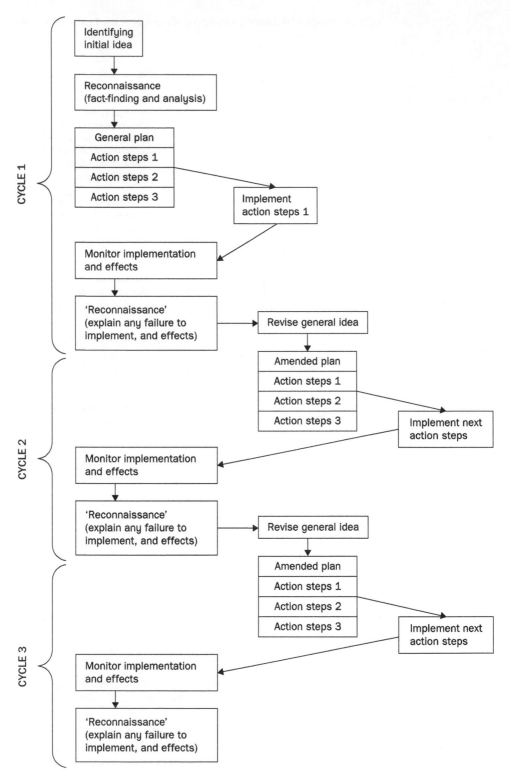

Figure 4.2 Elliott's action research model.

(from Elliott 1991: 71).

general idea' can be fixed in advance, that 'reconnaissance' is merely fact-finding and that 'Implementation' is a fairly straightforward process. But I would argue that:

- The general idea should be allowed to shift.
- 'Reconnaissance' should involve analysis as well as fact-finding, and should constantly recur in the spiral of activities, rather than occur only at the beginning.
- 'Implementation' of an action-step is not always easy, and one should not proceed to evaluate the effects of an action until one has monitored the extent to which it has been implemented.

Dave Ebbutt (1985), a colleague of Elliott, provides us with another variation on Kemmis's model and makes these comments about it:

> It seems clear to me that Elliott is wrong in one respect, in suggesting that Kemmis equates reconnaissance with fact finding only. The Kemmis diagram clearly shows reconnaissance to comprise discussing, negotiating, exploring opportunities, assessing possibilities and examining constraints – in short there are elements of analysis in the Kemmis notion of reconnaissance. Nevertheless I suggest that the thrust of Elliott's three statements is an attempt on the part of a person experienced in directing action research projects to recapture some of the 'messiness' of the action-research cycle which the Kemmis version tends to gloss.

But Ebbutt (1985) claims that the spiral is not the most useful metaphor. Instead, the most

> appropriate way to conceive of the process of action research is to think of it as comprising of a series of successive cycles, each incorporating the possibility for the feedback of information within and between cycles. Such a description is not nearly so neat as conceiving of the process as a spiral, neither does it lend itself quite so tidily to a diagrammatic representation. In my view the idealized process of educational action research can be more appropriately represented [as shown in Figure 4.3].

A number of other similar models have recently been developed, most of which build on Lewin's original idea or Kemmis's interpretation of it. For example, James McKernan (1996) has suggested a 'time process' model (see Figure 4.4) which emphasizes the importance of not allowing an action research 'problem' to become too rigidly fixed in time, and of rational problem solving and democratic ownership by the community of researchers.

My purpose in presenting these practical models of action research is twofold. First, my aim has been to provide an overview of action research to help the reader gain an understanding of the whole process. Second, it is to demonstrate that despite the proliferation of eponymous 'models', they do, in fact, share more similarities than

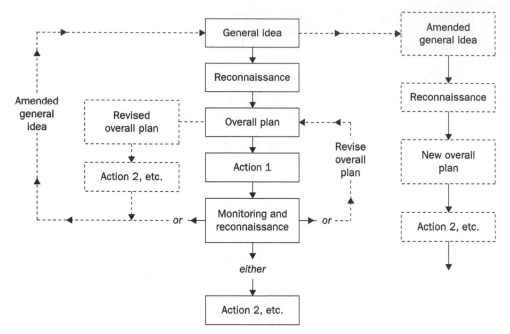

Idealized representation of the process of action research

Figure 4.3 Ebbutt's model.

(from Ebbutt 1985).

differences. There is a high degree of consensus among those who write on the subject about overall method and purpose. There are, however, some problems inherent in these models, and to these I now turn.

Critique of educational action research

There are three main areas of concern that I have with the action research models developed by Kemmis, Elliott, Ebbutt, McKernan and others. Although this is not the place for a thorough critique, a brief discussion of these concerns is necessary because the problems may lead teacher researchers into possible confusion. Also, the critique will help explain the form and structure of the rest of the book.

My first concern is that there may be a misunderstanding of the nature of Lewinian action research. As I mentioned earlier, the term 'action research' was coined as a useful label to describe what teacher-researchers were doing. Much energy has been devoted to setting out the intellectual basis for action research as it derived from Lewin. Lewin's concept of action research is, however, very different in some respects from what goes on in the name of teacher research. Lewin's concept of action research was (1) as

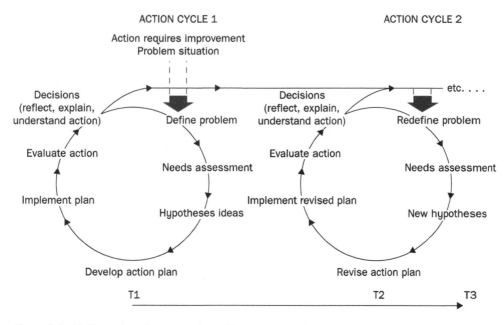

Figure 4.4   McKernan's action research model

(from McKernan 1996: 29).

an externally initiated intervention designed to assist a client system, (2) functionalist in orientation and (3) prescriptive in practice. None of these features apply to what I assume to be the nature of classroom research by teachers which is characterized by its practitioner, problem-solving, and eclectic orientation.

We should take care that what began as a useful label to describe teacher research for professional development purposes does not assume a different character as a result of a quest for intellectual credibility.

My second concern relates to the specification of process in the action research models. There are three interrelated points. The first is that the tight specification of process steps and cycles may trap teachers within a framework which they may come to depend on and which will, consequently, inhibit independent action. The original purpose of teacher research was to free teachers from the constraints of prespecified research designs. It is useful to have a guide for action; my concern is when it becomes, or appears to become, prescriptive. Second, the models outline a process rather than a technology. They delineate a sequence of stages, but say little about the 'what' and the 'how' within these stages. Third, the models may appear daunting and confusing to practitioners. Ebbutt himself admits that Elliott's framework tends to 'mystification'.

Unfortunately, models and frameworks cannot mirror reality: they are one individual's interpretation of reality. Consequently, they impose upon the user a prespecified analysis of a process that the user may quite rightly interpret differently. At best, they provide a starting point, an initial guide to action. At worst, they trap the practitioners within a set of assumptions that bear little relationship to their reality and, consequently, constrain their freedom of action.

The line between specifying principles of procedure that encourage informed action, and prescribing activities that determine behaviour and limit outcomes, is a fine one indeed. There is a real danger that teacher research will assume the character of the objectives model, which 'is like a site-plan simplified so that people know exactly where to dig their trenches without having to know why' (Stenhouse 1980). To use Jean Rudduck's felicitous phrase, it seems that already 'the elusive butterfly of teacher research has been caught and pinned'.

My third concern is a semantic one. There is a tendency for some 'action researchers' to overuse words and phrases such as 'problem', 'improve' and 'needs assessment'. This could give the impression that action research is a deficit model of professional development: 'something is wrong, so do this to make it better'. I know that this is not the intention, and I am as guilty of this as anyone in this regard, but it does behove all of us to talk (and write) about classroom research in as positive a way as we can. At the present time, the teaching profession in the UK is suffering from low morale largely as a result of ill-informed public and political criticism. Action research is one way of restoring and enhancing professional confidence.

These concerns notwithstanding, the importance of action research is not to be underestimated. Action research provides teachers with a more appropriate alternative to traditional research designs and one that is, in aspiration at least, emancipatory. We must, however, be aware of the problems associated with too prescriptive a framework for action and the values that are embedded within it. Consequently, I tend to use terms such as 'classroom research by teachers' rather than 'action research'. This is not a fundamental point of difference with those colleagues I have cited earlier. It does, however, serve to emphasize the importance of the acquisition of skills and techniques that become part of a teacher's repertoire and which are then subject to the exercise of their professional judgement.

The student perspective

The importance of students' participation in research and action research has been highlighted more recently. The late Jean Rudduck's work has been particularly influential (e.g. Rudduck and Flutter 2004), as has been the importance given to the role of the student in the IQEA programme (Beresford 2003).

The research by Jean Rudduck (Rudduck and Flutter 2004) has shown that there is considerable potential in consulting students not only to strengthen their commitment to learning but also to contribute to the classroom research process. This involves a range of impacts that student voice has, such as:

- developing their capacity to reflect on learning, leading to a greater control over how they learn and how to improve it;
- making students feel respected and listened to in the school and developing a positive sense of self;
- developing new capacity to take up more roles and responsibilities;

- giving students a sense of belonging and a positive membership of the school and the classroom;
- seeing teachers more positively.

Such potential, however, is very much dependent on successful implementation. Activities that involve students in decision-making have to be well thought through, rather than treated as just another task to be completed. They also have to move beyond the tokenism that sadly often accompanies efforts to secure student voice.

This emphasis on involving students in classroom research has led to the development of models where students are seen not only as 'data sources' or 'active respondents' but also as 'co-researchers' with teachers or as 'researchers' themselves (Fielding 2004). The work of Michael Fielding (2004) on student voice is relevant here (we explore student voice a bit further in Chapter 8). He advocates that transformation is more likely to be realized through the active participation of students in the research process and believes that students can be radical agents of change. Although his work is not a step-by-step model of action research such as the ones described above, he provides a clear conceptual framework on how student participation in action research for transformation can occur.

Fielding sees 'students as co-researchers', as partners in the inquiry to be conducted and in the development of instruments and analysis. However, teachers are the driving force and the research lies predominantly with them. The following example explains the process:

> Thus, a primary school teacher keen to develop more independent learning with her Year 1 students asked them their view of independence in learning, what it meant, what it felt like, what it looked like. She and the class discussed these matters, developed an observation schedule, jointly videoed lessons, sat down and looked at the video data, discussed what it meant to them, and developed new learning and teaching practices together. Here the teacher learned things about independence in learning from her engagement and dialogue with her student co-researchers that she could not have done from traditional action research. Similarly, her students as co-researchers learned things about independence in learning, about their individual and collective agency that they could not have learned in other ways.
>
> (Fielding 2004: 306)

As implied, the notion of 'students as researchers' places students/pupils in the role of the researcher. Students are trained in research and attend the same training sessions as their teachers and are responsible for identifying the topic of the investigation and selecting the methods of data gathering and analysis. Teachers assist students in the process, but 'student leadership is constitutive and distinctive of this approach' (Fielding 2004: 307). Fielding argues that the premise of this model is that students have a different standpoint from that of teachers and so different understandings of similar issues and their importance. This can result in innovation and renewal. Table 4.1 demonstrates the principles and values for this model.

Table 4.1   Levels of student (pupil) involvement in school self-review and school improvement (Fielding 2001: 136–7)

Students as DATA SOURCE	Students as ACTIVE RESPONDENTS	Students as CO-RESEARCHERS	Students as RESEARCHERS
(a) Rationale & engagement			
Rationale Teachers need to know about students' prior learning/ perceptions of their learning in order to teach effectively	**Rationale** Teachers need to engage students in order to fully enhance both teaching and learning	**Rationale** Teachers need to engage students as partners in learning in order to deepen understanding and learning	**Rationale** Students need to engage with their teachers and peers in order to deepen understanding and learning
What Kind of Knowledge is Used Knowing about student performance and attitudes towards learning	**What Kind of Knowledge is Used** Knowing how students learn	**What Kind of Knowledge is Used** Knowing what students might be able to contribute to deepen understanding	**What Kind of Knowledge is Used** Knowing what teachers and peers might be able to contribute to deepen understanding
How Teachers Engage with Students Acknowledging	**How Teachers Engage with Students** Hearing	**How Teachers Engage with Students** Listening in order to learn	**How Teachers Engage with Students** Listening in order to contribute
Student Role Recipients	**Student Role** Discussants	**Student Role** Co-researchers	**Student Role** Initiators
How Meaning is Made Dissemination	**How Meaning is Made** Discussion	**How Meaning is Made** Dialogue (teacher led)	**How Meaning is Made** Dialogue (student led)
(b) Classroom (pedagogy), Department/Team, School			
Classroom e.g. • data about student past performance	**Classroom** e.g. • shared lesson objectives • explicit assessment criteria	**Classroom** e.g. • feedback techniques on pedagogy (teacher led) • developing metacognition	**Classroom** e.g. • feedback techniques on pedagogy (student led) • developing metacognition & shared responsibility for learning
Department/Team e.g. • looking at samples of student work	**Department/Team** e.g. • department agenda based on student perception data/ suggested by pupils	**Department/Team** e.g. • students co-research aspects of pedagogy/learning with teacher	**Department/Team** e.g. • students run session for staff on how to engage with particular learning styles

- teacher-led action research (ask students for feedback)
- pupils involved in evaluation of unit of work

- student suggestions for new units of work

Classroom research by teachers

My preference for the phrase 'classroom research by teachers' rather than 'action research' will not lead me to produce an alternative step-by-step model. Instead, I will present a series of methods and techniques that teachers can use in their classroom research efforts. In particular, I will discuss:

1   ways in which classroom research projects can be identified and initiated (Chapter 5);
2   principles and methods of classroom observation and of other ways of gathering data on classroom behaviours (Chapters 6–8);
3   ways of interpreting and analysing the data gathered from classroom research (Chapter 9);
4   ways in which classroom research can be reported (Chapter 10);
5   ways in which classroom research methods can be linked to a focus on teaching and learning (Chapter 11);
6   how staff development activities and networking can support teacher and school development (Chapter 12).

My purpose in tackling classroom research in this way is to give teachers an introduction to the variety of methods available to them as a means of extending their repertoire of professional practices and of encouraging flexibility in professional development. These are methods and approaches that teachers can put into use, that will empower them, and make them increasingly competent and 'autonomous in professional judgement'.

Criteria for classroom research by teachers

The essence of what I am advocating is the development of a teacher's professional skill, expertise and judgement. Although many teachers are in broad agreement with this general aim, some are quite rightly concerned about how far involvement in classroom research activity will impinge upon their teaching and on their personal time. Concerns are also raised as to the utilitarian or practical value of classroom research. With these concerns in mind, let me suggest the following six principles for classroom research by teachers.

The first is that the teacher's primary job is to teach, and any research method should not interfere with or disrupt the teaching commitment. This rule of thumb should serve to quell immediate concerns. I am prepared to stand behind the teacher's judgement, particularly if the teacher is involved in activities focused on improving the teaching and the learning experience of his or her students. The research focus undertaken by the teacher should also be one to which he or she is committed. Although this sounds self-evident, it is difficult enough, given all the pressures on a teacher's time, to sustain energy in a project even if it is intrinsically interesting and important to the teacher's professional activities. As a corollary, the problem must in fact be a problem; that is, the problem must be capable of solution, else by definition it is not a problem. In becoming a teacher-researcher, the individual teacher is deliberately and consciously expanding his or her role to include a professional element. It is almost inconceivable, then, that he or she would do this and at the same time ignore the primacy of the teaching/learning process.

The second criterion is that the method of data collection must not be too demanding on the teacher's time. As a consequence, the teacher needs to be certain about the data collection technique before using it. The reasons for this are obvious. Teachers already consider themselves overworked and there are continuing demands for increased preparation and professional development time. It is naive to assume that the adoption of a research role will make no inroads on a teacher's private time. This can be reduced, however, by judicious use of specific data collection techniques, and the utilization of easily analysed diagnostic methods. For example, take the contrast between the use of the tape-recorder and the iPad as tools for the classroom researcher. It takes approximately 50 per cent longer to listen to a tape than to make it, and on top of that transcription (which is necessary if full use is to be made of the method) is both time-consuming and expensive. The iPad is a much more flexible method for broad-spectrum diagnosis and for assessing the narrative and flow of a lesson. It is best to use the iPad initially and then perhaps use other methods for more specific and finely focused enquiries. A number of techniques for classroom observation are discussed in Chapter 7 and a taxonomy of data collection techniques is presented in Chapter 8.

The third principle is perhaps the most contentious. The methodology employed must be reliable enough to allow teachers to formulate hypotheses confidently and develop strategies applicable to their classroom situation. Traditional researchers hold a poor opinion of action research. In many cases, that opinion is well founded, particularly if it is based on individual pieces of research. It behoves all researchers, be they psycho-statisticians engaged in large-scale research or primary teachers testing Piaget's theoretical hypotheses, to be rigorous about their methodology. It is no excuse at all to claim that rigour is unnecessary because the research is practitioner oriented, small scale or used solely to improve individual practice. If a change in teaching strategy is to be made, then that decision needs to be based on reliable data. These issues form the substance of Chapter 9.

The fourth criterion is the importance of involving students in the classroom research process. As we have seen, developing the role of the 'student as a researcher' and the 'student as a co-researcher' can not only produce significant data for the classroom research, but also support students' thinking and learning, and leadership skills significantly. This approach is also consistent with the UN Convention on the Rights of the Child (1989). The four basic principles include the child's right to be heard (Article 12 – The views of the child). This justifies, I believe, the emphasis in this book on personalized learning and in particular the importance of student voice.

The fifth criterion refers to the need for teacher-researchers to pay close attention to the ethical procedures surrounding their work. Ethical standards for classroom researchers were worked out during the 1970s and 1980s by researchers associated with the Centre for Applied Research in Education (e.g. MacDonald and Walker 1974; Simons 1982, 1987). A summary of ethical procedures for teacher-researchers can be found in at the end of this chapter.

The sixth criterion is that as far as possible classroom research should adopt a classroom exceeding' perspective. What I mean by this is that all members of a school community actively build and share a common vision of their main purpose. Teachers are now increasingly relating the teaching and learning focus of their classroom research efforts to whole-school priorities through the use of classroom observation techniques. They adapt educational ideas and policies to suit their own context and professional needs. The main focus for action is the teaching and learning in classrooms, in order that all students develop 'the intellectual and imaginative powers and competencies' that they need in as personalized a way as possible. Such classroom practice can only be sustained through ongoing staff development. These principles characterize an approach to teacher and school development that builds on the methods and philosophy of classroom research. In Chapters 11 and 12 we see how this can fit into an overall strategy for school and system improvement.

In the chapters that follow, these criteria will be dealt with in more detail. In the next chapter, the ways of developing a focus for classroom research projects are discussed. Before this however, we need to review the ethical procedures to be followed by classroom researchers.

Ethics for classroom research

It is paramount that classroom research teachers, as part of the wider research community, are fastidious in taking into consideration and meeting ethical standards posed by such communities. First, in this section, we will briefly refer to a framework established for social researchers before examining the ethical principles and considerations that apply specifically to classroom research.

There are a number of approaches to research ethics. According to the Economic and Social Research Council (ESRC 2012: 40), research ethics 'refers to the moral principles guiding research, from its inception through to completion and publication of results and beyond – for example, the curation of data and physical samples after the research has been published'.

The six key principles underpinning ethical research, wherever applicable, should include (ESRC 2012: 2–3):

1   Research should be designed, reviewed and undertaken to ensure integrity, quality and transparency.

2   Research staff and subjects must be informed fully about the purpose, methods and intended possible uses of the research, what their participation in the research entails and what risks, if any, are involved. Some variation is allowed in very specific and exceptional research contexts for which detailed guidance is provided in the policy guidelines.

3   The confidentiality of information supplied by research subjects and the anonymity of respondents must be respected.

4   Research participants must take part voluntarily, free from any coercion.

5   Harm to research participants and researchers must be avoided in all instances.

6   The independence of research must be clear, and any conflicts of interest or partiality must be explicit.

The ESRC guidelines, as one can easily recognize, are intentionally vague so that researchers are able to interpret them in ways that fit the needs of the specific research they are undertaking (Smyth and Williamson 2004: 10), also allowing researchers to make ethical decisions based on their own morality and the issues raised by their research project. And classroom researchers should do exactly that.

Action researchers must trust the ethical decisions they take, when these do not come in conflict with the above key principles, but also with those of their particular organization. As Kemmis and McTaggart (1988: 43–4) remind us, classroom researchers' 'actions are deeply embedded in an existing social organization and the failure to work within the general procedures of that organization may not only jeopardize the process of improvement but existing valuable work'. Principles of procedure for action research accordingly go beyond the usual concerns for confidentiality and respect for the persons who are the subjects of enquiry and define, in addition, appropriate ways of working with other participants in the social organization. The principles outlined below reflect the commitment implicit in the methods of action research to participation and collaborative work, and negotiation within, and ultimately beyond, existing social and political circumstances.

Observe protocol: Take care to ensure that the relevant persons, committees and authorities have been consulted, informed and that the necessary permission and approval has been obtained.

Involve participants: Encourage others who have a stake in the improvement you envisage to shape the form of the work.

Negotiate with those affected: Not everyone will want to be directly involved; your work should take account of the responsibilities and wishes of others.

Report progress: Keep the work visible and remain open to suggestions so that unforeseen and unseen ramifications can be taken account of; colleagues must have the opportunity to lodge a protest to you.

Obtain explicit authorization before you observe: For the purposes of recording the activities of professional colleagues or others (the observation of your own students falls outside this imperative provided that your aim is the improvement of teaching and learning).

Obtain explicit authorization before you examine files, correspondence or other documentation: Take copies only if specific authority to do this is obtained.

Negotiate descriptions of people's work: Always allow those described to challenge your accounts on the grounds of fairness, relevance and accuracy.

Negotiate accounts of others' points of view (e.g. in accounts of communication): Always allow those involved in interviews, meetings and written exchanges to require amendments which enhance fairness, relevance and accuracy.

Obtain explicit authorization before using quotations: Verbatim transcripts, attributed observations, excerpts of audio and video recordings, judgements, conclusions or recommendations in reports (written or to meetings).

Negotiate reports for various levels of release: Remember that different audiences demand different kinds of reports; what is appropriate for an informal verbal report to a faculty meeting may not be appropriate for a staff meeting, a report to council, a journal article, a newspaper, a newsletter to parents; be conservative if you cannot control distribution.

Accept responsibility for maintaining confidentiality.

Retain the right to report your work: Provided that those involved are satisfied with the fairness, accuracy and relevance of accounts which pertain to them; and that the accounts do not unnecessarily expose or embarrass those involved; then accounts should not be subject to veto or be sheltered by prohibitions of confidentiality.

Make your principles of procedure binding and known: All of the people involved in your action research project must agree to the principles before the work begins; others must be aware of their rights in the process.

Classroom researchers have also to acknowledge their ethical responsibility towards their own personal biases. Our own background, values and beliefs and cultural understandings inevitably have an impact on our decisions about the research. We construct reality through our own ideas and 'truths' which many, and justifiably, would argue is 'our truth'. However, research needs to be as objective as possible, and as any claim to objectivity or to a 'value-free' position is an illusion, personal biases have to be identified throughout the research process and strategies to minimize them have to be employed.

If we were to match the classroom researchers' ethical considerations with each of the research stages, as at any stage during research ethical issues could materialize (Cohen *et al.* 2011), then we should be able to confidently answer the following questions:

Preparation stage

1   Should you do the research at all?
2   What ethical issues may arise from your research?
3   If your research includes children, what ethical issues could arise from the ages of the children involved?
4   Whose interests is the research serving?

Before the data collection

1   Whose consent do you need?
2   Have you fully explained to the participants the reasons for the research, its methods and possible implications?
3   Have you made clear to participants that they have the right to withdraw at any stage of the research?
4   Are participants assured confidentiality?
5   How have you made sure that the participants have understood the above? Have you used language that they comprehend?

During the data collection

1   Are you true to your promises to participants?
2   Is the research causing participants the minimum disruption?
3   Are you storing confidential data safely so that they are not accessible by others?
4   Are the data reliable and valid?

During the data analysis

1   Are findings reliable and valid?
2   Have you been reporting parts of your findings periodically to stakeholders?

During the report writing and dissemination

1   Are you writing the truth?
2   Have you ensured that none of the participants can be identified?
3   Have you considered the different audiences and dissemination approaches for your research?

From Kemmis and McTaggart (1988) with permission of Deakin University.

Further reading

One of the earliest examples of teacher-based research was the Humanities Curriculum Project, and the approach is still worth considering (Stenhouse 1970, 1983). Of similar interest are the accounts of the Ford Teaching Project (Elliott and Adelman 1976) and the materials from Deakin University, for example their *Action Research Reader* (1998). There are a number of well-known articles on Lewinian action research which, although rather technical and specialized, may be of interest (see Corey 1953; Lewin 1946; Rapoport 1970; Sandford 1970). The literature on action research and critical theory is growing. Carr and Kemmis's (1986) *Becoming Critical* provides an extensive rationale for action research. See also Carr and Kemmis's (2005) article, 'Staying Critical', in which they revisit their book and identify the need in any new edition to demonstrate the possibility and desirability of 'staying critical' in the postmodern world. Elliot's (2005) retrospective critique of their book is also of interest. Rex Gibson's (1986) *Critical Theory and Education* provides an excellent introduction, while Young's

(1989) *A Critical Theory of Education* is more theoretical. A discussion of how critical theory underpins school improvement is found in *School Improvement For Real* (Hopkins 2001: Chapter 2). Of much interest is the work of Stephen Kemmis. His articles on action research (Kemmis 1983, 1988, 2005, 2006) provide an excellent overview of the topic, and the revised *Action Research Planner* (Kemmis and McTaggart 1988) not only contains a step-by-step guide, but also has useful introductory essays on action research. Background reading on the teacher-researcher movement and its educational context can be found in Stenhouse's (1975) *An Introduction to Curriculum Research and Development* and John Elliott's (1991) *Action Research for Educational Change.*

5 Developing a focus

Engaging in classroom research is often, initially, an unnerving and occasionally threatening experience. Trying anything new involves uncertainty, and this is particularly true of teacher research. Increasingly, however, teachers are regarding the 'researching of practice' as part of their professional responsibilities. It is important, therefore, that the first criterion mentioned in the previous chapter – that of identifying and being committed to a topic for classroom research which is stated in workable terms – is adhered to. But even when this is the case, it is often difficult to establish a precise focus for the inquiry. For these reasons, in this chapter I review some ways in which teachers can develop a focus for classroom research, establish research questions and engage in theorizing. In short, this chapter deals with how to get started on classroom research.

Developing your research focus

Teacher research does not necessarily start with the setting of precise hypotheses! As Kemmis and McTaggart (1988: 18) point out in their first edition of *The Action Research Planner*:

> You do not have to begin with a 'problem'. All you need is a general idea that something might be improved. Your general idea may stem from a promising new idea or the recognition that existing practice falls short of aspiration. In either case you must centre attention on:
>
> - What is happening now?
> - What could be improved?
> - What can I do about it?
>
> General starting points may be:
>
> - I would like to improve the . . .
> - Some people are unhappy about . . .

- What can I do to change the situation?
- I am perplexed by . . .
- . . . is a source of irritation. What can I do about it?
- I have an idea I would like to try out in my class.
- How can the experience of . . . be applied to . . .?
- Just what do I do with respect to . . .?

This approach is consistent with contemporary approaches to educational change and development. In his recent book, but with a more action orientation, Michael Fullan (2011a: 12) concurs with our inductive approach: 'don't try to figure out someone else's theory but rather use practice to get at theory, and more directly use practice to discover strategies that work'. Building on Duggan's (2007) argument in *Strategic Intuition: The Creative Spark in Human Achievement*, he suggests the following sequence:

- **Step 1**. Examine your own practice and results and identify what might be lacking.
- **Step 2**. Look in the laboratories of other practitioners in similar circumstances who seem to be achieving success.
- **Step 3**. Building on Steps 1 and 3, try out something new in your own practice.
- **Step 4**. If it works, draw a conclusion – your new theory – and do more of it, learning as you go.

Fullan (2011a: 13) then comments:

> In short, the new theory is the product of considered practice. It is not just that the change leaders immerse themselves in action, but rather they use it as the best source of evidence and insights. They do analyse, but their analysis is based on substance.

Given that this approach is so generic, as you read these extracts, no doubt certain ideas or topics for classroom research come to mind. These ideas may also relate to the priorities on the school's improvement plan, or to the school's values, targets or mission statement. More likely they will relate to practical and immediate concerns, such as a particular aspect of a scheme of work, or a troublesome individual or class. It is worth taking a few minutes to jot down these ideas. Do not worry about how well they are formed; at this stage it is more important to generate a list of topics from which you can work. Having produced a list, the next step is to evaluate the usefulness, viability and/or importance of the individual issue. There are a number of guidelines that can be of use here.

First, do not tackle issues that you cannot do anything about. For example, it may be impossible in the short or medium term to alter the banding or streaming system in your school or to change the textbook that you are using. Because you cannot do anything about it, either avoid the issue or rephrase it in a more solvable form. So, although you cannot change the textbook, it may be possible to experiment with different ways the text could be used as evidence in your classes.

Second, only take on, at least initially, small-scale and relatively limited issues. There are several reasons for this. It is important to build on success, and a small-scale project satisfactorily completed in a short space of time is reinforcing and encouraging. It is also very easy to underestimate the scale and amount of time a project will take. It is very discouraging to have found after the initial flush of enthusiasm that you have bitten off more than you can chew.

Third, choose an issue that is important to you or to your students, or one that you have to be involved with anyway in the course of your normal school activities. The topic that you focus on needs to be intrinsically motivating. If not, then again after the initial flush of enthusiasm and when the difficulties begin to build up, you will find that motivation will begin to evaporate.

Fourth, as far as possible try to work collaboratively on the focus of your classroom research. Professional partnerships, as is seen in the examples throughout the book, are a powerful form of staff development and personal support. They are also a way of reducing the isolation that some teachers work in.

Finally, make connections between your classroom research work, teaching and learning, and the school's improvement plan priorities or the school's values. Although there need not be a direct relationship, it is important to relate one's individual professional inquiry to whole-school initiatives and the direction in which the school is moving.

In summary, it is necessary to select an initial focus for classroom research that is viable, discrete, intrinsically interesting, involves collaboration and is related in some way to teaching and learning and whole-school concerns.

Performance gap

There is a body of research in education that suggests: (1) there is often incongruence between a teacher's publicly declared philosophy or beliefs about education and how they behave in the classroom; (2) there is often incongruence between the teacher's declared goals and objectives and the way in which the lesson is actually taught; and (3) there is often a discrepancy between a teacher's perceptions or account of a lesson, and the perceptions or account of other participants (e.g. pupils or observers) in the classroom (see Elbaz 1983). All of these discrepancies reflect a gap between behaviour and intention. The Ford Teaching Project also monitored the 'performance gap' between teachers' aspirations and their practice. These issues have more recently been commented on in contemporary reports on the state of primary education. The 'performance gap' therefore forms an important starting point for classroom research enquiries and represents an important tradition in classroom action research.

Dave Ebbutt (1985) writes about 'the performance gap' as follows:

> It is via the notion of a performance gap – a gap between espoused theory and theory in action – by which advocates of action research locate its niche as an

appropriate mode of research in schools and classrooms. For instance Kemmis in his *Planner* [Kemmis and McTaggart (1988)] uses this illustrative example:

> There is a gap between the idea and the reality of inquiry teaching in my own classroom. Recognising this gap, I must develop a strategy of action if improvements in this kind of questioning are to be achieved . . .

If you now return to the list of possible classroom research topics that you have just generated, there is probably implicit in each of the topics a description of what is currently happening (that provides a basis for reflection) and an indication of some new action connected to the existing behaviour that will lead to improvement. So, for example, in the case studies in Chapter 2, the teachers identified an existing teaching behaviour and at the same time thought of ways in which this aspect of their teaching could be improved. It is this gap between what is and what could be that is an important source of motivation in classroom research by teachers.

Ebbutt (1985) also illustrates the notion of the performance gap by posing six simple questions to demonstrate the gap between the curriculum in action and the curriculum as intention:

1   What did the pupils actually do?
2   What were they learning?
3   How worthwhile was it?
4   What did I do?
5   What did I learn?
6   What do I intend to do now?

The concept of the performance gap is useful in refining your list of topics for classroom research. The identification of a gap between what is and what could be provides motivation for change and indicates a direction for improvement. Action leads out of existing behaviours towards a new articulated goal.

Contemporary educational research has given increasing sharpness to the concept of the performance gap in reflecting on classroom practice. As an educational community we are becoming increasingly secure about our understandings of the impact of a range of teaching behaviours on the performance and achievement of students. We have already noted Hattie's (2009) synthesis of over 800 meta-analyses on the influences on achievement of school-aged students in *Visible Learning*. Hattie's 'barometer of effects' provides a tool for predicting the impact of a wide range of teaching practices of student learning. So, for example, we have already seen in Chapter 3 the effect size (0.73) associated with higher-order questioning. If a teacher is using higher-order questions according to a research-based specification and her students are not performing close to the 65th percentile, then she has to ask why. This discrepancy – performance gap – becomes the focus of her classroom research inquiry.

In this connection reference should also be made to the Sutton Trust–Education Endowment Foundation *Teaching and Learning Toolkit* (see http://educationendow-mentfoundation.org.uk/toolkit/). The Toolkit is an accessible summary of educational research which provides guidance for teachers and schools on how to use their resources to improve the attainment of disadvantaged pupils. Although the Sutton Trust, one of the partners in the project, has a principal focus on students from disadvantaged backgrounds, the techniques and strategies apply equally well to all students. The Toolkit currently covers 33 topics, each summarized in terms of their average impact on attainment, the strength of the evidence supporting them and their cost. It is a live resource that is being updated on a regular basis as findings from EEF-funded projects and other high-quality research become available. As such the Toolkit provides another predictive tool that teachers can use to enhance their effectiveness and to focus inquiries for classroom research.

Open and closed questions

Implicit in much of what I have written so far is the idea that a research focus emerges out of a teacher's critical reflection on classroom experience, which is then explored through the use of the classroom research procedures.

In other words, both the formation and resolution of the research inquiry are grounded in the teacher's experience. The formation of a research focus or question occurs within either an open or closed context. Open questions take as their starting point a teacher's critical reflection on their teaching. This reflection culminates in a decision to utilize classroom research techniques to understand more fully and then develop their teaching (using the techniques discussed in the following four chapters). A number of the teacher-researchers whose work is cited in Chapter 2 started from an open position and developed hypotheses about their teaching by using classroom research procedures. Having identified a focus, they then developed a plan for action. The open approach, then, is one where teachers engage in classroom research as a reflective activity. From this reflection they derive questions that can be researched and that subsequently provide a basis for action.

The closed approach deviates from the open in so far as many teachers have already identified a specific issue or hypothesis before engaging in classroom research. In this instance, their classroom research begins with the testing of a hypothesis or exploring a specific activity. So with other examples in Chapter 2, teacher-researchers, having heard about a new teaching method that applied to their subject area, used classroom research to investigate the effectiveness of the approach. In this case, the focus on teaching strategies had immediate and direct relevance for classroom practice.

Later in this chapter, there is a more extensive discussion of formulating evaluation questions. Although the purpose there is specifically evaluation, rather than classroom research more generally, the same principles apply. The *open* approach is characterized as follows:

- Take a broad area of inquiry.
- Carry out the initial inquiry.
- Gradually focus the inquiry.

By way of contrast, the *closed* approach typically follows this sequence:

- Take a specific issue.
- Derive research questions.
- Choose an appropriate methodology.

The difference between open and closed reflects the derivation of the focus. In the first instance, the hypothesis or question emerges as a result of critical reflection; in the second, it is a given, and the teacher, having refined it, proceeds to the inquiry. Both approaches reflect classroom research as it is defined in this book, because in both instances the research is controlled by the teacher for the purpose of improving practice. The contrast between open and closed questions or hypotheses can also be represented in diagrammatic form as in Figure 5.1.

Dillon (1983) has produced a similar (if rather more academic) schema for conceptualizing 'problem formation'. He writes:

> Three existential levels of problem and three corresponding psychological activities can be identified as forming part of those events which may be appropriately designated as problem finding. In existential terms, a problem can be existent, emergent or potential. An existent problem has fully-developed being and appearance in the phenomenological field of events facing the observer. In psychological terms, the problem is evident and the observer perceives, recognizes, and identifies it. At a second, less developed level an emergent problem exists which is implicit rather than evident. After probing the data – nosing about in the field of events, so to speak – the observer discovers or 'finds it'. At a still less developed level, a potential problem exists. No problem in an ontological sense exists *qua* problem, but constituent elements are present, striking the observer as an inchoate problem. By combining these and other elements in some way, the observer creates, produces or invents a problem. These descriptive terms relate the existential and psychological dimensions of problem finding activity at three levels, as [shown in Figure 5.2].

Type	Hypothesis
Open	Generating
Closed	Testing

Figure 5.1 Open and closed questions.

Problem level (existential/ psychological)	Problem ——————	Activity ——————	Solution
1 existing/evident	... as problematic	Perceiving the situation (Recognition)	... as resolved
2 emergent/implicit	... for elements of a problem	Probing the data (Discovery)	... for elements of a solution
3 potential/inchoate	... a defined problem	Producing the problem-event (Invention)	... a defined solution

Figure 5.2 A conceptual scheme for comparing levels of problem finding and solving.

My purpose in going into such detail about developing research questions, or what others call 'problem formation', is simply to legitimize the position of teachers who want to engage in classroom research just to find out about their teaching. Classroom research is not solely about exploring specific 'problems' or testing explicit hypotheses. It is appropriate for teachers to use classroom research as a means of critically reflecting on their teaching and developing hypotheses about it.

Formulating hypotheses

Whether or not teachers are initially involved in open or closed problems, they will have to formulate hypotheses or questions at some stage. It is essential that the teacher-researcher, either as an individual or as a member of a group, defines their problem clearly, for it is this definition that determines what data are collected and analysed. It is inevitable that our observations tend to be theory-laden, so consequently it is important to formulate as explicitly as one can the hypotheses that are being tested or the research questions one wishes to explore. If, for example, a group of teachers are concerned about the problem of initiating classroom discussion, they may first hypothesize that asking more open-ended questions would encourage freer responses; a number of different hypotheses could be developed and tested around this contingency. The hypotheses, however, need to be extremely clear and precise. Because there are so many variables in the complex art of teaching, even a carefully worded hypothesis can sometimes only be reported as tentative and provisional. Pring (2012) gives some examples of classroom research hypotheses taken from the Ford Teaching Project:

> In order to cut out 'the guessing game' and move from a formal to an informal pattern, teachers may have to refrain from the following acts:

1 Changing topic
Hypothesis. When teachers change the topic under discussion, they may prevent pupils from expressing and developing their own ideas, since pupils tend to interpret such interventions as attempts to get conformity to a particular line of reasoning.

2 Positive reinforcers
Hypothesis. Utterances like 'good', 'interesting', 'right', in response to ideas expressed can prevent the expression and discussion of alternative ideas, since pupils tend to interpret them as attempts to legitimate the development of some ideas rather than others.

Following Popper's answer to the problem of induction (see Magee 1973: Chapter 2), it is more appropriate to formulate hypotheses as unambiguously as we can, so as to expose them as clearly as possible to refutation. For as Popper pointed out, although empirical generalizations are in principle not verifiable, they are falsifiable and, consequently, they can be tested by systematic attempts to refute them.

The case of curriculum evaluation

Many of the issues related to 'developing a focus' for classroom research have been paralleled in recent years by developments in curriculum evaluation. Although many curriculum evaluations were initially 'externally funded', increasingly much of this evaluation activity became school-based. Unfortunately, this approach to evaluation, instead of building on the traditions of classroom research, has remained wedded to an academic view of evaluation that is based on the ubiquitous evaluation report. Yet evaluations that have an improvement perspective provide a structure for teachers and others to subject a particular curriculum change to their own professional judgement and, in so doing, to improve the programme and make further plans for implementation. In this way, an evaluation can, like classroom research, provide a means for translating an educational idea into practice as well as monitoring and enhancing curriculum development. This was the central theme of my book *Evaluation for School Development* (Hopkins 1989), where I tried to outline an approach to evaluation that was:

- built on the best practice of classroom research in so far as it supported development and was linked to classroom practice;
- sufficiently pragmatic to serve the decision-making purposes of evaluation; and
- as far as possible fitted into the day-to-day life of the school.

The reason for discussing curriculum evaluation at this point is twofold. The first is that one of the approaches to school-focused evaluation described in the evaluation book was based around the use of the evaluation or research question that is one of the themes of this chapter. The second is that the structure of curriculum evaluation provides another model or format for conducting whole-school teacher research. Although this book is now some decades old, I maintain that the strategies it describes and the arguments it makes for educational evaluation are still relevant today. This is particularly the case in my opinion with curriculum evaluation. The debate on school-based curriculum development has been moribund for too long, and as I intimate in Chapter 3, I believe that its time is coming again.

In the following example, I describe two approaches to the formulation of questions in an evaluation we did of 'technology across the curriculum' (TAC; see Figure 5.3). Although the example is specifically about TAC, the approach is applicable across the range of curriculum subjects.

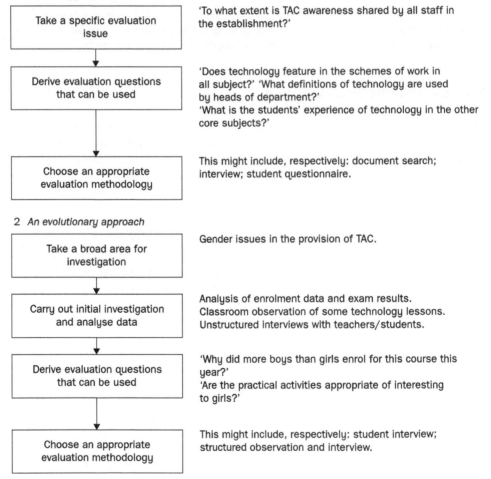

1 *A linear approach*

| Take a specific evaluation issue | 'To what extent is TAC awareness shared by all staff in the establishment?' |

| Derive evaluation questions that can be used | 'Does technology feature in the schemes of work in all subject?' 'What definitions of technology are used by heads of department?' 'What is the students' experience of technology in the other core subjects?' |

| Choose an appropriate evaluation methodology | This might include, respectively: document search; interview; student questionnaire. |

2 *An evolutionary approach*

| Take a broad area for investigation | Gender issues in the provision of TAC. |

| Carry out initial investigation and analyse data | Analysis of enrolment data and exam results. Classroom observation of some technology lessons. Unstructured interviews with teachers/students. |

| Derive evaluation questions that can be used | 'Why did more boys than girls enrol for this course this year?' 'Are the practical activities appropriate of interesting to girls?' |

| Choose an appropriate evaluation methodology | This might include, respectively: student interview; structured observation and interview. |

Figure 5.3 Formulating evaluation questions.

An evaluation question is, simply, a question that can be answered by some form of structured investigation or research. In this context, it is important to:

- avoid grandiose questions outside the scope of formative evaluation, such as 'is TAC a "good thing"?';
- avoid long-term questions outside the time frame: 'are this year's students getting a better experience of technology?';
- avoid questions that are only answerable by large-scale or very technical research;
- aim for suitably defined questions that can be addressed through the limited quantity of data you can be expected to collect.

Although the formulation of questions is often quite challenging, this should not deter us from confronting tough 'bottom-line' issues that reflect the various stages in the change process. Obviously, not all the following questions will apply to every evaluation, but they are examples of the types of questions that will help us assess the impact of a curriculum change on student achievement and the process of school improvement:

- What changes have occurred in teachers' or students' knowledge base?
- What changes have occurred in teachers' or students' skill level and use?
- What changes have occurred in teachers' or students' opinions and feelings?
- What changes have occurred in the culture or organization of the school?
- What changes have occurred in student tests or examinations?

This general approach to evaluation includes four major activities:

1 *Agree on evaluation questions*. Generating questions helps focus the evaluation. Often the questions will relate to the school development plan priorities. It is important not to be too ambitious about the number and scope of the questions asked.
2 *Determine information needs and collection methods*. Once the questions are generated, clarified and prioritized, some way of answering them has to be devised. Potential information sources and collection methods should be identified for each evaluation question. The more sources and methods used, the greater the likelihood that the information will be valid. One way of structuring this important stage in the design of the evaluation is to use a simple worksheet as outlined in Figure 5.4. As you begin to formulate your evaluation question(s) and devise appropriate data-gathering methods, it is helpful to 'cost' them in terms of the time it will take to complete the work, and the time and people available to you. The plan shown in Figure 5.4 is an example of an evaluation schedule for TAC.
3 *Collect and analyse information*. This activity should coexist with data collection. Early checks allow evaluators to seek new information sources if necessary and to identify emerging and unanticipated outcomes.

4   *Reports*. Feedback should normally occur as soon as possible, be tailored to its audience and include follow-up activities if required. This may include reporting to governors and parents and providing information for the school's next development plan. The reports need not be written; they may be given orally with handouts containing summaries of data as 'back-up' material. Often, reduced data are sufficient to act as a basis for discussion. When reports are written they should be short; usually data summaries can be prepared on one side of A4. They should also distinguish clearly between the presentation of data and any interpretation that may be made of the results.

An overview of this evaluation process is given in Figure 5.5. This figure is of course far more linear than the action research cycle described in the previous chapter, and in reality, a number of these steps coexist and timelines tend to merge. It may also be that questions have to be refined and unanticipated logistical problems may occur during the evaluation. An obvious precaution is to ensure that timelines are realistic, that one is not expecting too much too soon, and that as many problems as possible are anticipated.

Two further points need to be made about this process. The first is that there needs to be a logic or flow between the evaluation question, the data collected, analysis, feedback and the resulting action. In that way, the evaluation develops a power of its own because each stage builds on the other. The second is to make certain that the

Question	Source	Collection method	Responsibility	Time-line
How was the plan for the delivery of TAC formulated? Was the process effective?	TAC co-ordinator; school co-ordinator	Interviews	Evaluator	Oct.–Dec.
What is the plan? Why was this method of delivery chosen?	TAC/school co-ordinators; staff	Review documents; questionnaires; interviews	TAC co-ordinator; evaluator	Jan.–Mar.
Have students received 10% balanced TAC? Does the reality reflect the plan?	Staff; students	Interviews; questionnaires	Co-ordinator; evaluator	Easter onward

Figure 5.4 A practical evaluation schedule.

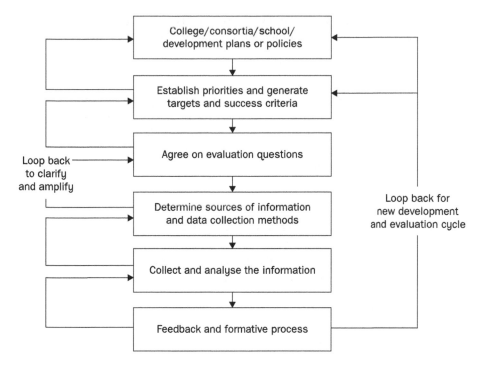

Figure 5.5 The evaluation process.

evaluation questions are important to the school and staff concerned. Evaluation is so time-consuming that its results should not be gratuitous, but feed real need and be able to provide useful and pertinent information.

Appreciative inquiry

One of the approaches we have recently been using in our more general approach to school improvement that offers significant advantages for developing a focus for classroom research is *appreciative inquiry* (AI). Developed most notably by David Cooperrider (see Cooperrider *et al.* 2003), AI is the search for the best in people, their organizations – schools and classrooms – and the world around them. AI involves searching out what gives 'life' to a living system when it is most alive, and most effective. Successful organizations focus on strengths, the things that work for them and young people. They have strategies and approaches to focus the organization, staff and young people on asset-based, strength-focused work.

The organizational impact of AI is to establish a community of people committed to change, enthusiastic about the possibilities of the future, and pledged, in one sense or another, to work for it. AI is a particular approach to asking questions and envisioning the future that fosters positive relationships and builds on the basic assets of a person, a situation, or an organization. In doing so, it enhances a system's capacity for change and collective working.

AI utilizes a four-stage process focusing on:

- *Discovery*: the identification of organizational processes that work well. Discovery is what gives life to an organization and acknowledging the best of what it is now. The discovery phase involves data collection and narrative exploration. It begins the process of revealing the positive and successful experiences of the individual and the collective. Through carefully developed interview questions based on the affirmative topic, the focus is to explore and enliven the stories that are shared through interviewing the defined group within the organization.
- *Dream*: the envisioning of processes that would work well in the future – dreaming of what might be to create a clear results-oriented vision for the future. Participating groups discuss their individual visions of the ideal organization and describe what would be happening some years into the future. From this discussion, the group's collective vision is developed. The strategic focus becomes articulated as a vision of a better organizational world and a compelling statement of strategic intent
- *Design*: planning and prioritizing processes that would work well, by collaboratively co-creating action plans. Provocative propositions are developed as bold statements of the organization of the future as if it had already happened. Implementation plans are then developed by small working parties. To ensure comprehensiveness, the design phase can focus on specifics like leadership, strategy, culture, business practices, capabilities, professional development and systems.
- *Delivery*: the implementation of the proposed design – delivering the results through implementation and review. At an organizational level, if the AI process of positive transformation is supported through empowering employees to connect, co-operate and co-create, the results will continue to surface in new, innovate and bold ways.

The basic idea is to build organizations around what works, rather than trying to fix what does not. It is the opposite of problem-solving, and the method aims to create meaning by using real success stories. We have used it as a methodology for developing an image of what teachers and students envision for their future school or classroom in concrete, optimistic and realizable terms. It is flexible is so far as it can focus on the whole school, a classroom and even an individual. It has a positive and optimistic philosophy and as such is well tuned into the values of action and classroom research. It involves all participants, in our case leaders, teachers and students in taking responsibility for personal and organizational change and improvement. AI's positive approach and staged development process make it particularly appropriate for developing a focus for classroom research.

Theory and theorizing

Finally, a word about theory. So far, I have used the word in two distinct senses. The first refers to a set of personal assumptions, beliefs or presuppositions that individuals hold. Our view of the world, our individual construction of reality, is at one level essentially theoretical. The second use of the word is in the more traditional or 'grand' sense, where theory refers to a coherent set of assumptions, which purport to explain, predict and be used as a guide to practice. This is the sense in which the word was used when the teacher-researchers in Chapter 2 turn to theory in order to inform their classroom research problem.

Unfortunately, all too often educational theory in this second sense is not all that useful in telling us in a practical way how to behave in the classroom. In many instances, the gap between theory and practice is so large that it prevents any useful connection. This occurs because our theories are often not specific enough, or the propositions they contain are not easily generalized to individual situations. This, of course, is an unsatisfactory situation, and one that argues for a different approach to educational theory.

A viable alternative is to theorize about practice, and theorizing is a third way in which we can understand theory. Theorizing approaches theory through practice (the reverse of grand theory, which goes from theory to practice), much in the same way as the hypotheses, assumptions and constructs we develop from classroom research procedures emerge from data gathered from actual classroom experiences. The discussion of grounded theory in Chapter 9 illustrates how theory can be generated from data gathered in a substantive situation. And Chapter 12 gives an extended example of how in the Northern District Schools in Melbourne, Australia, we developed a composite set of 'theories of action' about teaching and learning from a series of classrooms observations based on the instructional rounds approach (see Chapter 6). We refined the theories of action through testing them against John Hattie's (2009) research and then developed an overarching theory of teaching and learning the 'curiosity and powerful learning' approach that became a theory in action for the region as a whole (Northern Metropolitan Region 2011). This is an excellent example of theorizing about practice at scale within an unrelenting improvement frame.

When we are engaged in classroom research, we can be said to be engaged in educational theorizing because we are reflecting systematically and critically on practice. As Richard Pring (2012: 244–5) writes:

> Such systematic and critical examination will involve philosophizing, appealing to evidence, reference to . . . theories. But there is no reason for saying that it will add up to a theory. [Classroom research is about] helping the practitioner to theorize, i.e. think more systematically, critically and intelligently about his or her practice.

You will remember that Stenhouse (1975), in his discussion of the teacher-researcher, illustrates this attitude when he suggested that the teacher, instead of accepting uncritically what a particular theory claims, implements it in the form of a working hypothesis or curriculum proposal. This thought captures two of the fundamental aspects of what Donald Schön (1991) has called the 'reflective practitioner'. In educational terms, such professional teachers stand in control of knowledge rather than being subservient to it, and by doing this they are engaged in the process of theorizing and achieving self-knowledge.

The idea of 'self-knowledge' is an important one in this context. It refers to the individual internalization of ideas that empowers the person. It refers to those moments of clarity and power that occur when we understand a concept and see how we can use it in our personal or professional lives. It is an exciting and exhilarating moment and one which, for teachers and pupils alike, is too rare in our schools. This, as I understand it, is the basis of Polanyi's (1973) writing on *Personal Knowledge*. Personal knowledge is that which is mediated through subjective experience and subsequently owned by the individual. The most pertinent feature of Polanyi's work is the concept of tacit knowledge, the knowledge we cannot articulate. He suggests that we know a great deal more than we can put into words, and that we sense and understand more than we can describe or explain. An aspiration of the approach to classroom research adopted in this book is for teachers to gain more clarity on their 'tacit knowledge' and to incorporate this in their teaching. Walt Whitman (1855/1959) captures a similar thought in this evocative passage from *Leaves of Grass*:

> You shall no longer take things at second or third hand . . . nor look through the eyes of the dead . . . nor feed on the spectres in books, You shall not look through my eyes either, nor take things from me. You shall listen to all sides and filter them from yourself.

In this chapter, I have discussed the challenges involved in developing a focus for classroom research by teachers. I have been at pains to point out that the focus of an inquiry can be either open or closed in so far as the teacher is engaged in hypothesis generation or testing. I have also pointed to some ways in which the focus of classroom research can be clarified and made more specific, and I then linked the whole discussion to a notion of theorizing and self-knowledge. The underlying theme is that through developing a focus for their research, teachers gain more control over their professional lives.

The advice in this chapter obviously applies to teachers working both alone and in collaboration. For reasons already rehearsed in previous chapters, I believe that collaborative efforts at teacher research are to be preferred. Talking to others, for example, is an excellent way of clarifying the focus of a research inquiry. In the next three chapters, we discuss practical ways in which data about the focus of a classroom research inquiry can be gathered.

Further reading

The third edition of *The Action Research Planner* by Stephen Kemmis and Robin McTaggart (1988) contains detailed and helpful advice on 'finding a theme' for classroom research. Other helpful sources for 'getting started' are Judith Bell's (2010) *Doing Your Research Project*, Jean McNiff's (2013) *Action Research: Principles and Practice* and McNiff and Whitehead's (2011) *All You Need to Know about Action Research*. More specific foci for classroom research inquiries are comprehensively illustrated in Good and Brophy's (2007) *Looking in Classrooms*. A description of evaluation techniques and approaches similar in aspiration and application to the strategies described in this book is found in *Evaluation for School Development* (Hopkins 1989). For a discussion of hypothesis generation, it is useful to look at some of the Ford Teaching Project materials (see Elliott 1976). The article by Dillon (1983) on problem finding is very informative. Bryan Magee's (1973) monograph on Popper is a paragon of clarity and neatly summarizes Popper's solution to the problem of induction. Donald Schön's (1991) *The Reflective Practitioner*, although not specifically about education, echoes many of the themes of this book, particularly with regard to how professionals develop and learn through reflection and action. Cooperrider *et al.* (2003) provides an introduction to and practical advice on the appreciative inquiry approach.

6   Principles of classroom observation

Observation of teachers and teaching in the classroom plays a crucial role not only in classroom research, but also more generally in supporting the professional growth of teachers and in the process of school development. In my experience, it seems to be the pivotal activity that links together reflection for the individual teacher and collaborative inquiry for pairs or groups of teachers. It also encourages the development of a language for talking about teaching and provides a means for working on developmental priorities for the staff as a whole. This chapter is therefore of central importance. I begin by outlining five criteria crucial to the successful practice of classroom observation, then describe the generic three-stage cycle of classroom observation and its specific application to partnership teaching, and conclude by making some suggestions for training activities. In discussing the principles underlying observation, the emphasis is not just on classroom research, but also more generally on teacher and school development. The next chapter is devoted to a description of four methods of undertaking classroom observation: open, focused, structured and systematic observation.

Before we launch into the substantive discussion on classroom observation it is important to enter a caveat for English audiences, although the phenomenon to be described is in my experience, prevalent in many other countries as well. Simply put, it is the increasing association of classroom observation with various approaches to educational accountability, particularly inspection such as OFSTED and performance management such as performance-related pay. This has resulted in three probably unintended consequences that have a seriously negative effect on the practice of classroom observation for the developmental purposes described in this book. First. the association has created a climate of fear around observation. Many teachers become fearful when observation is suggested and become resistant to engaging in what should be a formative experience because of the climate within which observation is usually conducted. Second, the association encourages a rush to judgement that creates a power imbalance between the observer and the observed and tends to create defensiveness that gets in the way of development. Third, observation for accountability creates a superficial appreciation of what constitutes an effective teaching and learning process. There also seems to be a relatively high degree of unreliability between observation judgements that compounds the issue. All of these tendencies have fundamentally reduced the positive impact that classroom observation can have on school improvement and professional development. It is, however, this more positive formative and developmental approach to classroom observation that is described in this and following chapters.

Key features of classroom observation

One of the ways of guarding against the negativity currently associated with classroom observation is to develop the specific skills associated with the developmental and formative aspects of the practice. The main problem, as seen above, is that often we jump too quickly to conclusions about the behaviour of others. As I note in Chapter 9, the philosopher Karl Popper claims that 'observations . . . are [always] interpretations in the light of theories' (Magee 1973: 107). Although we constantly need to use our personal theories to construct our worlds (and without doing so would not survive long in the classroom!), this uniquely human intuition is not the greatest asset during classroom observation. Moving to judgement too quickly is one of the main characteristics of poor observation. There are at least five key features of classroom observation that need to characterize our approach if the process is to lead to professional growth.

Joint planning

A joint planning meeting is of crucial importance, especially if it precedes the first in a series of observations. There is a need to establish at the outset a climate of trust between observer and observed, to agree on a focus that both regard as worthwhile, to discuss the context of the lesson, to sort out the 'ground rules' – time and place of the observation, where to sit, how to interact with the pupils, how long to spend in the classroom, etc. The more specific and focused the observation, the more there is a need for joint planning. Once the observer and the observed become familiar with each other's style and the roles are reversed, then the time spent in the initial meeting can be reduced. It may also be possible during an ongoing cycle of observations to combine feedback and planning meetings.

Focus

There are two broad ways of categorizing the focus of classroom observation activities: general and specific. The terms are self-explanatory: the former indicating an approach where 'everything counts' and therefore could be commented on; and the latter where the observation is confined to a particular or well-defined classroom activity or teaching practice. When the focus is broad, the observer, who may have no criteria to turn to, is more likely to rely on 'subjective' judgements to interpret what is going on in the classroom. Although these judgements may be perfectly valid, they most probably will be of little use to the teacher being observed unless the basis for them has been discussed and agreed on in advance. The danger in this situation is that the teacher being observed is subject to a series of 'mini-judgements' on their teaching that tell you more about the educational values of the observer than the teacher whose classroom practice is under scrutiny. The more specific and negotiated the focus of the classroom observation, the more likely it is that the data so gathered will be useful for developmental purposes. If the focus for classroom observation relates to the improvement plan, then the observation could contribute both to teacher and school development.

Establishing criteria

The contribution of classroom observation to professional development is greatly enhanced if, during the initial discussion, criteria for the observation are established. I remember vividly during an interview on our evaluation of the School Teacher Appraisal project, asking an appraiser, the head of a primary school, what criteria she used when observing her colleagues. 'We don't use checklists in this school', she replied angrily. 'Come on', I said, 'what were you looking for when you went into the classroom?' 'Oh', she said. 'Were the children smiling and engaged in their work? Was the classroom environment attractive? Was the work they were doing appropriate for their ability?' and so on. Before long she had given me a fairly sophisticated description of 'good primary practice'. What a pity, I thought, that the staff of that primary school had not had that discussion before the start of the appraisal process. Criteria are nothing to be frightened of, particularly if they are negotiated and agreed *before* the start of an observation. It may be helpful for the staff as a whole to agree and develop criteria on a particular classroom observation before the cycle of observation begins. It is also important that such criteria are subject to ongoing review as those involved refine their definitions of good practice. When viewed in this way, the discussion of criteria can act as a 'road map' for development as well as providing standards by which to discuss the outcomes of an observation. There is a strong link here to the research based practices discussed in the previous chapters associated with the *Visible Learning* approach of John Hattie (2009), the Sutton Trust–Education Endowment Foundation *Teaching and Learning Toolkit* (http://educationendowment-foundation.org.uk/toolkit/) and the establishing of the 'theories of action' described in Chapter 12.

Observation skills

There are three main 'skills' involved here. The first is guarding against the natural tendency to move too quickly into judgement. This can be achieved to some extent, as we have seen already, by having a clear focus for the observation and agreeing the ground rules beforehand. Second, there are the interpersonal skills involved when 'invading another person's space'; this includes creating a sense of trust and being supportive in situations where the other person may feel threatened. The third skill area is more technical. It is knowing how to design schedules that will allow the observer to gather appropriate information on classroom behaviour or transactions, or knowing which are the most appropriate checklists or aide-memoires to use in a particular situation. This latter point is especially important, as one obviously wishes to avoid having the values underlying an observation schedule imposing themselves on the outcomes of the feedback discussion.

Feedback

The benefits of classroom observation will only be realized if appropriate feedback is given. Put another way, poor feedback is characterized by being rushed, judgemental, one-way and impressionistic. As has already been implied, feedback appears to work best if:

- it is given within 24 hours of the observation;
- it is based on careful and systematic recording;
- it is based on factual data;
- the factual data are interpreted with reference to known and agreed criteria;
- the interpretation comes in the first instance from the teacher who has been observed;
- it is given as part of a two-way discussion; and
- it leads to the development of strategies for building on what has been learnt.

The three-phase observation cycle

These key features lay the basis for a professional development approach to classroom observation. The 'three-phase observation cycle', originally called 'clinical supervision', was initially developed in North America as a method of supervising student teachers, but it is well suited for use in classroom research situations.

The three essential phases of this classroom observation process are a planning meeting, the classroom observation itself and a feedback discussion. The *planning meeting* provides the observer and teacher with an opportunity to reflect on the proposed lesson, and this leads to a mutual decision to collect observational data on an aspect of the teacher's classroom practice. During the *classroom observation* phase, the observer watches the teacher in the classroom and collects objective data on that aspect of the teaching or learning they agreed upon earlier. It is during the *feedback discussion* that the observer and teacher share the information gathered during the observation, decide on appropriate action, agree a record of the discussion, and often plan another round of observation (see Figure 6.1). It is important to realize that to be effective, all three phases of the process need to be gone through systematically.

There are a number of principles that are important to consider in this approach to classroom observation. First, the climate of interaction between teacher and observer needs to be non-threatening, helpful and one of mutual trust. Second, the focus of the activity should be on improving classroom practice and the reinforcing of successful strategies, rather than on criticism of unsuccessful patterns of behaviour, or changing the teacher's personality. Third, the process depends on the collection and use of objective observational data, not unsubstantiated value judgements. Fourth, teachers are

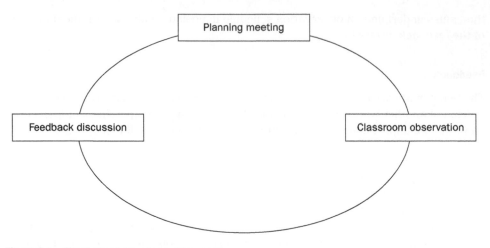

Figure 6.1 The three-phase observation cycle.

encouraged to make inferences about their teaching from the data, and to use the data to construct hypotheses that can be tested out in the future. Next, each cycle of observation is part of an ongoing process that builds on the other. Finally, both observer and teacher are engaged in a mutual process of professional development that can lead to improvement in teaching and observational skills for both. In all these ways, classroom observation can support both specific purposes, as well as the more general aspirations of teacher and school development.

Case Study 6.1 gives an example of the three-phase approach to classroom observation.

CASE STUDY 6.1

The three-phase approach to classroom observation

Marsha had already observed several of George's Year 8 history classes. During a planning conference, they went over George's lesson plan. George identified his objectives, one of which was to involve as many pupils as possible in discussing a particular historical event. They decided to focus the observation on the type of questions George asked and the pupils' responses. Marsha suggested she use a seating plan on which to 'tally' the voluntary and solicited comments from the pupils. George agreed and also requested that she jot down his questions verbatim.

During the lesson, Marsha recorded information for the 20 minutes George had planned for the discussion. Afterwards, as they went over the data, patterns began to emerge. George noticed that, although the discussion had been lively, only 12 out of the 28 pupils had participated (he had thought during the lesson that more were involved). Also, certain types of questions tended to elicit more complete responses.

They both decided that it might be useful if George sequenced his questions from factual types (to establish a common knowledge base) to more open-ended, opinion questions. Also, now that he knew which pupils were reticent, George would attempt to involve them more in class discussions. Marsha suggested a couple of techniques that worked for her, and George was excited about trying them out. The feedback conference ended with both agreeing to use the same observation focus in the near future to compare the results of George's new strategies.

Partnership observation

The three-phase cycle provides a general framework for classroom observation which is particularly relevant to 'partnership' teaching or collaborative observation. I try to encourage teachers to engage in classroom research in pairs or small groups for a number of reasons. Among them is the emotional support they gain from each other, particularly as this activity is initially threatening. It is now fairly well established that teachers learn best from other teachers, and take criticism most easily from this source. It is ideal if teachers in cross-hierarchical groups can act as observers for each other, and this mutual exchange of roles quickly breaks down barriers which otherwise may be monolithic.

The observer in the partnership can play any number of differing roles. They can observe a lesson in general, focus on specific aspects of the teaching and talk to pupils all during one observation period. This lightens the teacher's problem of analysis and tends to increase the objectivity of the data gathered. In addition, the observer may also be able to note incidents that the teacher would ordinarily miss.

Colleagues involved in the University of Cambridge Institute of Education and Bedfordshire Education Service Developing Successful Learning Project refined an approach to classroom observation that emphasizes the partnership role. The following description is taken from their work.

This approach to partnership observation assumes that:

- all teachers can develop their practice; and
- all students can learn successfully.

It is based on the following principles:

- Practice can only be improved in the contexts in which it normally occurs.
- Individuals need the support of colleagues as they seek to develop their practice.

The central strategy is to create partnerships of teachers who are committed to helping one another develop their classroom practice. These partnerships usually involve two or three colleagues who, for the purposes of this work, regard one another as equals. A partner must be somebody with whom you can work comfortably.

Before the observation, a number of issues have to be considered and decisions made by the partners:

- the role of the observer in the classroom;
- the confidentiality of discussions;
- commitment to the programme;
- date/time place of observation;
- date/time place of *review* – this should be set as near to the observation as possible (within 24 hours); the place must be one without interruptions, on or off site, and needs to be non-threatening; it is best to allow a minimum of 40 minutes for the review;
- how often observation is to take place – this is dependent on the timetable and the availability of cover;
- which classes and lessons are to be observed;
- whether this is to be a focused or unfocused observation; and
- methods of observation to be used.

During the observation, the observer should only record what is seen or heard and not be judgemental or intrusive. Time should also be found for one or two minutes of positive discussion at the end of the observation period. This will allow the observed teacher to release any tension that may have developed during the lesson. The observer may also give the class teacher a copy of the observation notes.

During the review discussion, feedback should be non-threatening, supportive and based on the information gathered during the observation. *Target setting* evolves from feedback, and once this has been given it is time to identify one area of learning to be developed. Targets must be realistic and attainable within the designated time-span. This does not, however, preclude the developments continuing over an extended period. If successful, these changes often become an integral part of effective class teaching, thus enhancing the learning experience of students.

Action planning for development is based on the answers to a series of questions that need to be addressed before modifying teaching practice:

- What do I want to achieve?
- How am I going to achieve this?
- How will this improve the quality of learning?
- How will this development be evaluated?
- Will I involve the pupils in the process of monitoring and evaluation?
- Are there adequate resources to implement the proposed development?

If, after carrying out the action plan, the outcomes were not successful, do not be discouraged! Try to discover why. This is where assistance and advice from a third person could be invaluable. Perhaps you were too ambitious in your objectives; if so, return to target setting. If the objective was realistic, it may have been the way in which it was developed in the class; if this was the case, return to the action plan. If the outcomes were successful, why were they? Always reflect on practice.

The partnership may now wish to continue with the original target, or a new target may be set.

Case Study 6.2 is an example of partnership observation from the work of the Developing Successful Learning Project, prepared by Pamela Hughes of Sharnbrook Upper School. It focuses on involving students in the observation process.

CASE STUDY 6.2

Partnership observation and student involvement

This classroom project placed particular emphasis on the idea of student involvement. There are 29 students in the class. The project included the following steps:

1   Initially the students in the two classes involved were given letters to take home, to explain their involvement and to give parents an opportunity to contact us if they wished.
2   The students, working in groups, discussed and then listed things which (a) helped their learning and (b) hindered their learning within the class. (This took 10 minutes in one class and 30 in the other where it was used as an oral exercise.)
3   After the observation, the students in my class were very keen to be involved further. They knew that the focus would be evaluating group work, but they did not know the specific areas.

We discussed ways of evaluating our learning, but not in those terms! The outcomes, from the students, were recorded by further observation, videotaping and by questionnaire (testing was not mentioned). I explained that I had already designed a questionnaire. Somebody asked if the class could compile their own – we debated time, costs, what it would include, how to go about it, etc.

I decided to let them try during the following lesson. I was able to do this because they were Year 9 and the task was suitable for an English lesson. I think this would have been more difficult to organize in other areas of the curriculum. They were also keen to video the lesson and one student was made responsible for setting it up in the corner of the room before the beginning of the lesson.

I began to think of my action plan when they undertook the task, i.e. using the board for key points and ensuring a better mix within groups.

The lesson

The video

It was difficult to decide where to focus as we did not want it to be intrusive. The students decided that they would focus the camera on one side of the room and that halfway through a designated person would change its direction. The lesson followed afternoon registration and so there was no difficulty in setting the camera up prior to the class arriving.

The observation

This was unscheduled. We were just about to begin the lesson when a member of the class asked if one of them could observe as the other teacher had. I 'thought on my feet' and could not see any objection. I asked for a volunteer and chose the first hand that shot up. I knew that I did not have time to explain about how to do observation, so placed him in a position from where he could see most of the class and told him to write down anything that he thought might be affecting our learning. This would by nature be judgemental and for 'my eyes only'.

The task

The aim was for each group to produce a questionnaire which would be used by a group, not an individual. Whole-class discussion (using the board for key points), followed by paired friendship groups. Further brainstorming as a class, followed by each pair joining another. I chose the groupings.

Follow-up

I used the student observation notes and the video with my teaching partner, Christine. We were both surprised at the candid nature of the observation notes. Groups of students have also seen extracts from the video (during lunchtimes) and this has led to further discussion. One 'spin-off' from the student involvement has been greater tolerance of individuals within the class and the building of a more positive class identity.

Notes made by the class member

Beginning of lesson: Everybody is chatting quietly. Then group task is explained. Groups are scattered around the room. (Group task in pairs.)[1]
Same groups (pairs) as they are sitting in. They begin the group discussion. One pair messing around.
Everybody works with somebody of the same sex.
Groups talking.
People at the back of the class are working more than the people towards the front.
Another member of staff enters – pupils cease to work and then get back to what they were doing before they entered.

Class discussion: Most people are contributing to the questions.
Some people had very good questions.
Some doodling in their notebooks while class discussion.
Nobody talked between themselves during this part of class discussion.
A couple of people are chewing pencils, pens.
Some people seem to be getting bored.

Groups combine: People only joined in a mixed group when there was no other choice.

[1] The comments in parentheses have been added by Pamela Hughes.

Once the groups had been rearranged there was new discussion.

People who did not want to really work together in groups are working better than groups made up of just friends.

The people working best are the people with the camera directed towards them.

Most of the groups seem to have forgotten about the camera.

People who are messing around at the beginning seem to have calmed down a bit.

When the camera was moved for a second time people who had been fairly quiet up until now suddenly started moving and talking.

The people who are not in the picture now relax and start playing the fool to the camera. (I collated the group tasks some had not finished. Those who finished quickly began designing the layout.)

Quick response from all to correct teacher. (I cannot remember what this was – it may have been homework.)

Bell goes, chattering began and people started to pack away, but Mrs Hughes stopped them straight away.

Training for observation

Classroom observation can be a sensitive issue for teachers unused to regular or systematic observation since their teacher training and early days in the profession. As discussed earlier, it is also associated in many teachers' minds with accountability procedures such as inspection, appraisal, evaluation and performance management. As I am arguing in this book, however, observation is something that can be valuable in its own right and used for a variety of staff development and school improvement purposes. Experience suggests that initial apprehension disappears once the process of observation is under way, providing appropriate procedures are used. I have already discussed some of the main principles of classroom observation, and it now may also be useful to briefly describe some training activities that can be used to promote good practice.

The first activity is designed to acquaint participants with the three-phase cycle of classroom observation. The activity utilizes video examples to provide 'action images' which participants can relate to their own experience. The session could be divided into five parts:

1   Overview of benefits of the three-phase cycle.
2   Video example of the planning meeting. In discussing the video, participants may wish to consider:
   •   How important is negotiation in the whole process?
   •   What skills are involved?
   •   What is the relationship between the participants?
   •   How realistic is the agreed focus?
3   Video example of the classroom observation. During the video, participants should be encouraged to keep in mind the agreed focus of the observation and

make notes on it as if they were in the classroom. In discussing the video, participants may wish to consider:
- What other areas of focus could have been identified?
- How feasible was it to obtain information on the agreed focus?
- What skills are needed by the observer?
- What are the relative benefits of open or focused observation?

4 Video example of the feedback discussion. In discussing the video, participants may wish to consider:
- How far do you agree with the points raised in the discussion?
- What is the balance between judgement and reflection in the discussion?
- How far can this discussion lay the basis for professional growth?
- What skills are required by an observer in promoting the developmental nature of such a discussion?

5 Review the classroom observation process in relation to the five key issues discussed earlier.

The second activity is designed to aid thinking about which areas to focus on in classroom observation and suitable data collection methods. Each group member should in turn select an aspect of their work as a possible focus for classroom observation and outline it to the group. The remainder of the group should then discuss the following questions:

- What information could be gathered through classroom observation?
- How would the observer collect it?
- How would the observer record it?
- What are the criteria that could most helpfully be applied to this particular aspect of the teacher's work?

As each member of the group presents an example and the others respond to it, the group should build up an aide-memoire using the box below. The aide-memoire may then be helpful in designing appropriate observation instruments or schedules and for identifying the most appropriate criteria to inform the feedback discussion.

If possible, back in school, participants should ask a colleague to use the approach devised during this exercise in their classroom and then to report back to other colleagues on how well it worked. Experience suggests that dry runs such as this assist enormously in the process of acquiring the skills of, and allaying fears about, classroom observation.

Area of focus	Information needs	How to collect	How to record	Criteria

Classroom observation as professional learning

In concluding this chapter it may be instructive to broaden the discussion a little to emphasize the role that classroom observation can play in professional development and school improvement. This is an antidote to the somewhat negative associations classroom observation has assumed of late as a consequence of its use by inspectors, evaluators and performance managers. Indeed, one of the key themes of this chapter has been to stress the positive aspects of classroom observation. Now we briefly describe its use in three specific professional learning contexts: lesson study, peer coaching and instructional rounds. These are key strategies for using classroom observation to link together professional learning and school improvement (Hopkins 2013).

Lesson study

This approach to professional development was popularized by the National Strategies in England during the 2000s (Department for Education and Skills 2007). It is well known as a key element of continuing professional development of Japanese and Chinese teachers.

Key features of the model

A pair or small group of teachers work to improve an aspect of teaching which evidence tells them could improve in relation to children's learning and progress. They identify 'focus children' who are to be the focus of the study. Together they plan a 'research lesson' with some new element designed to improve the focus of children's learning (who may be higher-, middle-, or lower-attaining). One person teaches the lesson while others observe the progress of the focus children. They discuss the learning of each child – what worked as planned, what did not and why. They plan another lesson to address the identified learning issues. Over a series of lessons they develop techniques that strengthen learning and progress for each of the focus children. They share learning with other teachers via video, coaching or a public research lesson. Children can participate at this feedback stage.

Strengths of the model

- Strongly grounded in 'lessons' and improving hard aspects of teaching.
- Focuses exclusively on specific children's learning with progress as an indicator of success.
- Peer ownership of the research lessons and focus on learning not the teacher.
- Encourages risk-taking in a supportive context and incisive observation.
- Multiple views of the lesson allow more to be seen and so 'dissect' the learning,
- Collaborative honing of techniques then sharing the new approach boosts impact for all children.

Constraints and risks associated with the model

- Works well when careful analysis is made of a good range of progress information before research lessons are planned.
- Releasing groups of teachers to observe a research lesson can present difficulties and requires resourceful leadership.
- Care needs to be taken to ensure that this is not felt to be performance management oriented or less will be learned.
- Learning can be lost without opportunities to share what was learned.
- Avoid creating research lesson groups entirely made up of inexperienced teachers whose observation of learning is limited.

This approach is most useful when . . .

- Improving the teaching of concepts that are important stepping-stones in learning and present identified barriers to progress, e.g. securing children's understanding of fractions in mathematics.
- Eliciting the views of children on teaching that works and to identify the learning gains, e.g. how the use of peer assessment in writing improve confidence and skills.
- Looking at how to secure learning in areas that are hard to teach and hard to learn, e.g. scaffolding the skills of inquiry into mathematics.

Peer coaching

Bruce Joyce and Beverly Showers's (2002) work on staff development, in particular their peer coaching strategy, has in recent years transformed our thinking on staff development. It is here that there is the closest link with classroom research techniques, especially observation. Joyce and Showers identified a number of key training components which, when used in combination, have much greater power than when used alone. The major components of training are:

- presentation of theory or description of skill or strategy;
- modelling or demonstration of skills or models of teaching;
- practice in simulated and classroom settings;
- structured and open-ended feedback (provision of information about performance); and
- coaching for application (hands-on, in-classroom assistance with the transfer of skills and strategies to the classroom).

Based on this analysis, Joyce and Showers (1984: 85) summarized the 'best knowledge' we have on staff development like this:

- the use of the integrated theory-demonstration-practice feedback training programme to ensure skill development;

- the use of considerable amounts of practice in simulated conditions to ensure fluid control of the new skills;
- the employment of regular on-site coaching to facilitate vertical transfer; and
- the preparation of teachers who can provide one another with the needed coaching.

A key element in all of this is the provision of in-classroom support. It is the facilitation of peer coaching that enables teachers to extend their repertoire of teaching skills and to transfer them from different classroom settings to others.

During the implementation of our various school improvement projects we have emphasized the use of peer coaching to support student learning (see, for example, Hopkins 2002). When the refinements noted below are incorporated into a school improvement design, peer coaching can virtually assure 'transfer of training' for everyone:

- Peer coaching teams of two or three are much more effective than larger groups.
- These groups are more effective when the entire staff is engaged in school improvement.
- Peer coaching works better when heads and deputies participate in training and practice.
- The effects are greater when formative study of student learning is embedded in the process.

Instructional rounds

The best-known current approach in what I have called (Hopkins 2013) the 'inductive mode' of staff development is the use of 'instructional rounds'. The application of the 'rounds' approach in medical training to the work in classrooms has been popularized by Richard Elmore (City *et al.* 2009). Essentially this is training in the workplace rather than the lecture theatre and involves, in Elmore's words, 'learning the work by doing the work'. It also engages participants in practising the two essential skills of the professional – diagnosis and treatment. In educational terms, these might be phrased as 'What are the necessary educational goals for this student?' and 'How can we bring to bear the most powerful curriculum and instructional strategies to achieve them?'

Instructional rounds imply a four-step process: identifying a problem of practice, observing, debriefing and focusing on the next level of work. The approach is based around the use of networks of teachers and leaders who have agreed to schedule significant and systematic time to explore a problem and develop a practice. The process works something like this:

1   The network convenes in a school for an instructional round visit hosted by a member or members of the network (principal, headteacher or teachers, regional or local authority officers). The visit starts with a process of reviewing

a teaching and learning focus that the school is currently wrestling with and would like the network's feedback on.

2   The network divides into smaller groups that visit a rotation of four to six classrooms for approximately half an hour. In each classroom, network participants collect descriptive evidence related to the teaching and learning focus.

3   After completing the classroom observations, the entire group assembles in a common location to work through a process of description, analysis and prediction. The group analyses the evidence for patterns and looks at how what they have seen explains (or does not explain) the observable student performance in the school. From this, they develop a series of constructs that provide a logical and analytic description of what they have observed and then develop appropriate 'theories of action' for each construct.

4   Finally, the network discusses the next level of work recommendations for the school and system to make progress on the problem of practice. No comments are made about the behaviours of individual teachers; the focus is unrelentingly on describing the practice and how it can be enhanced. The resulting report is shared with all.

The purpose of this discussion is twofold: first, to emphasize that the essential ingredient of professional learning and school improvement is peer-to-peer observation between teachers; and second, that different strategies are required for different objectives and contexts.

The constellation of staff development activities just described makes the structural link between the collaborative and reflective work of teachers and enhanced levels of student achievement clear and achievable. The staff development focus has the potential to unite both the focus on teaching and learning and capacity building. In highly effective schools it is this that provides the essential infrastructure for school improvement.

Conclusion

As the discussion and examples in this chapter demonstrate, classroom observation can provide powerful insights into classroom practice, as well as being a means of professional development and a major tool for the classroom researcher. In the chapter, I have described some of the main principles involved in doing classroom observation as well as providing a series of examples which hopefully give a feel of the method in practice and some suggestions for training activities. I have emphasized the partnership approach to observation because I feel that it is here that the link between teacher and school development lies, especially if the focus of the observation is related to whole-school issues. In the following chapter, we look more closely at the methods available to the classroom observer committed to enhancing classroom practice.

Further reading

The 'clinical supervision' approach to classroom observation, on which this three-phase approach was based, is described in a practical way by Acheson and Gall (1997) in their *Techniques in the Clinical Supervision of Teachers*. The other classic texts on clinical supervision are by Goldhammer *et al.* (1993) and Cogan (1973). The work of Jean Rudduck contains a number of examples of teachers in partnership (Rudduck 1982, 1991; Rudduck and Sigsworth 1985). Colin Hook's (1995) *Studying Classrooms* contains a detailed discussion of the place of classroom observation in teacher research, and Judith Bell's (2010) helpful book on research in general contains a rationale for a more traditional approach to classroom observation. More generally, the role of classroom observation in school improvement is found in a number of my other books, particularly *Improving the Quality of Education for All* (Hopkins 2002), *Exploding the Myths of School Reform* (Hopkins 2013) and *The New Structure of School Improvement* (with Bruce Joyce and Emily Calhoun: Joyce *et al.* 1999). *Instructional Rounds in Education: A Network Approach to Improving Teaching and Learning* (City *et al.* 2009) describes the approach in detail.

7 Methods of observation in classroom research

Within the general framework of the three-phase classroom observation or partnership teaching approach discussed in Chapter 6, there is no one best method to use. When teachers observe each other teach, all they often require are simple ways of gathering information on basic topics, such as questioning techniques, on- or off-task behaviour, and classroom management. It is usually preferable for teachers to devise their own observation schedules, to invent them for a specific purpose. By doing this, there is usually more ownership developed over the subject of the observation and a better fit between the focus of the observation and the data-gathering method.

Before devising the observation checklist, it is often useful to ask some organizing questions in order to clarify the purpose of the observation. These questions are illustrative:

- What is the purpose of the observation?
- What is the focus of the observation?
- What teacher/student behaviours are important to observe?
- What data-gathering methods will best serve the purpose?
- How will the data be used?

These and similar questions should help the teachers involved clarify how easy it is to use the chosen approach, how much the observer looks at and how far the observer makes judgements.

The next step is to decide on the observation method. Although there are many approaches, it is possible to categorize them into four main groups. Each of them could involve the use of 'pencil and paper', audio or video recording. They are *open* observation, *focused* observation, *structured* observation and *systematic* observation.

As the various editions of this book have progressed, so the technology available to the classroom researcher has advanced and become more sophisticated. Now, for example, high-definition video cameras are small, easy to use and relatively cheap. The iPad has become widely available in education and offers audio and video recording as well as the possibility of electronic input from learners and note-making capabilities. The material gathered is also much more easily analysed than previously, with the increased accessibility of computers, tablets and appropriate software.

In our current work in the UK and Australia we are finding that teachers are using iPads to record their teaching, thus obviating the need for the presence of an observer or colleague in the classroom. They can then 'observe' the lesson for themselves using one of the four observation methods described in this chapter. Given the perceived threat, discussed in Chapter 6, that is often at least initially associated with classroom observation, this has the advantage of allowing the teacher to retain control over the recording. They can do the initial analysis themselves and then share with others only what they want colleagues to see. This can help teachers build their confidence in the early stages of engaging with classroom observation.

Open observation

In this approach, the observer literally uses a blank sheet of paper (or its electronic equivalent) to record the lesson. The observer either notes down key points about the lesson or uses a personal form of shorthand for making a verbatim recording of classroom transactions. For example:

> *Teacher:*   Turn 2 p. 46. Mary give us y. ans. to q. 1.
> *Mary:*   WW II was partly t. result of unresolved conflicts of WW I.
> *Teacher:*   That's 1 pt. of the ans. John give us y. ans.

The aim is usually to enable subsequent reconstruction of the lesson. A variation of this approach is to agree to record only those events that fit into certain broad categories or under certain headings, as shown in Figure 7.1.

A problem with the open observation approach is that it can be unfocused and can lead to premature judgements. The best way to handle this approach is to make open recording as factual as possible and leave interpretation until a discussion after the lesson. Because of its general nature, it is important to stick closely to each component of the three-phase cycle (planning, observation, feedback); otherwise what began as a mutual approach to observation could result in a one-way critique.

The observer should aim to record factual and descriptive information.
Teaching skills

(i) Presentation
(ii) Indirect teaching
(iii) Direct teaching
(iv) Voice
(v) Questioning strategies
(vi) Feedback
(vii) Subject matter
(viii) Expectations

Figure 7.1   An example of open observation.
(from Bollington and Bradley 1990).

In Case Study 7.1, Heather Lockhart describes how she went about observing her colleague Maureen's teaching in a focused observation.

CASE STUDY 7.1

Maureen has recently begun to doubt the effectiveness of her questioning techniques. She asked me to observe a review lesson on a 'plants and seeds' unit she had recently completed. We decided to concentrate on observing the effectiveness of her questioning techniques rather than the lesson content.

We also decided that I would be in the classroom strictly as an observer. I would not participate in the lesson in any way. We felt that, as many of the children in the room had been former students of mine and because I work with her class two periods every week, the children were familiar with me and comfortable in my presence.

We also decided not to use a tape-recorder or videotape so that the children would not be inhibited by them. Maureen and I discussed the most effective way of monitoring and decided on a checklist. I made a checklist and showed it to Maureen. Maureen agreed that it should give us the information we needed.

I positioned myself in the room within the children's immediate sight but slightly separated from the group. As I was within the field of their vision, I would not be causing distraction through children turning to check to see what I was doing. By separating myself slightly from the group, I was implying that I was not participating in the lesson. Maureen reinforced this by telling the children that I was going to watch because I didn't believe that they knew anything about plants and seeds. As we had predicted, outside of an occasional quick glance or smile, the children tended to ignore my presence.

When we first sat down, Maureen allowed the class about a minute of 'wriggle time' before she began to speak. She quickly explained my presence, then went directly into the lesson. She began by giving the children 'fact' questions that they could answer directly from the pictures. The responses were slow to come. Few children volunteered to answer the first few questions. As Maureen continued with the 'fact' questions, the children became more excited and eager to answer.

Maureen then began to inject 'inference questions'. The children were experiencing such success with 'fact questions' that they experienced no trouble in making inferences from the pictures. She then interspersed questions which required the children to form opinions. Again, the children responded freely and confidently. The children began to get restless after about 15 minutes and their attention began to wander. Maureen realized what was happening and quickly ended the lesson.

Looking at the checklist after the observation, my reactions to Maureen's questioning techniques were confirmed. The questions were asked clearly and concisely. The children had full understanding of the type of response that was being elicited. As they understood the questions, they were comfortable and eager to respond.

Maureen's interaction with the children was warm and caring. She listened carefully and respectfully to each response, whether the response was correct or incorrect. She encouraged hesitant children by smiling at them, giving verbal encouragement or nodding while the child was speaking. She was careful to ensure that each child had the opportunity to respond at least once during the lesson.

I feel that Maureen has excellent questioning techniques. This includes the variety in the type of questions she asks, the manner in which she uses her voice, the positive reinforcement she employs, the pace of the lesson and the warmth she shows towards the children.

I feel that Maureen's main problem with questioning techniques is that she doesn't recognize her expertise in this area. I would suggest she tape the lessons that use intensive questioning methods and analyse the results for her own benefit.

Focused observation

When a pair of teachers have decided on a focus for an observation (e.g. questioning technique), they need to define exactly what to look at or for. In these situations, it may be helpful to draw on some external resources to help focus the observation. For example, they may need to identify or research the range of higher-order/lower-order questions. In another situation, they may have decided to look at 'praise' in their classrooms, but find it difficult to describe all the different possible forms of praise. Or again even with a phrase as commonplace as 'effective teaching', what exactly is it that we are looking for? The teachers who were focusing on 'questioning' may find a form like that illustrated in Figure 7.2 of some help; or the teachers interested in praise may find the lists of effective and ineffective praise in Table 7.1 illuminating. Similarly, the teachers who were discussing effective teaching may find the observation schedule, distilled from the research evidence of teacher effectiveness, a useful classroom research tool (see Table 7.2).

As we have discussed previously, all of these specifications of practice, aide-memoires and summaries of research can be of help as long as they are subject to the teacher's own judgement. Problems arise when the checklist controls the focus of the observation, or encourages the observer to become judgemental. They are there to help focus and refine the teacher's judgement and extend their professional practice. It should also go without saying that such specifications and observation schedules should be agreed and negotiated beforehand. Ideally they are part of the overall professional development of the staff in the school and an integral aspect, as seen in Chapter 12, of the school's approach to improvement.

Structured observation

Although the aide-memoires described in the previous section are helpful in some situations, often all that an observer requires is fairly simple information that can be collected by either using a *tally system* or a *diagram*. I call this approach 'structured observation'. With a tally system, an observer puts down a tally or tick *every time* a particular event occurs, e.g. every time the teacher asks a question or gives praise. The resulting record is factual rather than judgemental and can be made more detailed by being based on aide-memoires such as those described earlier. The aim of a diagram is to produce a record of what happens in the classroom. It records in diagrammatic form a series of classroom interactions.

FORM 10.6 Questioning techniques

Use: When teacher is asking class or group questions
Purpose: To see if teacher is following principles for good questioning practices

For each question, code the following categories:

Behaviour catagories

A **Type of question asked**
   1 Academic: Factual, Seeks specific correct response
   2 Academic: Opinion, Seeks opinion on a complex issue where there is no clear-cut response
   3 Non-academic: Question deals with personal, Procedural, or disciplinary matters rather than curriculum

B **Type of response required**
   1 Thought question. Student must reason through to a conclusion or explain something at length
   2 Fact question. Student must provide fact(s) from memory
   3 Choice question. Requires only a yes-no or either-or response

C **Selection of respondent**
   1 Names child before asking question
   2 Calls on volunteer (after asking question)
   3 Calls on non-volunteer (after asking question)

D **Pause (after asking question)**
   1 Paused a few seconds before calling on student
   2 Failed to pause before calling on student
   3 Not applicable; teacher named student before asking question

E **Tone and manner in presenting question**
   1 Question presented as challenge or stimulation
   2 Question presented matter-of factly
   3 Question presented as threat or test

Record any information relevant to the following:
Multiple Questions. Tally the number of times the teacher:
   1 Repeats or rephrases question before calling on anyone 11
   2 Asks two or more questions at the same time 0

Sequence. Were questions integrated into an orderly sequence or did they seem to be random or unrelated?

Teacher seemed to be following sequence given in manual (led up to next history unit).

Did students themselves pose questions?   No

Was there student-student interaction?
How much?   None

When appropriate, did the teacher redirect questions to several students or ask students to evalute their own or other's responses?   No

	Codes				
	A	B	C	D	E
1	1	2	2	1	2
2	1	2	2	1	2
3	1	3	2	1	2
4	1	2	2	1	2
5	1	2	2	1	2
6	1	3	2	1	2
7	1	2	2	1	2
8	2	1	2	1	1
9	1	2	2	1	2
10	1	2	2	1	2
11	1	2	2	1	2
12	1	2	2	1	2
13					
14					
15					
16					
17					
18					
19					
20					
21					
22					
23					
24					
25					
26					
27					
28					
29					
30					
31					
32					
33					
34					
35					
36					
37					
38					
39					
40					

Figure 7.2 Questioning techniques.

(from Good and Brophy 2007).

Table 7.1   Guidelines for effective praise

Effective praise	Ineffective praise
1 Is delivered contingently	1 Is delivered randomly or unsystematically
2 Specifies the particulars of the accomplishment	2 Is restricted to global positive reactions
3 Shows spontaneity, variety and other signs of credibility; suggests clear attention to the student's accomplishment	3 Shows a bland uniformity that suggests a conditioned response made with minimal attention
4 Rewards attainment of specified performance criteria (which can include effort criteria, however)	4 Rewards mere participation, without consideration of performance processes or outcomes
5 Provides information to students about their competence or the value of their accomplishments	5 Provides no information at all or gives students information about their status
6 Orients students towards better appreciation of their own task-related behaviour and thinking about problem-solving	6 Orients students towards comparing themselves with others and thinking about competing
7 Uses students' own prior accomplishments as the context for describing present accomplishments	7 Uses the accomplishments of peers as the context for describing students' present accomplishments
8 Is given in recognition of noteworthy effort or success at difficult (for *this* student) tasks	8 Is given without regard to the effort expended or the meaning of the accomplishment
9 Attributes success to effort and ability, implying that similar successes can be expected in the future	9 Attributes success to ability alone or to external factors such as luck or low task difficulty
10 Fosters endogenous attributions (students believe that they expend effort on the task because they enjoy the task and/or want to develop task-relevant skills)	10 Fosters exogenous attributions (students believe that they expend effort on the task for external reasons – to please the teacher, win a competition or reward, etc.)
11 Focuses students' attention on their own task-relevant behaviour	11 Focuses students' attention on the teacher as an external authority figure who is manipulating them
12 Fosters appreciation of, and desirable attributions about, task-relevant behaviour after the process is completed	12 Intrudes into the ongoing process, distracting attention from task-relevant behaviour

Source: Reproduced with permission from Brophy (1981).

Table 7.2 IQEA observation schedule relating to features of effective teaching

An effective teacher	Check when observed
achieves eye contact with pupils during lessons	
allows pupil practice after each learning step	
allows short breaks where pupils move about	
allows pupils thinking time	
asks a large number of questions	
attributes ownership of ideas to initiating pupils	
attributes pupils' successes to their efforts	
avoids digressions/ambiguous phrases	
calls pupils by first names	
checks for pupil understanding	
conveys sense of enthusiasm in presentation of tasks	
discourages pupil–pupil verbal abuse	
gets a high percentage of correct answers from pupils	
gets pupils to restate answers	
gives clear/detailed instructions/explanations	
gives concrete, varied examples	
gives hints, clues	
gives moderate amount of praise	
gives short review of previous learning	
guides pupils during initial practice	
has brief contacts with individual pupils (maximum 30 seconds)	
has pupils asking questions/initiating verbal interactions	
highlights main points of lesson	
is knowledgeable about subject matter	
monitors pupils' work when necessary	
moves around class and approaches all pupils	
obtains responses from all pupils	
organizes break when pupils' energy wanes	
organizes short transitions between activities	
presents new material in short steps	
provides answers, asking pupils to restate in own words/give other examples	
provides systematic feedback/corrections	
rephrases questions	
responds positively to incorrect answers, identifying correct parts	
restates questions	
specifies expected pupil performance on tasks	
specifies what pupils did to achieve success	
teaches with pace	
uses anecdotes, asides relating to task	
uses humour	

Source: Beresford (1998: 85–6).

This structured approach lends itself to a factual or a descriptive record. It should be noted that all of these approaches can fit a wide range of concerns. They can focus on aspects of the teacher's work, pupil–teacher interaction or the work of one or more pupils. The following examples of structured observation involve both tally systems and diagrams. They were developed by teachers who were interested in gathering data on questioning techniques and on- or off-task behaviour.

Observing questioning techniques

1   *Question distribution*: In Box 7.1 the circles represent pupils. When they answer a question, the number of the question is entered into their circle; blank circles indicate pupils who have not answered a question.

Box 7.1

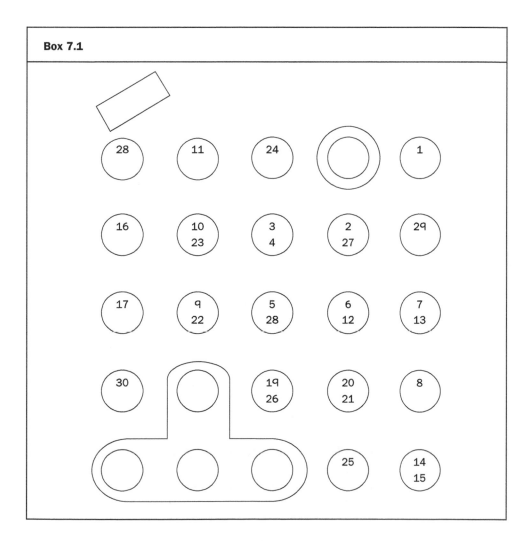

2   *Volunteered and solicited answers*: In Box 7.2 the circles again represent pupils. Use a 'V' for pupils who volunteer answers and an 'A' for those who are asked to answer. Placing a number beside the 'V' or 'A' will indicate the sequence of the questioning (e.g. V1, A2, V3, V4, A5, A6, . . .).

3   *Teacher response to questions answered*: Indicate how the teacher responds to answers by using the following abbreviations. Tally scores as in Box 7.3.
V = verbal response
NV = non-verbal response
+ = indicated positive response
0 = indicated no response
− = indicated negative response.

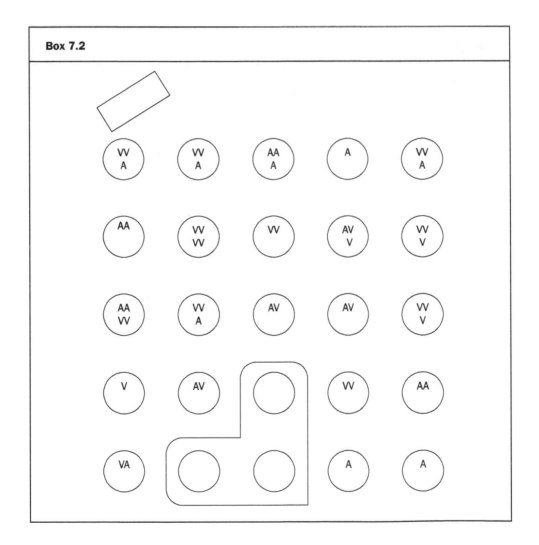

Box 7.2

Box 7.3					
Question	**Response**				
	V	NV	+	0	−
1	√		√		
2	√		√		
3		√	√		
4	√				√
5		√		√	
6	√		√		
7	√		√		
8	√			√	
9		√	√		
10		√		√	
Totals	6	4	6	3	1

Observing on-task/off-task behaviours

- Identify, by scanning the classroom, all of the students who appear to be off-task every 2 minutes. Number each scan, using the same number for all pupils who appear to be off-task during that scan. For example, during scan 7, five pupils appeared to be off-task as in Box 7.4.
- Tally on-task/off-task behaviour: list in the off-task column the number of pupils off-task at each scan (say, every 2 minutes). Subtract the off-task from the class total to determine on-task pupils. Work out the percentages as in Box 7.5.
- Tally observable off-task behaviour by using the following code:
  1   talking not related to task assigned;
  2   doodling;
  3   daydreaming;
  4   wandering around;
  5   working at other tasks;
  6   physically bothering other pupils;
  7   attempting to draw attention;
  8   pencil-sharpener, fountain, washroom;
  9   other.

Box 7.4

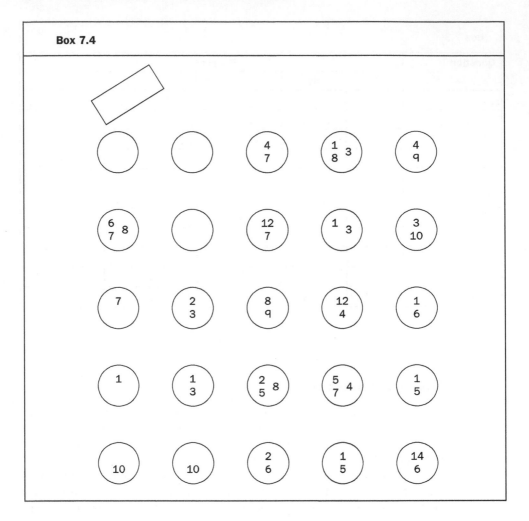

Box 7.5					
Scan	Off-task			On-task	
	Number	%		Number	%
1	4	16		21	84
2	6	24		19	76
3	1	4		24	96
4	0	0		25	100
5	3	12		22	88
6	3	12		22	88
7	6	24		19	76
8	5	20		20	80
9	4	16		21	84
10	4	16		21	84
Total	36			214	
Average		15			85

This observation is easiest to do if you concentrate on a small number of pupils over an extended period of time, rather than trying to observe a whole class at once. During each scan, observe the off-task behaviour and place the appropriate number in the space. If the student is on-task during the scan, the space is left blank as seen in Box 7.6.

Box 7.6											
Student	Scan										
	1	2	3	4	5	6	7	8	9	10	%
Jeroen	3	4				3		8			40
Jessica	2	2		3	3		4	2	3	2	80
Marloes	6	7			6	6		7			40
David		5	5			5	5		5		50
Dylan	1	1	1	8				8	1		70

Systematic observation

The research approach that relies entirely on the use of observation coding scales is known as 'systematic classroom observation'. Coding scales have long been used by social scientists to analyse behaviour and collect quantitative information about behaviour. The observer uses a scale or code to record the type of behaviour as it occurs and/or the number of instances of specific types of behaviour.

Classroom observations using coding scales are generally appropriate where a range of behaviours, too numerous to record in an open observation and too complex to collect in a structured observation, need to be mapped. Recording the on- and off-task behaviour of students, *along with their causes*, would require such an approach, as would an audit and categorization of teaching strategies used in a range of lessons.

Although it may be preferable for teacher-researchers to devise their own observation scales, sometimes they may not have the time, or they may already be familiar with an existing coding scale previously invented. In this section, I will discuss a variety of coding scales that can be utilized in specific situations by teachers, and give a more detailed illustration of one interaction scale – the Flanders interaction analysis categories.

The impetus for coding scales and checklists has come from North America where there is, and has been for some time, a concern with 'scientific' approaches to teaching (Gage 1978). But there is also a strong British tradition of systematic classroom observation; for example, the Oracle Project in primary education, which was the first large-scale study of classroom interaction in Britain (Galton *et al.* 1980). I appreciate that I am drawing on somewhat dated sources here, but am doing this because the principles and procedures they demonstrate still have a contemporary application to the practice of observation in teacher research.

There are some potential problems in the use of coding or interaction scales. The first problem is that most scales were not designed for use by teachers. Their original intent was as research tools for analysing classrooms. Given the aspirations of this book, however, it is important to stress that these are tools teachers can use to enhance their practice. The teacher-researcher's orientation is always action.

The second difficulty is that each scale represents the author's concept of a situation. One is looking at classrooms through someone else's eyes: their purposes and perceptions could be very different from one's own. It is easy, therefore, to get trapped within the intentions of the researcher who designed the scale. Consequently, it is important for teacher-researchers to match their needs closely to the intent and focus of the scale. In that way, they can maintain control over the situation.

Third, there is a heavy emphasis on quantitative methods in systematic observation. This frequently results in a conflict between statistical rigour and analytical richness. In my opinion, this inevitably leads to abstraction rather than reflection on (or in) action. This approach often leads away from the classroom rather than into it. To misquote T.S. Eliot, systematic observers may well have the experience, but in so doing they are in danger of losing the meaning.

Because of the 'scientific' bias in this approach it is unsurprising to find that most coding scales available are American in origin. As Galton (1978) comments:

> The obvious starting point for any classification of interaction analysis systems must be *Mirrors for Behaviour* (Simon and Boyer, 1975). The current edition of this anthology contains some 200 observation schedules. Most are

American and only two are British. In their collection the observation instruments are classified under eight main headings:

1. the subject of observation (teacher, pupil),
2. the setting under which the instrument is used (subject area),
3. the number of targets observed,
4. the coding unit used,
5. the collecting method employed,
6. the number of observers required,
7. the dimensions of the system (affective, cognitive), and
8. the uses reported by the author.

One of the problems with many of the American scales is that they are overly concerned with the formal teaching situation. British researchers have also been developing their own coding scales which, in general, stand in contrast to the American models. Galton (1978) comments again:

> A feature of British research has been the wide variety of different organisational contexts within which classroom observation has been carried out. Much criticism has been directed at American systems because they often seem appropriate only to the more formal type of teaching situation. One of the most interesting features of the British research is the emphasis on observation in informal settings at one extreme and the variety of schedules suitable for use in the microteaching setting for the purpose of evaluating performance in questioning and lecturing skills at the other.

These quotations from Galton (1978) are taken from his book *British Mirrors*, which is a collection of 41 classroom observation systems that are British in origin. The majority of these instruments are junior and secondary school oriented, but some are specifically designed for infant or higher education settings. Their target is almost exclusively teachers and pupils, most require only one observer and they are almost exclusively concerned with descriptions of classroom practice. The four major foci of the instruments are: classroom climate, organizational learning, the management and control of routine activities, and knowledge content. In general, they are applicable across all curriculum areas.

One of the earliest coding systems is the Flanders interaction analysis categories (FIAC). Although it may not necessarily be the most effective of the systems available, it is probably the best known. It is widely used and has influenced the design of many other category systems.

FIAC is based on ten analytical categories that reflect Flanders's conceptualization of teacher–pupil verbal interaction (see Table 7.3). Each of the categories has a number, but no scale is implied. In his book *Analysing Teaching Behaviour*, Flanders (1970) described the ten categories in detail, but for our purposes the descriptions given are sufficient. In order to help memorize the categories and make coding easier, one can shorten the descriptions of the categories as shown in Box 7.7.

Table 7.3 Flanders interaction analysis categories

Teacher talk Indirect influence	1 *Accepts feelings*: accepts and clarifies the feeling tone of the student in a non-threatening manner. Feelings may be positive or negative. Predicting and recalling feelings are included.
	2 *Praises or encourages*: praises or encourages student action or behaviour. Jokes that release tension, not at the expense of another individual, nodding head or saying 'uh huh?' or 'go on' are included.
	3 *Accepts or uses ideas of student*: clarifying, building or developing ideas or suggestions by a student. As teacher brings more of his own ideas into play, shift to category 5.
	4 *Asks questions*: asking a question about content or procedure with the intent that a student answers.
Direct influence	5 *Lectures*: giving facts or opinions about content or procedures, expressing his own idea; asking rhetorical questions.
	6 *Gives directions*: directions, commands or orders with which a student is expected to comply.
	7 *Criticizes or justifies authority*: statements, intended to change student behaviour from non-acceptable to acceptable pattern; bawling someone out; stating why the teacher is doing what he is doing; extreme self-reference.
Student talk	8 *Student talk-response*: talk by students in response to teacher. Teacher initiates the contact or solicits student statement.
	9 *Student talk-initiation*: talk by students, which they initiate. If 'calling on' student is only to indicate who may talk next, observer must decide whether student wanted to talk. If he did, use this category.
	10 *Silence or confusion*: pauses, short periods of silence, and periods of confusion in which communication cannot be understood by the observer.

Source: Open University (1976).

Box 7.7		
Teacher talk	1	accepts feelings
	2	praise
	3	accepts ideas
	4	question
	5	lecture
	6	command
	7	criticism
Pupil talk	8	solicited
	9	unsolicited
	10	silence

Source: Open University (1976).

School _____   Teacher _____
Class _____   Subject _____
Date _____   Observer _____
Lesson (1st, 2nd, etc.) _____

TALLY ACROSS

01																				
02																				
03																				
04																				
05																				
06																				
07																				
08																				
09																				
10																				
11																				
12																				
13																				
14																				
15																				
16																				
17																				
18																				
19																				
20																				
21																				
22																				
23																				
24																				
25																				
26																				
27																				
28																				
29																				
30																				

Figure 7.3 FIAC lesson observation sheet.
(Open University 1976).

The procedures for using the Flanders system are quite straightforward. Observers are first trained until they show a high level of agreement with other trained observers. Once they have been trained, they watch a lesson and apply the technique as follows using a coding sheet such as that illustrated in Figure 7.3.

1   Every 3 seconds the observer writes down the category best describing the verbal behaviour of the teacher and class.
2   The numbers are written in sequence across the data sheet.
3   Each line of the data sheet contains 20 squares, thus representing approximately 1 minute of time.
4   Separate 'episodes' can be identified by scribbled margin notes, and a new line commenced for a new 'episode'.
5   In a research project, the observer would have a pocket timer designed to give a signal every 3 seconds, thus reminding them to record a tally (a mobile phone or a pager can be used).

Two main advantages of the Flanders system are that it is fairly easy to learn and apply, and that the ten categories describe a number of behaviours which many would agree are important, such as the teacher's use of praise and criticism and the pupil's solicited and unsolicited talk. Also, the tallying of events every 3 seconds enables considerable information to be collected and analysed. There is usually a high level of agreement between trained observers.

On the other hand, much information is lost, especially non-verbal aspects of communication. In particular, some categories are too broad (e.g. category 4: Asking questions) and others discriminate insufficiently. For example, category 5 (Lectures) does not discriminate between giving information which is correct and that which is incorrect. Category 10 (Silence) can represent both the silence achieved by an autocrat and the chaos which occurs when a teacher has lost control. Also, there are too few pupil categories, and it is difficult to use in informal classrooms, where two or more members may be talking at once.

For our purposes, FIAC is most appropriately used as a means for gathering classroom data that can then be used as a basis for action. So, for example, if after using FIAC a teacher discovered that he or she was talking too much, then that becomes an identifiable problem upon which action can be taken and monitored by classroom research procedures.

CASE STUDY 7.2

Case Study 7.2 illustrates the first few seconds of an exchange occurring in the twelfth minute of a lesson.

The teacher tells children to look at a map on page 60 of their books and asks the name of the country coloured green. There is a short pause and then a child replies. The text of this exchange and the data sheet would look like that shown in Box 7.8.

Box 7.8

		Category number tallied by observer
Teacher:	'Look at the map on page 60'	6 (command)
Teacher:	'What is the country coloured green?'	4 (question)
	three second pause	10 (silence)
Pupil:	'I think it's Finland, but I'm not sure.'	8 (solicited pupil talk)

Data sheet entry

(minute 12 of the lesson)

12		6	4	10	8

Source: Open University (1976).

Further reading

Rob Walker's (1989) *Doing Research* and Colin Hook's (1995) *Studying Classrooms* both contain exemplary and sound advice on methods of classroom observation that are sympathetic to the theme of this book. Walker and Adelman (1990), Wragg's (2011) *An Introduction to Classroom Observation*, Daniels *et al.*'s (2001) *Understanding Children: Interview and Observation Guide for Educators* and Reed and Bergemann's (2004) CD-ROM *Guide to Observation, Participation and Reflection in the Classroom with Forms for Field Use* also provide useful information on classroom observation. Hitchcock and Hughes (1995), in their *Research and the Teacher*, provide extensive advice but from a more traditional perspective. Good and Brophy's (2007) *Looking in Classrooms* contains many schedules for assessing classroom behaviour; this book is an important resource for teacher-researchers as it provides a range of material on teaching skills and ways of measuring their impact in the classroom. Sara Delamont's (1983) *Interaction in the Classroom* is a balanced and introductory account of the domain of classroom observation research. The second edition of Paul Croll's (2000) book *Systematic Classroom Observation* contains a fairly sustained argument for the centrality of systematic observation in quantitative research. This book also provides a detailed introduction to the large-scale 'Oracle' and 'One in Five' classroom interaction research studies. The approach taken in this book, however, tends to lead away from the classroom rather than into it, and Croll overemphasizes, in my opinion, the distinction between teachers and researchers rather than the benefits of collaboration between them. In the same tradition, the two collections of classroom observation scales by Simon and Boyer (1975) and Galton (1978) are primary resources for teacher-researchers wanting examples of coding scales. Critiques of these various approaches to classroom interaction and observation are to be found in Sara Delamont's (1984) *Readings on Interaction in the Classroom* and Martin Hammersley's (1993) *Controversies in Classroom Research*. John Beresford (1998), in his *Collecting Information for School Improvement*, provides a range of instruments for school-based and classroom research, as well as useful hints on how to administer them. Matt O'Leary's (2013) book *Classroom Observation: A Guide to the Effective Observation of Teaching and Learning* provides a good overview of classroom observation, including FIAC. For those who want a more detailed text on using systematic observation, Yoder and Symons's (2010) book *Observational Measurement of Behavior* details how to develop coding scales, though not specifically in the classroom environment.

8 Data gathering

In this chapter, I discuss a variety of techniques other than observation that teachers can use to gather information about their teaching. I will observe a similar format in discussing each of the approaches, briefly describing the technique, considering its advantages and disadvantages, stating appropriate uses and giving an example of the technique in practice. At the end of the chapter, I will present a taxonomy of teacher research methods.

The Ford Teaching Project (Elliott and Adelman 1976) in general, and the booklet *Ways of Doing Research in One's Own Classroom* (Bowen *et al.* n.d.) in particular, provided the inspiration for this chapter. The idea for the boxes illustrating the advantages/disadvantages of the data collection methods came from the appendix to the Bowen *et al.* booklet, and a number of the points made there are reproduced here verbatim. Also, all the methods of data collection mentioned below, with the exception of sociometry, were used by the Ford Teaching Project. Once again I am very grateful to the Ford Teaching Project for allowing me to use their material in this chapter. It is a great pity that their work is no longer in print. There are now, however, a number of excellent more recent books that contain such practical advice and they are referred to in the further reading section at the end of the chapter.

Before describing these methods in more detail, two caveats have to be entered. The first is that describing the techniques individually may give a false impression of orderliness and discreteness. In practice, these techniques are more often than not used eclectically and in combination. Second, we need to remember the criteria established earlier which cautioned that the method employed should not be too demanding on the teacher's time.

Field notes

Keeping field notes is a way of reporting observations of, reflections on and reactions to classroom problems. Ideally, they should be written as soon as possible after a lesson, but can be based on impressionistic jottings made during a lesson. The greater the time-lapse between the event and recording it, the more difficult it becomes to reconstruct problems and responses accurately and retain conscious awareness of one's original

Table 8.1 Advantages and disadvantages of field notes

Advantages	Disadvantages
• Very simple to keep; no outsider needed	• Need to fall back on aids such as question analysis sheets, tapes and transcripts for specific information
• Provide good ongoing record; used as a diary, they give good continuity	
• First-hand information can be studied conveniently in teacher's own time	• Conversation impossible to record by field notes
• Act as an aide-memoire	• Notebook works with small groups but not with a full class
• Help to relate incidents, explore emerging trends	• Initially time-consuming
	• Can be highly subjective
• Very useful if teacher intends to write a case study	

thinking. Many teachers I know keep a notebook open on their desk or keep a space in their daybooks for jotting down notes during the lesson and as the day progresses. Keeping a record in this way is not very time-consuming and provides surprisingly frank information that is built up over time. It also provides a fascinating biographical record of our development as teachers.

Field notes can be of a number of different types. They can be 'issue-oriented' in so far as the observations focus on a particular aspect of one's teaching or classroom behaviour and constitute an ongoing record. On the other hand, they can reflect general impressions of the classroom, its climate or incidental events. Field notes can also be used to provide case study material of a particular child. This information should be descriptive rather than speculative, so that a broad picture amenable to interpretation can be built up.

The main advantages and disadvantages of field notes are listed in point form in Table 8.1. Four uses of field notes in classroom research are:

1   They can focus on a particular issue or teaching behaviour over a period of time.
2   They can reflect general impressions of the classroom and its climate.
3   They can provide an ongoing description of an individual child that is amenable to interpretation and use in case study.
4   They can record our development as teachers.

In Case Study 8.1, taken from a series of teacher-researcher reports on children's thinking in Hull *et al.* (1985), Ian uses field notes to build up a picture of the work ethic in a low academic set of 12–13-year-olds. At a later date, the teacher might use such notes as 'evidence' in discussions with his students about their progress and aspirations.

CASE STUDY 8.1

I started making observations, keeping a notepad on the desk. I chose not to take a particular focus. After making initial observations on movement, posture and seating arrangements, and after some interviews of a general nature concerning the pupils' attitudes to the teaching of language and the organization into sets that the pupils had to submit to, a picture of the work ethic of a low academic set was gradually built up.

For each distinct activity that goes on in the English language lesson (story writing, grammar skills, etc.), the working environments and climates are different. In language work, for example, there is always an initial rush to complete one card – the minimum requirement. When this is completed, although another card is often collected, intensive work ceases and chatting about the weekend, with some desultory work, is the norm (the lesson is first period Monday). This ritualized behaviour has the function of reaffirming certain social groups, and talk is, interestingly enough, voluntarily kept to quite a quiet level. The various friendship groups have distinct topics of conversation which don't vary much over the year. Changes to the seating, which I have tried, cause a much higher level of noise. All the other English activities – each one has one lesson a week – have different structures and patterns of social interaction, attitudes and noise levels which have built up over time.

I noted that the pattern of work throughout the term – and the year – is affected by traditional school rituals. The arrangement of pupils into sets is reviewed at the end of each term and this ritual always influences work rate and conversation:

Girl: You 'eard about moving up yet, sir?
Teacher: No, I've been asked to make three recommendations to go up and down. Mr . . . will make the decision. [chorus of enquiries]
Girl: Shut up you – you're thick. If you move, it'll be down. I hope I move up – we do no work in 'ere. 'Alf of 'em can't even write [looking at the boys]. [cheers from boys]

The low status of the set is always a factor in the pupils' perceptions of their ability and in their attitude to work.

Audio recording

Audio recording is one of the most popular teacher research methods. Transcripts are excellent for those situations where teachers require a very specific and accurate record of a limited aspect of their teaching, or of a particular interaction, say, between a specific teacher and child or between two children. An increasing number of teachers are using audio as one further way of gathering data to support other forms of assessment, albeit on an incidental basis. Also, simply playing back recordings of one's teaching can be very illuminating and provide useful starting points for further

Table 8.2   Advantages and disadvantages of the audio recorder

Advantages	Disadvantages
• Very successfully monitors all conversations within range of the recorder • Provides ample material with great ease • Versatility – can be transported or left with a group • Records personality developments • Can trace development of a group's activities • Can support classroom assessment	• Nothing visual – does not record silent activities • Transcription largely prohibitive because of expense and time involved • Masses of material may provide little relevant information • Can disturb pupils because of its novelty; can be inhibiting • Continuity can be disturbed by the practical problems of operating

investigation. In our digital age the equipment has become increasingly sophisticated and you can use a mobile phone for this purpose.

Playing back recordings or making transcripts can be very time-consuming and expensive, however, unless the method is used judiciously. The Ford Teaching Project teachers and staff were very enthusiastic about this method, but they, like funded research projects, did have secretarial support for making transcripts. Most teachers do not, and for that reason I advise against it as a broad-spectrum diagnostic tool. Note that if you do need to transcribe a digital recording, there are applications that will allow you to slow down the recording and stop and start it easily for transcription purposes.

On the practical side, the use of an audio recorder requires some technical knowledge, so make certain you can use it before taking it into class and that the device is charged! It is important when recording to ensure that the microphone is picking up what is intended, and this also may require practice. Pupils often find the presence of an audio recorder in the class disturbing and have to be introduced to the technique over time. Always check with the pupils and other teachers or adults that they do not mind you recording the conversation or discussion.

The main advantages and disadvantages of the audio recorder are listed in point form in Table 8.2. Three uses of the tape-recorder in classroom research are:

1   as a general diagnostic tool for identifying aspects of one's teaching;
2   for providing detailed evidence on specific aspects of teaching through the use of transcripts;
3   as an additional source of evidence for classroom assessment.

In Case Study 8.2, again taken from Hull *et al.* (1985), Val uses an audio recorder as an aid to understanding children's thinking in relation to sketch maps in geography. What she learned from this helped her adapt her teaching style with more able pupils.

CASE STUDY 8.2

The class (of very bright 11-year-olds) was arranged in groups of four or five pupils and each group was given copies of the four maps and asked to discuss them and decide which they thought was 'best'. I only had access to one audio recorder and was only able therefore to record one discussion. When I listened to the recording, I realized that discussion clearly had potential as a research tool and that this strategy for gaining access to pupils' critical thinking was worth repeating. Pupils were realistic in their criticisms and were to some extent impersonal. The discussion helped me to see what criteria they were using and how the range of their considerations might be extended.

In my next attempt . . . (there was only one audio-recorder available), there were several groups responding to the maps, so each group chose a leader and he or she gave a report to the class at the end of the discussion and it was the final reports that were recorded. Some of the spontaneity of the original discussion was lost, but nevertheless some interesting points emerged.

It seemed that the brighter pupils were more methodical and precise in their criticism:

Simon: Our verdict on map 1 was that a ruler could have been used and some of the buildings had doors missing and that there wasn't any scale . . . title, key or north direction.

Map 3 – it's a drawing, it's not a map.

Map 4 – that's quite good, that's more of a map, they have got a key and direction and a suitable title.

Sarah: We thought map 1 wasn't very good because the writing is too small.

Map 3 wasn't very good – too artistic.

Valerie: Map 2 was the best because it showed all the roads and railways and bridges.

Pupil diaries

It is common practice in many schools for pupils to keep a daily log. This is also a quick way of obtaining information, as teachers normally check pupil diaries as a matter of course. Also, pupil diaries provide an interesting contrast to the field notes kept by the teacher on the same topic. Once the pupils have been taken into the teacher's confidence and are aware of the teacher's concern to research their teaching, these diaries are an excellent way of obtaining honest feedback, particularly when the pupils retain the right to decide whether the teacher has access to the diary. The teacher can use pupil diaries as feedback on a particular teaching episode, to gain an indication of the general class climate or to assess the progress of an individual pupil. When pupils feel comfortable with the approach, they may feel free to write about other teachers and aspects of the school. Sometimes the ethical issues raised by this may be difficult to resolve, particularly when the use of pupil diaries is not commonplace in the school.

There are a number of other methods for gathering data on the pupil's perspective, such as learning logs and peer assessment records. The use of pupil drawings is discussed later in this chapter, for example. There is a good discussion of this in Baumfield *et al.* (2013).

The main advantages and disadvantages of pupil diaries are listed in point form in Table 8.3. Three uses of pupil diaries in classroom research are:

1 to provide a pupil perspective on a teaching episode;
2 to provide data on the general climate of the classroom; and
3 to provide information for triangulation.

In Case Study 8.3, Judy is using pupil diaries as part of her strategy for reorganizing her maths class.

Table 8.3 Advantages and disadvantages of the pupil diary

Advantages	Disadvantages
• Provides feedback from pupil's perspective • Can be either focused on a specific training episode or related to the general classroom climate • Can be part of a lesson • Can help in identifying individual pupil problems • Involves pupil in improving the quality of the class • Provides a basis for triangulation	• May not be an established practice in the school • Difficult for younger children to record their thoughts and feelings • Pupils may be inhibited in discussing their feelings with the teacher • Pupil's accounts are obviously subjective • May raise ethical dilemmas

CASE STUDY 8.3

I used the diaries mainly as immediate feedback for myself and as an aid in monitoring the daily progress of the students. The following are samples of information that I gathered from the various student diaries during a four-week period:

1 There were explanations as to why they hadn't completed a number of assignments for my substitute while I was at a convention.
2 Throughout the four weeks the students used the logs to tell me when they were having trouble with an assignment and to ask to see me the next day for help.
3 A number of students suggested that I put in a centre containing mazes and logic puzzles that they could go to when they had completed all their assignments.

4   Occasionally, a pupil would ask me to change their seating arrangement as they weren't able to work near a certain person.

5   Many of them began to use the log to establish a private conversation between us.

6   I used the logs to indicate when I was disappointed in a student's performance or behaviour and to question them about it. I found that they were more open since they weren't put on the spot in front of their classmates.

7   Some of them mentioned when they felt I had let the noise level get too high or when they had been able to do more than usual because it had been exceptionally quiet.

8   They pointed out when they had wasted time waiting for me to get their books marked so they could finish off their corrections.

9   I found it especially helped me monitor the progress of my less assertive students.

10   The students would indicate when they felt I had given too heavy a workload for the week.

11   Students twice pointed out that they had come to me for assistance and I had been too busy to help them.

I felt that these logs were one of the most valuable aspects of my research project. They weren't always relevant to my actual research, but the personal contact I managed to establish with each of my students was of more importance to me than keeping them on target concerning their work in the maths programme.

Interviews

Interviewing in classroom research can take four forms: it can occur between teacher and pupil, observer and pupil, pupil and pupil and, occasionally, teacher and observer. This latter activity, however, normally occurs as a consequence of peer observation (see Chapters 6 and 7). Because teacher–pupil interviews are very time-consuming, it may be more profitable to devote that time to general classroom meetings, and only talk individually with pupils (for research purposes) when a specific instance warrants it. On the other hand, individual interviews are often very productive sources of information for a participant observer who wants to verify observations they have previously made. Like other researchers, however, I increasingly find group interviews with three or four students the most productive. Far from inhibiting each other, the individuals spark themselves into sensitive and perceptive discussion. I also find it helpful to audio-record my summary of the discussion with the students at the end of the interview. This enables them to correct or amplify my interpretation and provides me with a brief and succinct account of the interview that can easily be transcribed.

Pupil–pupil interviews can provide rich sources of data, particularly if the pupil interviewer keeps to an interview schedule prepared by the teacher. It is a good idea to audio-record these individual interviews for future reference, particularly if the encounters are relatively short.

Walker and Adelman (1990) make a number of points about effective interviewing:

1   Be a sympathetic, interested and attentive listener, without taking an active conservative role; this is a way of conveying that you value and appreciate the child's opinion.
2   Be neutral with respect to subject matter. Do not express your own opinions either on the subjects being discussed by the children or on the children's ideas about these subjects, and be especially careful not to betray feelings of surprise or disapproval at what the child knows.
3   Your own sense of ease is also important. If you feel hesitant or hurried, the students will sense this feeling and behave accordingly.
4   The students may also be fearful that they will expose an attitude or idea that you don't think is correct. Reassure along the lines of 'Your opinions are important to me. All I want to know is what you think – this isn't a test and there isn't any one answer to the questions I want to ask.'
5   Specifically we suggest that you:
    •   phrase questions similarly each time,
    •   keep the outline of interview questions before you, and
    •   be prepared to reword a question if it is not understood or if the answer is vague and too general. Sometimes it is hard not to give an 'answer' to the question in the process of rewording it.

The main advantages and disadvantages of interviewing are listed in Table 8.4. Three uses of the interview in classroom research are:

•   to focus on a specific aspect of teaching or classroom life in detail;
•   to provide general diagnostic information through teacher–pupil classroom discussion; and
•   to improve the classroom climate.

Case Study 8.4 consists of extracts from a conversation between three Year 9 students (S) at the Sanders Draper School, Havering, together with Mel Ainscow (MA), David Hargreaves (DHH) and myself (DH). Sanders Draper was involved in the Improving the Quality of Education for All school improvement project. The purpose of the discussion was to assess how far the school's development priority, 'resource based learning', had affected students' perceptions of the way they were taught and learned. We used this information in feedback to staff, who in turn incorporated it in their own developmental work. I have included such an extended illustration partly for its intrinsic interest, but also to show how classroom research can support whole-school development and to illustrate the power of the group interview.

Table 8.4   The advantages and disadvantages of interviews

(a) Teacher–pupil (individually or in groups of three or four)

Advantages	Disadvantages
• Teacher in direct contact with pupil • Pupil(s) familiar with teacher, therefore more at ease • Teacher able to seek information they want directly and not through a ream of irrelevant information • Can be done in lesson time or outside the class • Can follow up problems immediately when they arise and get information while minds are still fresh	• Time-consuming • May be carried out with some form of recording equipment, with attendant disadvantages • Frequently difficult to get younger children to explain their thoughts and feelings

(b) Observer–pupil (individually or in groups of three or four)

Advantages	Disadvantages
• Leaves teacher free as the interviewer discovers initial information from the pupil(s) • Pupil(s) are frequently more candid with the outsider than with class teacher or teacher from within the school • Outsider is likely to be more objective • Outsider can focus the information provided along predetermined lines of investigation	• Pupil(s) unfamiliar with observer may be reluctant to divulge relevant information • Mutual uncertainty • If the teacher is the primary agent in the research, then they will get their information second-hand and subject to the biases of the interviewer • The whole set-up is time-consuming as information goes from pupil(s) to interviewer to teacher • Difficult to obtain a skilled outsider

(c) Pupil–pupil

Advantages	Disadvantages
• Pupils may be more candid with each other • Leaves teacher free • Can occur during lesson time • May produce unanticipated/unusual perspectives	• Pupils may find the activity too unfamiliar • May encourage disruption • Has to be recorded and played to teacher

CASE STUDY 8.4

DH: What is it like to learn in this school?

S: It's changed now that we are able to use the library more, we are now using more visual/audio type stuff, videos, rather than just learning out of a textbook.

S: Also teachers tell you to get on with it, rather than them telling you what to do. You can come in here [the library], you find out all the information and you can say to a teacher I want to do this and that, and they say alright then.

S: Well we are more tending to get into things like, in maths for example, we tend to go into our own investigations where we can take a problem and we investigate it in our own way.

DH: Tell me a bit about how you actually find the information.

S: Well, if you find a book, look through the subject index, or there is a disk thing on the computer, it's got all newspaper things, you put the disk in and you say what subjects you want to find out about, type it in and it comes up with all the different things in the subjects. You choose what you want. There is also an encyclopaedia list on the computer.

DH: What happens when you've done all this and got some information on the subject you are dealing with, say four or five bits of information – what do you do then?

S: We either make it into like a folder of work, put it into graphs, or sometimes we get the chance to make a play out of it, but there is still a certain amount of written work to record it all. Things like – they'll tell a certain amount of detail. Like in science they were telling us about disease and then we had to write a newspaper report about it, so used the pictures.

DH: What happens if you get into the situation where you find that one bit of information disagrees with another piece of information. How do you make a decision?

S: Usually you put both of the arguments, both for and against, or you decide which you think, but explain that there are other sides to the idea. Put down what you thought what was right and what was wrong. Put both sides down.

MA: That's quite demanding, do some students struggle with that?

S: It depends if you are looking through hundreds of encyclopaedias for the one thing you are looking for; otherwise you might as well watch it on the video if you are looking for something about the Third Reich, see if they've got a video about it. That's easier. There will always be people who work at different speeds, are capable of different things. When we do learning in our own way, then it is better because they are not trying to keep up with the top students in the class.

DHH: You have given me the impression that this new style of learning, your relationship with the teacher is different.

S: Well it is in some ways because there are some teachers who are sitting there and want to teach you everything on the line, but there are others who think it best for us to work down here [in the library].

DHH: But is it? Is it best for you?

S: Yes, I think it is. I prefer it anyway. You are at your own pace. Not like a teacher dictating to you and you just sitting there with your mouth open.

DH: Some people say that the real way to be taught is to write down lots of notes, do exercises from the book.

S: But the two ways compensate each other. You learn at your own pace and then answer the questions from the book. Then you remember it, take it in rather than just taking notes. You sort of construct it your own way. No real way of learning, different people find it easier to do different things, so I don't think anyone can say it is a lot better to work out of a textbook or it is a lot better to watch a video.

DHH: If I understand you correctly when you take notes, you are not really learning anything.

S: You learn about half of it but if you are in control of your own learning, you are doing it the way you want to do it, you actually want to learn about it, you are taking it in, and remembering more because you are doing it your way.

[*The students then showed us some examples of work.*]

MA: Who produced this?

S: I decided to do it on a computer at home, then it would be easier to read.

MA: So this in a sense summarizes all the research that you did, you've put it into your own words and made an information sheet.

S: Yes, that's what they said, do it like a magazine article, then it comes out in your own words. More likely to remember something that way.

DH: You have been in the school now for three years, do you think there has been a change in the way that teachers teach over those three years?

S: [Since the new head arrived] the school has got more disciplined.

DH: More disciplined in the school, but at the same time a more open approach to teaching and learning?

S: Well we've been given the chance to like express ourselves, but because of that we've had to go by their rules.

DH: So there is a good response to this more open way.

S: Yes, you've got the responsibility of getting on with what you want to do, you've got to do it even if the teacher isn't watching you. It sort of works two ways, you respect the school rules and they'll respect you, they are trusting you to work on your own.

DHH: Somebody might say, from outside, that you might choose a very slow pace for yourself and the job of the teacher is to make you go at a faster pace. What do you say to that?

S: Well the teachers would like say to you, I don't think you have done enough work. If you have only done a couple of sentences of work for your whole

project, they will like give you a detention, or a series of detentions, or something like that. That will teach you to work more rather than at a faster pace.

S: You will always have to do a certain amount of work, you will never give in one
sheet of work for a project and it will be OK. That's never going to be told OK so
that's your pace then.

DHH: So you are not going to get away with that sort of thing.

S: No.

DH: So that is an example of the rules on the one hand and the flexibility on the
other.

S: Yes.

DHH: So it is tough in some ways but not in others.

S: Yes.

S: It's like the correct balance between lenience and strictness.
No good coming in one day and doing a little work and then saying that's enough,
then coming in the next day and doing nothing, you have to try to do as much
work as possible on both days.

[*We were then shown another piece of work.*]

DHH: Did you change your mind on anything when you were writing?

S: Yeah I did actually. At first I thought the approach was all wrong and it should
never be allowed. When I started researching into it and found out things, there
are fors and against. I really decided that it was a matter of individuals really, so
I put that in there. For and against, and then my own views.

DHH: It has a terrific ending to it. You went through the arguments, then you
made your own mind up personally at the end, and then it ends 'then I hope
you've decided what you think' – the reader is asked to decide for himself, or
herself.

S: Well really you've got to decide for yourself. There is no one who can say that
one thing is right and one thing is wrong, it's a matter of your own decision.

Video recorder and digital camera

The video recorder is increasingly being used by teachers as a means of gathering
general information about their teaching. We have also already noted how increasingly
many teacher-researchers are using their iPads to great effect to replace the
video recorder. This allows the teacher to observe many facets of their teaching
quickly, and provides heuristic and accurate information for diagnosis. After this,
the teacher may wish to use a different method to examine specific aspects of their
teaching.

Many of the teacher-researchers I know use the video on an intermittent but
regular basis to enable them to keep in touch with their teaching. If an observer
or student can be used to operate the video recorder, then more attention can be

Table 8.5 Advantages and disadvantages of the video recorder and digital camera

(a) Video recorder

Advantages	Disadvantages
• Enables all situations to be constantly reviewed • Origin of problems can be diagnosed • Behavioural patterns of teacher and pupils can be seen • Patterns of progress over long periods can be clearly charted	• Can be very conspicuous and distracting • If camera is directed by operator, it will only record that which they deem to be of importance; operator acts as editor

(b) Digital camera

Advantages	Disadvantages
• Advantage may be obtained by looking at images of kids working, or at end products of their work, and as a stimulus for discussion • Helps obtain observation and comment from other teachers who were not present at the time	• Shows isolated situations; difficulty of being in the right place at the right time; concentrates on small groups and individuals, not classes; records nothing in depth • Images may not truly depict activities of the children, if photographer is selective

paid to specific teaching episodes (identified beforehand) or the reaction of particular students.

The main advantages and disadvantages of the video recorder are listed in point form in Table 8.5(a). Three uses of video recorders in classroom research are:

1 for obtaining visual material of the total teaching situation;
2 acting as an aid to diagnosis; and
3 as a means of examining in detail a specific teaching episode.

Photographs, and the more recent use of the digital camera, are useful ways of recording critical incidents in classrooms or of illustrating particular teaching episodes. They can also be used to support other forms of data gathering (e.g. interviews or field notes) or as a means for providing reference points for interviews or discussions.

The main advantages and disadvantages of photographs and digital photography are listed in point form in Table 8.5(b).

In Case Study 8.5, I describe the first experience Geoff, a student on one of my in-service courses, had with the video recorder.

CASE STUDY 8.5

Geoff is a deputy headteacher in a special school. His pupils face many learning challenges, but the expectation is that they will eventually be able to cope by themselves in some limited way. To give his pupils that basic level of life skill is Geoff's main goal. Geoff used the video recorder to examine his teaching and to try and find an answer to the question 'why is everything so time-consuming?'.

Geoff decided to video the morning session from 9:30 to 10:15, which was the most structured and high-energy time of the day. During the lesson, the nursery nurse was also involved in the class. Before videoing, Geoff identified a series of topics on which he wanted to get information:

- maximum time worked by each pupil;
- time wasted by each pupil;
- time unavoidably lost;
- time to be spent with each pupil; and
- number of tasks accomplished in the 45-minute session by each pupil.

The video recording session went well. Geoff had had the camera in his room for a few days, so the pupils were used to having it around. With a wide-angle lens he was able to capture all the activity in the class. Geoff then began reviewing the recording. Besides gathering data on the points above, he also detailed the following:

- the amount of time he spent out of the class on administrative duties;
- the number of times he praised/reprimanded a pupil;
- how long the pupils were left unsupervised;
- time spent by nursery nurse with each pupil; and
- pupil's reaction to attention.

Geoff then analysed the recording for each pupil and produced a detailed analysis of how individual lessons were spent. From this information Geoff was able to derive a number of hypotheses concerning the class and set up a programme for utilizing the time more effectively.

Questionnaires

Questionnaires that ask specific questions about aspects of the classroom, curriculum or teaching method are a quick and simple way of obtaining broad and rich information from pupils. It is important, however, particularly in the primary grades, to be relatively unsophisticated in the structuring of the questions. Condense the usual five- point scale to two or three responses, keep the questions simple, and use the basic 'what did you like best?', 'what did you like least?', 'what would you do differently?' type of open-ended question.

Figure 8.1 Happy faces as a response to questions.

With younger (and older) pupils it is often more profitable to use a happy face as the criterion response to questions as in Figure 8.1. More imaginatively, cartoon pictures can be used, as in Figure 8.2 – the possibilities are endless!

Online/electronic questionnaires can be engaging to students and their results – depending on the types of questions asked – can be electronically analysed. There are free survey applications available on the Internet. Interactive whiteboards used with mobile devices or electronic voting systems can provide quick results (students transmit their answers to the whiteboard using the mobile or voting device), which can then be followed up with further questions if necessary.

The main advantages and disadvantages of the questionnaire are listed in point form in Table 8.6. The main use of the questionnaire in classroom research is to obtain quantitative responses to specific predetermined questions. Examples of questionnaires are given in Figures 8.2 and 8.3.

Sociometry

Sociometric analysis or sociometry is a technique used to measure the emotional structure of a group. As a diagnostic instrument, sociometry's purpose is to highlight the feelings of attraction, indifference and rejection that occur within a group and between its members. The approach has obvious applications to classrooms where teachers want to discover the social structure of the class for research and other purposes. The most important 'other purpose' is to identify pupils who are socially isolated in order to take remedial action.

Before administering a sociometric test, it is important to ensure that the pupils know each other fairly well, that confidentiality is established, and that action is taken as a consequence. Sociometry in this sense is a dynamic process that can lead to improvement in children's attitudes and relationships and the general enhancement of a classroom climate.

Congdon (1978: 6) describes a method for administering the sociometric test:

> Each child is handed a slip of blank paper and told to write his name at the top. Some teachers prefer to have the names of all pupils in the class written on the blackboard. It is always advisable to write up the names of any pupils who are absent. The test should be meaningful to the pupils. So, for example, the context of the test could be a project. After deciding on a project the pupils

Figure 8.2 Reading attitude survey.

Table 8.6 Advantages and disadvantages of questionnaires

Advantages	Disadvantages

• Easy to administer; quick to fill in
• Easy to follow up
• Provides direct comparison of groups and individuals
• Provides feedback on:
  – attitudes
  – adequacy of resources
  – adequacy of teacher help
  – preparation for next session
  – conclusions at end of term
• Data are quantifiable
• May be possible to collect answers and analyse them electronically
	• Analysis is time-consuming
	• Extensive preparation to get clear and relevant questions
	• Difficult to get questions that explore in depth
	• Effectiveness depends very much on reading ability and comprehension of the child
	• Children may be fearful of answering candidly
	• Children will try to produce 'right' answers

Inquiry/discovery follow-up questionnaire
Please put a ring round the answer you wish to give to each question. If you are not sure ring the nearest to what you think.

1 How much of the lesson did you enjoy?   All of it/Some of it/None
2 How much do you think you learnt?   Nothing/Something/A lot
3 How much did you understand?   Most of it/Some of it/Nothing
4 Could you find the books, information,   None/Some of it/Most of it
   equipment you needed?
5 Did other people help you?   A lot/A little/Not at all
6 Did other people stop you working?   A lot/Sometimes/Not at all
7 Did the teacher help you   Enough/Not enough
8 Did the lesson last   Long enough/Too long/Not long
                                               enough
9 Was the lesson   Boring/Interesting
10 Did you need anything you could   Yes/No
   not find?
11 Where did you get help from?   Teacher/Group/Someone else
12 Did you find this work   Easy/Hard/Just about right
13 Write down anything which made it hard for you to learn
14 Write down anything you particularly enjoyed about this lesson

Figure 8.3 A sample questionnaire designed by Roger Pols.

Reproduced with permission from Bowen *et al.* (n.d.).

could be told that they will be allowed to work in groups and that the groups would be made up according to their own choices.

On the left hand side of the sheet the pupils are asked to write the name of the person with whom they would most like to work in a group. Underneath they are asked to write the name of the one they would like next best, then the next and so on. They can be told to write as many names as they wish or none at all. The pupil is then asked to turn over the sheet and again down the left hand side of the page to write the names of any children with whom they do not wish to work. The teacher again tells them that they may write as many names as they wish or none at all. And what is more important, she tells them that the names will be known only to herself, i.e. the choices are made privately and no pupil should be told either who chose him or how many choices he received. In this way no one's feelings are hurt.

After the test has been administered, the pupil choices are analysed to establish the structure of relationships within the class. The best-known and easiest understood method of doing this is the sociogram. Congdon (1978: 7) continues to describe how a sociogram is constructed:

> In drawing a sociogram it is often useful to begin with the most chosen pupil and add the symbols for any pupils who reciprocate his or her choices. Next, pupils who have mutual choices with this group can be added. When these have been exhausted then a fresh group can be drawn up starting with the next most highly-chosen pupil and so on. The sociogram can be completed by filling in the unreciprocated choices.

Figure 8.4 is an example of a sociogram for a group of eight individuals with the symbols most commonly used marked on it. Clearly in Figure 8.4 pupils E, F and H are unpopular, and this information encourages the teacher to act to remedy this situation;

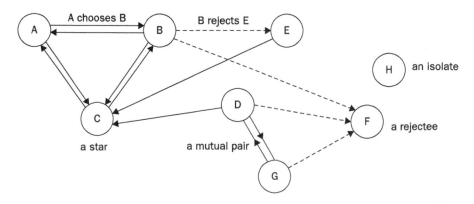

Figure 8.4   Example of a sociogram.

Table 8.7   Advantages and disadvantages of sociometry

Advantages	Disadvantages
• Simple way to discover social relationships in class • Provides guide to action • Can be integrated into class activity	• Possibility of compounding the isolation of some pupils

action can also be monitored through other classroom research techniques. The sociogram is a useful method for teacher-researchers who wish to explore the social structure of their class and the relationships between pupils. It also provides a starting point for action and further research. As sociometry emphasizes the class as a group, parallel efforts could focus on the perspectives of individual children, using, for example, self-concept inventories.

The major advantages and disadvantages of sociometry are listed in point form in Table 8.7. The main use of sociometry in classroom research is to disclose the social structure of the class.

In Case Study 8.6, Ann was using a behaviour modification 'game' to improve the level of assignment completion in her maths class.

CASE STUDY 8.6

Since I had scruples about such a game causing social rejection of the target pupils, a sociogram was done before and after the experiment. Pupils were each asked to name three children they would like to sit next to during art lessons or storytime. It was stressed that this would be a non-academic, non-competitive time. The first choices were assigned three points, the second two points and the third one point. Points were totalled and the results entered on a graph.

Pre- and post-use of the sociogram showed that the popularity of the target pupils was not detrimentally affected by the game. None of them were social isolates but they all fell into the lower half of the class.

Documentary evidence

Documents (memos, letters, position papers, examination papers, newspaper clippings, etc.) surrounding a curriculum or other educational concern can illuminate rationale and purpose in interesting ways. The use of such material can provide background information and understanding of issues that would not otherwise be available.

Table 8.8 Advantages and disadvantages of documentary evidence

Advantages	Disadvantages
• Illuminates issues surrounding a curriculum or teaching method • Provides context, background and understanding • Provides an easy way of obtaining other people's perceptions	• Obtaining documents can be time-consuming • Certain documents may be difficult to obtain • Certain persons may be unwilling to share 'confidential' documents

The main advantages and disadvantages of documentary evidence are listed in point form in Table 8.8. The main use of documents in classroom research is that they provide a context for understanding a particular curriculum or teaching method.

In Case Study 8.7, Gill used documents to understand the nature of the art curriculum.

CASE STUDY 8.7

During her work for a postgraduate degree, Gill, an art teacher, examined some of the influences on the art curriculum. Her reason for doing this was largely personal: increasingly she was feeling a tension between her aspirations for art teaching and the general approach to the art curriculum that she was being encouraged to adopt. Gill's approach to the teaching of art was essentially child-centred. She has a commitment to developing a pupil's artistic talents and her teaching style, and the activities she set her pupils were designed to achieve this goal. Her investigation involved examining a range of past papers and examiners' comments. To her chagrin, she found that the art curriculum in general was influenced not by pupil achievement or aspirations but more by the examiners' (rather traditional) comments. This discovery served at least to explain her tension. It also encouraged her to develop a scheme of work in painting for younger pupils and propose alternative syllabuses for examination pupils that integrated her own ideas on art teaching with the more traditional approach.

Case study

The case study is a relatively formal analysis of an aspect of classroom life. Some teachers may wish to produce case studies for a university course they are taking or as research towards a higher degree. These situations apart, it is unlikely that teachers will devote time to producing a formal case report of their teacher-researcher efforts every time they undertake a project. (For a more detailed discussion of case study research, see Stake 1995.)

Table 8.9 Advantages and disadvantages of the case study

Advantages	Disadvantages
• A relatively simple way of plotting the progress of a course or a pupil's or group's reaction to teaching methods • Tend to give a more accurate and representative picture than will any one of the research methods detailed above; case studies draw on data gathered by many methods	• In order for the case study to be of value it must be fairly exhaustive; this means that it will be time-consuming in its preparation and its writing • Feedback available to teacher only after considerable lapse of time

The main advantages and disadvantages of the case study are listed in point form in Table 8.9. The main use of the case study in classroom research is that it provides a relatively formal and fairly definitive analysis of a specific aspect of teaching behaviour or classroom life. Examples of teacher research case studies are given in Chapters 2 and 6.

Pupil drawings

Pupil drawings are a method of collecting students' perceptions and experiences on teaching and on their educational experience. This method is a fun activity, and one that students respond to, that can provide rich and informative data. Many researchers conduct follow-up interviews with the children and ask them to deconstruct their pictures. The advantages and the disadvantages of this method are illustrated in Table 8.10.

As an example, a student who participated in the *Working with Disaffected Students* research project (Riley and Rustique-Forrester 2002) describes his experience in the classroom through the drawing in Figure 8.5. He portrays himself as a mushroom.

Table 8.10 Advantages and disadvantages of pupil drawings

Advantages	Disadvantages
• An easy, fun and quick approach to gathering pupils' views and reactions to teaching and to life within the school • Information can be informative and could depict accurately students' views and experiences	• Analysis of the drawings could be challenging • Children who do not see this medium as their preferred way of expressing themselves could feel threatened and provide invalid data • Children could provide the 'right' answers

Figure 8.5   A student's experience of the classroom.

(from Riley and Rustique-Forrester (2002: 35), reproduced with the permission of Prof. Kathryn Riley).

He explains that whilst at school he hid in the background and as a result grew very little. He continues by stating that teachers had to look hard to find him in the classroom.

Mapping the 'process of change' in schools

The final data-gathering method refers to a battery of techniques rather than a single approach, so will therefore be described a little differently from the others. During our programme of research and development into school improvement, we have come to recognize that traditional research methods are sometimes too cumbersome and time-consuming in disclosing the intricacies of the change process. We felt that there was room for new, more user-friendly yet penetrating techniques for investigating and measuring the complex processes and relationships involved in school change. With a grant from the ESRC we developed six new techniques for mapping the process of change in schools. A comprehensive description, with advice on administration, of the techniques is found in the manual produced as a result of the research, *Mapping Change in Schools: The Cambridge Manual of Research Techniques* (Cambridge University 1994) and in a paper by Ainscow *et al.* (1995).

The six techniques in the series cluster around two key elements in the change process: the individual teacher and the school as an institution. Despite the proliferation of externally mandated changes, the success of many change initiatives remains attributable to the commitment of individual teachers. Certainly the impact of any change on student outcomes is heavily affected by behaviour in the classroom. At the same time, it is claimed that the school as a whole, especially its climate/ethos/culture, makes an important contribution to development and change. Three of the techniques focus on the *individual teacher* and tap data at that level. The other three focus on the *school as an institution*. Data from both levels are essential if the interaction between individual and institution in processes of change is to be better understood. The manual of techniques is accordingly divided into two series.

Series 1: Individual (teacher) level

- *Technique 1: The time line of change.* The aim of this technique is to record how individuals within a school perceive their experience of a particular change over a period of time.
- *Technique 2: The experience of change.* The purpose of this technique is to gather information about the feelings of individuals towards changes in their school.
- *Technique 3: The initiation of change.* This technique taps teachers' commitment to change and their sense of control over it. It differs from the previous two techniques in that it is concerned with change in general rather than a specific change.

Series 2: Institutional (school) level

- *Technique 4: The culture of the school.* The purpose of this technique is to generate data on teachers' perceptions of the culture of their school, the direction in which the culture is moving and their ideal culture (see Hargreaves 1995).
- *Technique 5: The structures of the school.* The purpose of this technique is to generate data on some of the basic social structures underlying school cultures.
- *Technique 6: The conditions of school.* This technique consists of a scale for measuring a school's internal conditions and potential for innovation. The 24 items are grouped under six headings that represent the key conditions necessary for school improvement.

There are a number of ways in which teacher-researchers can use the data generated by the techniques, and feed the data back to schools. First, because the techniques are amenable to rapid analysis and presentation, virtually immediate feedback can be given in some cases. This is especially true of the culture game (a technique for measuring school culture), school structures and responses to change techniques. When used with teachers as part of a training day or staff meeting, it is possible to give aggregate responses to the whole staff during the same session. This feedback has often aroused great interest and animated discussion.

The second method of feedback is to talk through the results from the administration of the whole battery with the senior staff of the school involved. There is a method for reducing the data onto one side of A4, and this makes the conveying of information much easier to handle. Our approach is to present the data in a sequential and descriptive way, and then on the basis of this to encourage discussion and interpretation of the results from the senior staff. This proves at times to be a delicate process. Occasionally our ethic of confidentiality is challenged, particularly when we are encouraged to be judgemental rather than descriptive. In these discussions it is vital to maintain confidentiality and not to go beyond the data.

The third approach to giving feedback is where the data are used as part of a school improvement process within a school. The techniques are now routinely used in IQEA schools as a basis for action planning. The experience we have had convinces us that the data emerging from the techniques have great heuristic power.

To summarize, when taken together the techniques provide a map of the process of change in a school. They can be used individually to investigate particular aspects of change processes or in combination for a more comprehensive analysis. The techniques can also be used to map changes in the school's conditions over time, and facilitate the process of change and improvement in schools.

Conclusion

In this chapter, I have described a variety of ways in which data can be gathered for the purpose of classroom research. The techniques described in this chapter are basically open-ended in so far as they are used most effectively for diagnostic purposes. Although I have described these techniques individually, it is important to realize that they can and are most often used eclectically and in combination. But each has a specific purpose and is best suited to a particular situation. A taxonomy of the main advantages, disadvantages and uses of the various techniques is given in Table 8.11.

Further reading

Additional information about the techniques of classroom research can be found in the publications associated with the Ford Teaching Project. Elliott and Adelman's (1976) case study of the Ford Teaching Project in the Open University curriculum course *Innovation at the Classroom Level* is informative and useful, as is the Ford Teaching Project booklet *Ways of Doing Research in One's Own Classroom* (Bowen *et al.* n.d.). Walker and Adelman's (1990) book *A Guide to Classroom Observation* is similarly helpful and contains advice on, and examples of, the use of photography in classroom

Table 8.11 Taxonomy of classroom research techniques

Technique	Advantage(s)	Disadvantage(s)	Use(s)
Field notes	simple; ongoing; personal; aide-memoire	subjective; needs practice	• specific issue • case study • general impression
Audio recording	versatile; accurate; provides ample data	transcription difficult; time-consuming; often inhibiting,	• detailed evidence
Pupil diaries	provides pupils' perspective	subjective	• diagnostic • triangulation
Interviews and discussions	can be teacher–pupil, observer–pupil, pupil–pupil	time-consuming	• specific in-depth information
Video recorder and digital photography	visual and comprehensive	awkward and expensive; can be distracting	• visual and diagnostic • illustrates critical incidents
Questionnaires	highly specific; easy to administer; comparative	time-consuming to analyse (unless this can be done electronically); problem of 'right' answers	• specific information and feedback
Sociometry	easy to administer; provides guide to action	can threaten isolated pupils	• analyses social relationships
Documentary evidence	illuminative	difficult to obtain; time-consuming	• provides context and information
Case study	accurate; representative; uses range of techniques	time-consuming	• comprehensive overview of an issue • publishable format
Pupil drawings	simple; quick accurate;	analysis can be challenging; can provide invalid data from some pupils; can encourage children to give the 'right' answer	• specific issue • diagnostic • specific in-depth information
Mapping techniques	comprehensive; easy to administer and analyse	requires whole-staff response; can be threatening; confidentiality sometimes challenged	• provides a map of the process of change in a school • can be used to promote development

research. Rob Walker's (1989) book *Doing Research* and Cohen *et al.*'s (2011) *Research Methods in Education* (7th edition) contains detailed advice about methods, as do James McKernan's (1996) *Curriculum Action Research* and Valsa Koshy's (2010) *Action Research*. Two additional practical texts are Colin Lankshear and Michele Knobel's (2004) *A Handbook for Teacher Research: From Design to Implementation* and Burton and Bartlett's (2005) *Practitioner Research for Teachers* which also includes best-practice case studies. Colin Hook's (1995) *Studying Classrooms* is extensive and practical and also contains a useful taxonomy of approaches similar to Table 8.11. Kemmis and McTaggart's (1988) third edition of *The Action Research Planner*, John Elliott's (1991) *Action Research for Educational Change*, Alan Bryman's (2004) *Social Research Methods* (2nd edition), John Beresford's (1998) *Collecting Information for School Improvement*, Sagor's (2011) *The Action Research Guidebook*, Briggs and Coleman's (2007) *Research Methods in Educational Leadership and Management* (2nd edition) and my *Evaluation for School Development* (Hopkins 1989) also contain helpful advice on data collection methods. For more details on case studies as a data gathering method I recommend Yin's (2013) fifth edition *Case Study Research: Design and Methods* (5th edition).

9 Analysing classroom research data

The third criterion for teacher research outlined in Chapter 4 was that the methodology employed must be reliable enough to allow teachers confidently to formulate hypotheses and develop strategies applicable to their own classroom situations. This is an area where teacher research in particular, and qualitative research in general, has traditionally not been conspicuously successful. Qualitative research procedures (i.e. where the emphasis is on expressing one's data and conclusions in the form of words) seem often to be shrouded in mystery. The findings of such studies are arrived at by usually unannounced procedures and techniques, thus creating methodologies which can be neither fully scrutinized nor usefully emulated. Consequently, it is important to establish a coherent methodology for analysing classroom research data. We have in recent years been assisted in this endeavour by methodological developments led by researchers such as Miles and Huberman's (1994) in their handbook on *Qualitative Data Analysis* as well as others referred to below. In this chapter, therefore, I first outline the problem in a little more detail, then suggest a framework for analysis and describe the four stages that comprise the process.

The problem

Action research, like most practitioner-oriented methodologies, has been widely criticized, but mainly by those who implicitly denigrate the method by criticizing individual research projects that have adopted classroom research techniques. It is illogical – not to say unfair – to judge the quality of a Shakespeare play by observing a performance by amateur actors. And so it is with classroom research as has already been argued, our preferred term for what others often term action research.

It is true, though, that classroom research has in the past often been done badly, mainly because of unarticulated procedures for analysis. By way of contrast, the rules for quasi-experimental research were cogently articulated some time ago by Campbell and Stanley (1963) and have a long and distinguished tradition. This tradition is so prevalent that research in education is commonly equated with studies carried out within this paradigm. This should not be surprising, for the rules are simple to apply and are consistent with the ubiquitous psycho-statistical research tradition. It is unfortunate, as we have seen, that this approach is ill-suited to the research needs of the classroom teacher.

In classroom research, the concern is more with cases than samples. This implies a methodology more applicable to understanding a problematic situation than one based on predicting outcomes within the parameters of an existing and tacitly accepted social system. The skills required of classroom researchers are, as Strauss and Corbin (1998) claim, 'The ability to step back and critically analyze situations, to recognize and avoid bias, to obtain valid and reliable data, and to think abstractly'.

Unfortunately, as Miles and Huberman (1984: 20) note in their paper 'Drawing Valid Meaning from Qualitative Data', there is an Achilles heel here: there are few agreed canons for the analysis of qualitative data, and therefore the truth claims and validity underlying such work are uncertain. They describe the problem as follows (1984: 20):

> Despite a growing interest in qualitative studies, we lack a body of clearly defined methods for drawing valid meaning from qualitative data. We need methods that are practical, communicable, and not self deluding: scientific in the positivist's sense of the word, and aimed toward interpretive understanding in the best sense of that term.

What follows is an attempt to rectify this situation, at least with regard to teacher-based classroom research. The situation is, however, not as dire as it was when this chapter was first written, as there have been a series of helpful methodological advances, many of which are noted in the discussion that follows.

A framework for analysis

Making sense of social situations has long been the task of sociologists, and it is from their (and anthropologists') methodological canons that much avant-garde work on educational evaluation was initially drawn (see Hamilton *et al.* 1977). It is this research tradition that provides a framework within which to consider teacher-based classroom research. Classrooms are also complex social situations that require understanding. We need to produce theory that is applicable to classrooms as well as within them.

Two of the classic statements on sociological fieldwork were made by Becker (1958) and Glaser and Strauss (1967). In his paper 'Problems of Inference and Proof in Participant Observation', Becker (1958: 653) described four stages in the analysis of fieldwork data:

> We can distinguish three distinct stages of analysis conducted in the field itself, and a fourth stage, carried on after completion of the field work. These stages are differentiated, first, by their logical sequence: each succeeding stage depends on some analysis in the preceding stage. They are further differenti-ated by the fact that different kinds of conclusions are arrived at in each stage and that these conclusions are put to different uses in the continuing research. Finally, they are differentiated by the different criteria that are used to assess evidence and to reach conclusions in each stage. The three stages of field

analysis are: the selection and definition of problems, concepts, and indices; the check on the frequency and distribution of phenomena; and the incorporation of individual findings into a model of the organisation under study. The fourth stage of final analysis involves problems of presentation of evidence and proof.

In a similar way, in *The Discovery of Grounded Theory*, Glaser and Strauss (1967: 105) describe the concept of the constant comparative method as a means of analysing sociological data:

> We shall describe in four stages the constant comparative method; 1. comparing incidents applicable to each category, 2. integrating categories and their properties, 3. delimiting the theory, and 4. writing the theory. Although this method of generating theory is a continuously growing process – each stage after a time is transformed into the next – earlier stages do remain in operation simultaneously throughout the analysis and each provides continuous development to its successive stage until the analysis is terminated.

Although Glaser and Strauss's notion of the constant comparative method is a more dynamic concept than Becker's linear sequence of stages, there are basic similarities in their approaches to the analysis of field data. Each envisage the analytical process as having four distinct generic stages: (1) data collection and the initial generation of categories, (2) validation of categories, (3) interpretation of categories and (4) action. These various stages are summarized in Table 9.1 and represent standard practice for the analysis of qualitative field data. My major point is that this same process can be used by teachers to analyse data emerging from their own classroom research efforts.

More recently, others have suggested similar approaches. Creswell (2014), for example, in his *Research Design: Qualitative, Quantitative and Mixed Methods Approaches* has proposed a helpful framework for the analysis and interpretation of qualitative data that follows the schema outlined here and below. Creswell's framework is reproduced in Figure 9.1. A useful discussion of Creswell's approach is also found in Koshy's (2010) *Action Research*.

Table 9.1 Fieldwork methodology

Classroom research	Becker	Glaser and Strauss
• Data collection • Validation • Interpretation • Action	• Selection and definition of concepts • Frequency and distribution of concepts • Incorporation of findings into model • Presentation of evidence and proof	• Compare incidents applicable to each category • Integrate categories and their phenomena • Delimit theory • Write theory

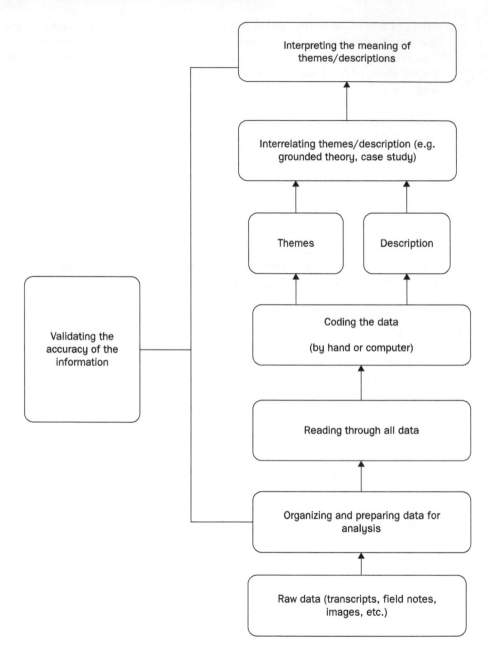

Figure 9.1   Analysing data and generating evidence.
(Cresswell 2014)

CASE STUDY 9.1

As part of the requirements for a course I taught on the 'Analysis of Teaching', Jane made a video of herself experimenting with various models of teaching. After reviewing the video, Jane felt that among other observations she had been rather abrupt in her questioning technique and had given the pupils little time to formulate responses to her questions. I suggested to Jane that she explore this observation a little further and ascertain whether this was a consistent behaviour or an aberration. She did this by taking a further video recording of her teaching, and by asking a colleague to observe her teaching. Jane also developed a short questionnaire on her questioning technique, which she administered to her pupils and subsequently analysed. As a result of this endeavour, Jane realized that she did in fact interject very quickly after asking a question, and quite often answered her own questions. All well and good, Jane thought, but what does this mean? Thinking that recent research on teaching might help, Jane did some reading and came across an article on think-time. The article reviewed a number of studies on the relationship between the amount of time that elapsed after questioning and the quality of pupil response. Jane felt that she was not allowing her pupils enough time to think after she had asked a question, to the detriment perhaps of their level of cognitive functioning. So she developed a plan to change and monitor her questioning technique. It took Jane some six months to complete these tasks (teaching is a time-consuming job!), but there was no pressure on her to complete the research. In fact, the longer time-frame allowed for more valid data, and she was pleased with the results. Not only did she find evidence of higher-level responses from her pupils, but also, by involving them in the evaluation of her teaching, the climate of her class was enhanced by the mutual and overt commitment of both teacher and pupils to the learning process.

Data collection

In the classroom research process, the first step is collecting data. With the use of, say, a video recorder, or any other of a range of methods (methods of data gathering were discussed in Chapter 8), the teacher gathers information about their teaching. Having collected the data, a sub-stage follows immediately or coexists with the collection of data – the generation of hypotheses. We are always generating ideas to explain classroom events. Even at the earliest stages of research, we are interpreting and explaining to ourselves 'why this is happening' and 'what caused that'. It is inevitable that as individuals we bring our experience and beliefs to bear upon situations that we wish to understand better. We have already noted the quote from Popper that, 'observations . . . are always interpretations of the facts observed . . . they are interpretations in the light of theories' (quoted in Magee 1973: 107). Popper's use of the word 'theory' implies, of course, not only 'grand' theory, but also personal theory – the presuppositions, assumptions and beliefs that guide our actions.

At the end of the data collection stage, not only have we collected our data, but we have also established a number of hypotheses, constructs or categories that begin to explain what is happening in the classroom.

These hypotheses (I am using the word broadly) usually emerge quite naturally from the data-gathering process. Jane, in Case Study 9.1, generated a number of ideas about her teaching from viewing the video recording. Among these was an observation that she was too abrupt in her questioning technique and had given her pupils too little time to answer questions. These hypotheses not only reflect the data but are also an interpretation of them. At this stage, the more ideas the better. The richer and more creative our thoughts, the more likely it is that the research will result in a coherent and complete interpretation of the problem. It is in the following stage that we begin to evaluate the hypotheses, so initially one should be as creative and as suggestive as possible.

Validation

The second stage in the process concerns the validation of the hypotheses. I will suggest a number of techniques for establishing the validity of a category or hypothesis. Of all these 'tests for trustworthiness', triangulation is most probably the best known, and so I describe it first.

The technique of *triangulation* was popularized by John Elliott and Clem Adelman during their work with the Ford Teaching Project. It involves contrasting the perceptions of one actor in a specific situation against those of other actors in the same situation. By doing this, an initial subjective observation or perception is fleshed out and given a degree of authenticity. Elliott and Adelman (1976: 74) describe the technique thus:

> Triangulation involves gathering accounts of a teaching situation from three quite different points of view; namely those of the teacher, his pupils, and a participant observer. Who in the 'triangle' gathers the accounts, how they are elicited, and who compares them, depends largely on the context. The process of gathering accounts from three distinct standpoints has an epistemological justification. Each point of the triangle stands in a unique epistemological position with respect to access to relevant data about a teaching situation. The teacher is in the best position to gain access via introspection to his own intentions and aims in the situation. The students are in the best position to explain how the teacher's actions influence the way they respond in the situation. The participant observer is in the best position to collect data about the observable features of the interaction between teachers and pupils. By comparing his own account with accounts from the other two standpoints a person at one point of the triangle has an opportunity to test and perhaps revise it on the basis of more sufficient data.

In Case Study 9.1, Jane validated her observations through triangulation. She had another teacher observe her teaching and she also gave her pupils a questionnaire on her questioning technique. From this evidence, she was able to validate and refine the observation from three different sources.

It must be admitted that triangulation is not always an easy process to engage in. Initially, it may be threatening for a teacher to involve students in the evaluation of their teaching, or it may prove difficult to obtain the services of a peer to act as a participant observer. Teachers with the personal openness and interest in their teaching needed to initiate such research will, however, eventually overcome these difficulties. As mentioned earlier, I believe that it is important for the teacher to involve their pupils in the research process as soon as their confidence allows. Rudduck *et al.* (2000) point out that the consultation of pupils about things that matter in school can provide a rich and powerful source of data that could be used by teachers to enhance pupil efforts and attainment. In England, 'pupil voice' – which requires pupils to play an active role in their schooling and has been a result of schools becoming more responsive to pupils' views (Hargreaves 2004) – is now considered one of the most powerful approaches for improving classroom practice. McIntyre *et al.*'s (2005) study on how teachers use data that pupils offer when consulted concluded that pupils commented – almost without exception – in polite, serious, thoughtful and constructive ways (p. 166). They did point out, however, the difficulty some students have in articulating their thoughts and providing feedback, which results in the voice of those students being silenced. They advocate that the students teachers find most difficult to consult are those whom they most need to hear.

Another well-known technique is *saturation*. Becker (1958) and Glaser and Strauss (1967) point to a similar process: Becker (1958: 653) refers to 'the check on the frequency and distribution of phenomenon' and Glaser and Strauss (1967: 67) to 'saturation', a situation where 'no additional data are being found . . . [to] develop properties of the category'. When applied to the classroom research situation, this implies that the hypothesis or category generated from observation is tested repeatedly against the data in an attempt to modify or falsify it.

It is difficult and perhaps reckless to suggest a frequency that ensures the validity of a category, for that will vary from case to case, but during this process a number of predictable events can occur. First, if on repeated testing the category is found wanting it is then discarded. Second, the category may have been conceptualized crudely and, through testing, the concept is modified, refined and amplified. Third, although the process of falsification (in the Popperian sense) is never complete, there comes a time when repeated observation leads neither to refutation nor amplification and only serves to support the hypothesis. At this point, when the utility of observation decreases, saturation can be said to have occurred and the hypothesis has been validated.

Referring to Case Study 9.1, having decided to explore her questioning technique further, Jane recorded herself again and found that, in fact, she was quite abrupt in her questioning and interjected far too quickly. In this way, she firmly validated the observation by saturating it.

There are a number of other techniques for establishing validity which I will describe more briefly.

In the same way as one triangulates the perception of various individuals, so too must we triangulate our *sources of data*. There are, as we have seen, many data sources open to the classroom researcher (e.g. surveys, questionnaires, observation, interviews and documents). The matrix shown in Figure 9.1 helps illustrate the range of data

Analysis	Information source				
	Surveys	Questionnaires	Observations	Interviews	Documents
1 Data collection and the generation of categories or hypotheses					
2 Validation of categories or hypotheses					
3 Interpretation by reference to theory, agreed criteria, established practice or teacher judgement					
4 Plan action for development					

Figure 9.2   A matrix for analysing classroom research data.

sources available at different levels of analysis. Although not every cell should be completed, a wide scatter should usually be employed. Each data source gives information of a different type which usually serves to complement and provide a check on the others.

Two other common techniques used at this stage of analysis are *rival explanations* and the search for *negative cases*. Michael Patton (2002) describes these techniques as follows:

> When considering rival hypotheses and competing explanations the strategy to be employed is not one of attempting to disprove the alternatives; rather, the analyst looks for data that *support* alternative explanations. Failure to find strong supporting evidence for alternative explanations helps increase confidence in the original, principal explanation.
>
> Closely related to the testing of alternative explanations is the search for negative cases. Where patterns and trends have been identified, our understanding of those patterns and trends is increased by considering the instances and cases that do not fit within the pattern.

I use the phrase '*call things by their right name*' to describe the next technique, which is nicely illustrated by Humpty Dumpty when he says: 'When I use a word it means just what I choose it to mean – neither more or less.' The point is an obvious one – we need to know what we are looking for. As classroom researchers, we have to do our conceptual work properly. We should beware, for example, of suggesting that a child who is looking intently at a teacher is in fact paying attention; or of dictionary definitions that define intelligence as mental ability; or of operational definitions that regard paying attention as not looking out of the window. None of these help us very much. Conceptualization involves articulating a full, clear and coherent account of what constitutes being an instance of something; that is to say, it necessitates elaborating the criteria that have to be met if, for example, a pupil is legitimately to be described as engaging in enquiry/discovery learning (Barrow 1986). This may be difficult to do at the outset, but the clarification of concepts should always be a major concern throughout the research process.

An *audit trail* is a technique used to increase the validity of one's data and which borrows its name from the concept of a financial audit. Schwandt and Halpern (1988: 73) describe the usefulness of an audit trail, or of establishing a chain of evidence, in this way:

> Preparing an audit trail is important for two reasons. First, it documents the inquiry in a fashion that facilitates a third-party examination. The audit trail contains information that describes the methods used to control error and to reach justifiable conclusions ... Second, an audit trail helps [classroom researchers] manage their record keeping. They find an organized trail useful when they need to retrieve information easily and when they prepare their final reports ... [it helps them] become more thoughtful, critical, and reflective.

Another widely used strategy for ensuring validity is having *key respondents* review drafts of one's research reports. This can either be the people involved in the research (one's colleagues or students), or those knowledgeable about the situation you are inquiring into. To the extent that those involved in the research do not recognize the description and analysis in the report, then its validity is suspect. Involving others in the research is also a worthwhile activity in itself.

In addition, and more recently, there has been the development of *computer-aided qualitative data analysis software* (CAQDAS) for the analysis and validation of qualitative data. This is a rapidly expanding field and a full discussion is beyond the scope of this chapter. A helpful overview however is found in Kelle's (2000) chapter on 'Computer-assisted analysis'. The most widely used CAQDAS program among educational researchers currently is NVivo, designed for the textual analysis of quantitative data (Bazeley and Jackson 2013).

Let me now restate the important methodological point. I am arguing that by employing analytical techniques such as triangulation and the other methods just described, teacher-researchers can produce hypotheses and concepts that are methodologically sound and to an extent generalizable.

By engaging in this process of hypothesis generation, teacher researchers are producing what Glaser and Strauss have called 'grounded theory', because it is theory grounded in data gathered from and applicable to a specific social situation. By utilizing this methodology, we can have confidence in our subsequent actions for, as Dunn and Swierczek (1977: 137) comment:

> The application of grounded theories promises to contribute to improvements in the degree to which findings

1   reflect conditions actually present in particular change efforts (internal validity);

2   typify conditions actually present in other change efforts (external validity);

3   contribute to the generation of new concepts by constantly comparing information obtained by different methods (reflexivity); and

4   promote understanding among groups with conflicting frames of reference.

Interpretation

The third stage in the research process is interpretation. This involves taking a validated hypothesis and fitting it into a frame of reference that gives it meaning. For the classroom researcher, this means taking a hypothesis and relating it to theory, the norms of accepted practice or the teacher's own intuition as to what comprises good teaching. This allows the teacher-researcher to give meaning to a particular observation or series of observations that can lead profitably to action. In doing this, the classroom researcher is creating meaning out of hitherto discrete observations and constructs. Jane in Case Study 9.1 gave meaning to her hypothesis by reading about 'thinktime'. That information not only helped her understand the implications of her behaviour but also suggested a direction for action. The previous discussion on specifications of practice and the frameworks for teaching presented in Chapter 11 are sources of meaning making for teacher researchers as they seek to make sense of their emerging hypotheses as well as extending and deepening their professional practice.

Action

The final step in the process is action. Having created meaning out of the research data, the teacher-researcher is in a position to plan for future action. Building on the evidence gathered during the research, the teacher is able to plan realistic strategies which are themselves monitored by classroom research procedures. Jane in Case Study 9.1 did just that. The interpretation stage gave her information on how to change her questioning technique, which after some planning she attempted to monitor and evaluate.

The ongoing process of data analysis

The analysis of data is a very important part of the classroom research process. It is only at this stage that the teacher can be certain that the results obtained are valid and trustworthy. When teacher-researchers fail to analyse their data adequately, they lack a secure platform for action. The four stages of classroom research are as follows:

1   *Data collection* and the generation of categories or hypotheses.

2   *Validation* of categories or hypotheses using the techniques for trustworthiness, such as triangulation.
3   *Interpretation* by reference to theory, agreed criteria, established practice or teacher judgement.
4   *Action* for development that is also monitored by classroom research techniques.

The four stages of classroom research, although based on sociological research methods, are, in fact, only organized common sense. These stages are also far more interactive than the linear description given so far in this chapter would imply. In fact, the whole process is in reality a very dynamic one. There are two aspects of this 'dynamism' that I want to mention in particular.

In Figure 9.2, the matrix illustrates the range of data sources available at each stage of analysis. As noted earlier, not every cell of the matrix needs to be completed. The point to be made here is that in the initial phase, one analyses the questionnaire or interview schedules, then uses the analysed data from a number of different sources to generate the categories or hypotheses. Having done that, one validates them in the second phase and then returns to the first phase to collect more data. This ongoing process of data collection and verification is a characteristic of the analysis of qualitative or naturalistic research data.

The second point is that the *whole* process is interactive. Matthew Miles and Michael Huberman, whose concern about the lack of agreement on methods for analysis we have already noted, have written a very practical and detailed book called *Qualitative Data Analysis*. In it they describe the interactive model of data analysis as follows (Miles and Huberman 1994: 21–2):

> *Data reduction*: Data reduction refers to the process of selecting, focusing, simplifying, abstracting and transforming the 'raw' data that appear in written up field notes. As data collection proceeds, there are further episodes of data reduction (doing summaries, coding, teasing out themes, making clusters, making partitions, writing memos). And the data reduction/transforming process continues after fieldwork, until a final report is complete.
>
> *Data display*: The second major flow of analysis activity is data display. We define a 'display' as an organised assembly of information that permits conclusion drawing and action taking. Looking at displays helps us to understand what is happening and to do something – further analysis or action – based on that understanding.
>
> *Conclusion drawing/verification*: The third stream of analytic activity is conclusion drawing and verification. From the beginning of data collection, the [classroom researcher] is beginning to decide what things mean, is noting regularities, patterns, explanations, possible configurations, causal flows and propositions. The competent researcher holds these conclusions lightly, maintaining openness and scepticism, but the conclusions are still there, inchoate and vague at first, then increasingly explicit and grounded.

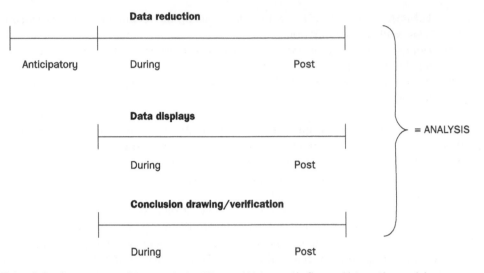

Figure 9.3   Components of data analysis: Miles and Huberman's flow and interactive models.

In this sense, qualitative data analysis is a continuous, iterative enterprise as seen in Figure 9.3. Issues of data reduction of display, and of conclusion drawing/verification, come into the process successfully as analysis episodes follow each other.

Enhancing validity

In the final section of this chapter, I wish to bring the discussion together by looking at the process of analysing data in a different way, using the concept of validity as the advanced organizer. Concepts of validity are of great importance for both quantitative and qualitative research. However, the latter has historically been charged as employing non-scientific methods in its analysis and thus, some would argue, as not being valid. Certainly this has been an argument made by policy-makers for many years, and most recently concerns about validity have increased internationally (see, for example, Bradbury and Reason 2001). On the one hand, quantitative research has elaborate statistical techniques at its disposal to ensure the trustworthiness of its data, although there is always a measure of standard error that is in-built and needs to be recognized. Qualitative researchers on the other hand, have traditionally addressed issues of validity through the honesty and richness of the data achieved. While this is still important, they have now, as we have seen in this chapter, an increasing range of methodological tools, techniques and processes to assist them. In general, most classroom researchers and those who use qualitative methods are concerned with validity rather than reliability, in so far as their focus is a particular case rather than a sample.

Validity is usually regarded as the degree to which the researcher has measured what they have set out to measure. I take a catholic view of the word 'valid'. My dictionary defines it as 'sound, defensible, well grounded . . . executed with proper formalities', and these are the general sense in which to use the term. Although there is a range of definitions and so of meanings of validity (Hammersley 1987; Patton 2002), one of the most useful and cited is that of Hammersley, who after reviewing a number of definitions of both reliability and validity asserted that there is an inconsistency in the usage of the terms. He defined validity as follows: 'An account is valid or true if it represents accurately those features of the phenomena, that it is intended to describe, explain or theorise' (1987: 79). McCormick and James (1989) give us a more traditional definition of validity, but in my opinion also a very useful one:

> Researchers are expected to demonstrate that the observations they actually record and analyze, match what they purport to be recording and analyzing. This is the concept of validity . . . Validity is concerned with errors that may occur in the research . . . the validity of a method is basically the extent to which the observations recorded are those that the researcher set out to record.

Although other authors identify a number of other types of validity (Cohen *et al.* (2011), for example, identify 21 types of validity), McCormick and James's (1989) six different types fit our purposes:

1 *Face validity* requires that a measure looks as if it measures what it purports to measure.
2 *Content validity* requires that data produced cover all relevant subject matter.
3 *Criterion-related validity* refers to the agreement between, for example, scores on a test and some other criterion such as teacher's estimates of ability.
4 *Construct validity requires* measurement to reflect the construct in which researchers are interested.
5 *Internal validity* refers to the soundness of an explanation – whether what is interpreted as the cause produces the effect.
6 *External validity* refers to the generalizability of results to the whole population.

However, this book is mainly concerned with the general notion of validity and with the threats to internal validity. Internal validity is the basic minimum without which classroom research is uninterpretable. If the various threats to validity are not taken into account, then one cannot claim that one's interpretation is correct. The existence of possible sources of invalidity potentially offer plausible, rival interpretations to our findings when we do not account for them.

Campbell and Stanley (1963) carefully documented the major threats to validity. Although their monograph was written some time ago, for those concerned with experimental and quasi-experimental research many of their threats to validity still apply. The original discussion of the these threats has been expanded in Cook and Campbell (1979) and Campbell and Russo (1999). Although it is probably impossible to take account of each of the variables, they do serve as a useful checklist and guide to good practice. Those that cannot be accounted for should at least be recognized and, if necessary, a rival explanation discussed. Although a discussion of each of these variables is redundant, some key examples may be of interest.

1 *History:* Over the time-span of data collection many events occur in addition to the study's independent variable. This threat to validity refers to the possibility that any one of these events may have changed rather than the hypothesized variable.

2 *Instrumentation:* Changes in the measurement process may be spuriously attributed to the dependent variable. For instance, where interviews or observations become increasing sloppy, fatigued, or more competent and experienced, results may subtly change.

3 *Differential mortality:* On any occasion that non-random subsets of subjects drop out of a study, comparison of the dependent variable across groups might be accounted for by these differential 'mortality' rates rather than by actual effects of the independent variable.

Although space precludes a full discussion, Miles and Huberman (1994) have two sections in their chapter on 'Making good sense: drawing and verifying conclusions' that are so pertinent to our theme that they need to be reported briefly here. They comment that a general strategy for analysis is a necessary but not sufficient condition, and that there is also a flow of specific analytic tactics, ways of drawing and verifying conclusions that need to be employed during the analytic process. They distinguish between 'tactics for generating meaning' (pp. 245–6) and 'tactics for testing or confirming findings' (p. 263).

A quick overview of the tactics for generating meaning, numbered from 1 to 13, and roughly arranged from the descriptive to the explanatory, and from the concrete to the more conceptual and abstract, includes: *noting patterns, themes* (tactic 1), *seeing plausibility* (2) and *clustering* (3), which help the analyst see 'what goes with what'. *Making metaphors* (4), like the preceding three tactics, is a way to achieve more integration among diverse pieces of data. *Counting* (5) is also a familiar way to see 'what's there'. *Making contrasts/comparisons* (6) is a pervasive tactic that sharpens understanding. Differentiation sometimes is needed, too, as in *partitioning variables* (7). We also need tactics for seeing things and their relationships more abstractly. These tactics include *subsuming particulars into the general* (8) and *factoring* (9), an analogue of a familiar quantitative technique, *noting relations between variables* (10); and *finding intervening variables* (11). Finally, how can we systematically assemble a coherent understanding of data? The tactics discussed are *building a logical chain of evidence* (12) and *making conceptual/theoretical coherence* (13).

After generating meaning we are confronted with issue of validity. Miles and Huberman (1994) identify 13 tactics for testing or confirming findings. These are numbered as before and begin with ones aimed at ensuring the basic quality of the data, then move to those that check findings by examining exceptions to early patterns, and conclude with tactics that take a sceptical, demanding approach to emerging explanations.

Data quality can be assessed through *checking for representativeness* (1); *checking for researcher effects* (2) on the case, and vice versa; and *triangulating* (3) across data sources and methods. These checks also may involve *weighting the evidence* (4), deciding which kinds of data are most trustable. Looking at 'unpatterns' can tell us a lot. *Checking the meaning of outliers* (5), *using extreme cases* (6), *following up surprises* (7) and *looking for negative evidence* (8) are all tactics that test a conclusion about a 'pattern' by saying what it is not like. How can we really test our explanations? *Making if–then tests* (9), *ruling out spurious relations* (10), *replicating a finding* (11) and *checking out rival explanations* (12) are all ways of submitting our beautiful theories to the assault of brute facts, or to a race with someone else's beautiful theory. Finally, a good explanation deserves attention from the very people whose behaviour it is about – informants who supply the original data. The tactic of *getting feedback from informants* (13) concludes the list. Some of these tactics have been described earlier, but this economical list of tactics provides a useful overview of the techniques in linking broad analytical strategies to more specific activities.

Although the style of research discussed in this book is, as noted earlier, inevitably concerned with validity, concerns about reliability should not be ignored. Reliability is concerned with consistency and generalizability and the use of standardized instruments. McCormick and James (1989: 188) describe it thus:

> Basically reliability is concerned with consistency in the production of results and refers to the requirement that, at least in principle, another researcher, or the same researcher on the same occasion, should be able to replicate the same piece of research and achieve comparable evidence and results.

In concluding this discussion I have attempted to draw together the various analytic techniques described in this chapter and link them to particular tests of validity and reliability (see Table 9.2). This is inevitably a somewhat arbitrary exercise as the various techniques overlap from category to category. The exercise does, however, demonstrate that just because one's data are qualitative does not mean that one's results need to be based on any less rigorous analysis than more traditional quantitative approaches.

Further reading

The territory covered in this chapter is complex, and I have tried to present it as simply as I can. Since the mid-1970s, there has been a growing interest in illuminative anthropological and ethnographic research approaches. Much of this literature is technical and not ideally suited for our purposes, however it is of interest: although the references in this section appear to be dated, they are by far the most important ones in qualitative analysis. The book by Hammersley and Atkinson (2007), *Ethnography: Principles in Practice*, provides an excellent overview of the field and an introduction to the literature. Lincoln and Guba's (1985) *Naturalistic Inquiry* is also

Table 9.2 Enhancing validity in qualitative research

Test	Analytic technique
Construct validity (i.e. the research must focus on the operational issues it purports to reflect)	• Use multiple sources of evidence • Call things by their right name • Establish a chain of evidence • Know what you are looking for • Have key informants review drafts • Use tactics for verifying conclusions
Internal validity (i.e. the integrity of the evaluation; that what is interpreted as cause produces the effect)	• Collect data at different points in time (time series design) • Seek alternative or rival explanations • Be clear and rigorous over all stages of analysis • Triangulation • Use tactics for generating meaning
External validity (i.e. the generalizability of findings from one case to others)	• Try to collect data from more than one site • Replicate the focus of evaluation during the period of the evaluation
Reliability (i.e. minimizing the errors and biases in a study so that another researcher could conduct the same evaluation study to arrive at the same conclusions)	• Protocol • Construct an audit trail • Huberman and Miles's (1994) interactive model of data analysis

Source: Adapted from Yin (2013: 42).

a useful source, as is Patton's (2002) *Qualitative Evaluation Methods. Beyond the Numbers Game* (Hamilton *et al.* 1977) is a comprehensive statement, albeit somewhat historical, on the illuminative (or new wave) tradition in educational evaluation and research, mainly from the UK perspective. One of the most helpful sections in this collection is the discussion of alternative methodology, especially the work of Louis Smith. Clem Adelman's book, *Uttering, Muttering* (1981), on linguistic research in classrooms contains a helpful chapter on triangulation. McCormick and James's (1989) book, *Curriculum Evaluation in Schools*, besides being an excellent general source, contains some very helpful sections on validity and reliability.

The references mentioned in the text should also be consulted, especially Becker (1958) and Glaser and Strauss (1967), although the latter may prove to be a little hard going. Fortunately, two books by Strauss (1987) and Strauss and Corbin (1998) are more accessible. The first chapter of Strauss's *Qualitative Analysis for Social Scientists* provides an exemplary introduction to grounded theory. Anyone seriously interested in educational research should also be familiar with Campbell and Stanley's (1963) classic

'Experimental and Quasi-experimental Designs for Research on Teaching'. Although written from a different perspective from this book, its discussion of research designs and the concepts of internal and external validity are essential knowledge for those involved in educational research. Cohen *et al.*'s (2011) *Research Methods in Education* (7th edition) also offers a useful source on qualitative data analysis as well as on reliability and validity. This is also the case with Colin Robson's (2011) exemplary *Real World Research* (3rd edition). It should be noted, however, that Miles and Huberman's (1994) *Qualitative Data Analysis* is the essential source book for anyone interested in the ideas and themes touched on in this chapter. Denzin and Lincoln's (2003) *Collecting and Interpreting Qualitative Methods Volume* 3 and Weinberg's (2002) *Qualitative Research Methods* complement the above reading. Auerbach and Silverstein's (2003) *Qualitative data: An Introduction to Coding and Analysis* provides a useful step-by-step guide to qualitative research, whilst Creswell's (2014) *Research Design: Qualitative, Quantitative and Mixed Methods Approaches* looks at mixed methods and has a useful chapter on ethics new to this fourth edition. Kelle's (2000) chapter in Bauer and Gaskell's edited volume on *Qualitative Researching with Text, Image and Sound* and Bazeley and Jackson's (2013) *Qualitative Data Analysis with NVivo* look at the analysis of non-numeric data.

10 Reporting classroom research

The link between research and action has been an implicit theme throughout this book. To teacher-researchers, research alone is necessary but not sufficient: research has to feed action and development. The classroom research process described in previous chapters has as its goal professional development and the enhancement of classroom performance. The fourth stage in the analytical framework discussed in this chapter is action, which itself is monitored and researched using classroom research procedures. This is the crowning achievement of the research process. In this chapter I want to look at some of the ways in which the action and information generated by the research process can be reported.

A classroom research report can in itself have significant impact. Technology in particular has provided the opportunity to teachers from all over the world to come closer together. This has opened up the prospect of substantive and sustained professional dialogues and the global exchange of ideas and good practice. These activities, in my opinion, are invaluable: classroom researchers should not only feel responsible for improving their own classrooms but also be concerned about the improvement of all classrooms and all schools in their own country and around the world. Hence, when classroom research reports are shared across a school, across a system and across systems they hold the potential to transform classroom practices around the globe and for the better.

In this chapter I will illustrate the various ways in which classroom research can be reported: first, by exploring literature on report writing; second, by discussing how one could write a report; third, by outlining other formats for reporting research; fourth, by identifying appropriate questions for evaluating your research report; fifth, by setting out criteria on how research can inform action; and sixth, by considering different approaches to the dissemination of results, before suggesting further reading for this chapter.

Reporting research

Accounts of research can never be a literal representation of events. Denscombe (2007: 285) provides us with a useful list of why envisioning a literal depiction is impossible:

- There are always limitations to the space available to provide the account of what happened, which means the researcher needs to provide an edited version of the totality. Decisions need to be made about what can be missed out of the account.

- The editorial decisions taken by the researcher are likely to be shaped by the researcher's need to present the methods in their best possible light. Quite rationally, the researcher will wish to put a positive spin on events and to bring out the best in the process. Without resorting to deceit or untruths, the account of research will almost certainly entail some upbeat positive filtering. The point, after all, is to justify the procedures as 'good' research.

- Although research notes will be used to anchor the description of what happened during the course of the research, the writing up of the research is inevitably a retrospective vision. Situations and data are likely to have a different meaning when viewed from the end of the research process from that at the time they occurred. They will be interpreted with the vision of hindsight.

- The impact of social norms and personal values on the way we interpret events pretty well guarantees that, to a greater or lesser extent, any account of research should be regarded as a version of the truth rather than a literal depiction of what happened. Within the social sciences, the idea of a purely objective position is controversial and a researcher would be naïve to presume that her/his account can stand, without careful considerations, as an 'objective' description of what actually occurred.

The end product, therefore, no matter how scrupulous it attempts to be, must always be recognized for what it is – an account of the research.

Bearing this cautious word in mind, we shall also see there are a number of different ways of reporting teacher research efforts. I have seen them range from loose anecdotal accounts to highly 'scientific' and formal research reports submitted for a higher degree. Brooker and MacPherson (1999: 210) confirm my argument in the previous chapter when they suggest that much published practitioner research is not rigorous in research terms but comes across as 'little more than picturesque journeys of self-indulgent descriptions of "this is what I did"'. According to them:

> Although 'insider accounts' focusing on personal experience are interesting, they have less meaning for the wider audience who aren't familiar with the context in which research took place. If such reports are to become more useful they must become more than exercises in self-indulgence where more is learned about the researcher than is learned about their interactions in the field . . . Practitioner researchers have a professional responsibility to ensure that sound precepts and practices inform their research efforts, and that these are clearly articulated in the reports of their research.
>
> (Brooker and MacPherson 1999: 209)

To avoid 'self-indulgent' descriptions and capitalize on the power of a research report, teacher-researchers need to put their data together in such a way that:

- the research could be replicated on another occasion;
- the evidence used to generate hypotheses and consequent action is clearly documented;
- action taken as a result of the research is monitored;
- the reader finds the research accessible and that it resonates with his or her own experience.

The process of setting a clear purpose, of using a methodology which provides valid results, and then using these as a basis for action, can be assisted if the researcher keeps a loose-leaf log or diary as the research progresses. An ongoing research diary like this also provides an invaluable basis for reflection and is great fun to look at with the wisdom of hindsight. It provides an excellent record of how one's views and attitudes evolve over time. The diary can also reveal the researcher's biases and how these impacted on decisions taken during the research and on the interpretation of events. Such information is invaluable when writing a report where personal biases should be highlighted and attempts to address them indicated, and their possible impact on the research results accounted for.

Writing a report

One of the first things one has to consider when preparing a research report is the intended audience. Teacher-researchers have to decide in advance who they are writing for and choose the most effective format and style to address their audience. The British Educational Research Association's (2000: 2) *Good Practice in Educational Research Writing*, identifies three major audiences for research writing – researchers, policy-makers and practitioners – and asserts that 'it is good practice in all research writing to aim for lucid prose which communicates effectively to the intended audience and avoids what that audience may perceive as jargon or obscurantism'.

The length of the report is also something that needs to be taken into account. Most people who read reports say that they are either too long to read or so short that there is insufficient evidence to be believable. The best bet is a report as short and condensed as you can make it (with detailed justification tucked away in appendices). The biggest temptation is to display your productivity in too many pages.

Formulating the report comes next. There are a number of guidelines and criteria available that are helpful at this stage. To begin with, there is the somewhat traditional approach that uses, as a guide, points similar to the following:

1   *Statement of intent*
    - clarify purpose
    - rationale

2   *Procedures and process*
  - research design
  - techniques of data collection
  - verification of concepts
  - what actually occurred
3   *Results and implementation*
  - outcomes of research
  - theoretical implications
  - action taken as a result
  - evaluation of action
4   *Meta-analysis*
  - review whole process
  - conclusions as to the usefulness of the research
  - what would you do differently next time?

A checklist of areas that need to be covered in such a conventional research report is provided in Box 10.1.

Box 10.1   Checklist for structuring a traditional research report

---

1   *Title.* Look for a general theme or a metaphor that will carry your main point without distorting it too much.
2   *Abstract.* Briefly outline the whole project. Locate the research and indicate the timescale and context within which it was conducted; provide an overview of the methods used for both collecting and analysing data; and convey to the reader the results of the research.
3   *Introduction.* Set out the reason why you decided to undertake the particular research project. What was significant about it?
4   *Literature review.* Provide an account of the literature written on the subject and highlight what can be learnt from it. (Many researchers compile the introduction and the literature review in one section. This is a question of opinion and audience.)
5   *Methodology.* Indicate the data collection and analysis methods you have adopted and explain why these seem to be the most appropriate. Also include in this section how reliable the data were in both the data collection and data analysis phases.
6   *Results/Findings.* Describe your results and use table and figures where appropriate.
7   *Discussion.* Answer the research questions posed; discuss everything about your results that is important and surprising; make recommendations and identify the next questions that arise.
8   *Conclusion.* Provide an overview of the project and review it.
9   *References.* Include all the references used, and preferably use the Harvard referencing system as it is the most accepted.
10 *Appendices.* Add all the material that would have taken too much space if you were to include them in the research and that are not directly relevant to the project, but help illustrate something refereed in the main report. Taber (2007: 185) provides us with some examples of appendices:

- sample questionnaires;
- sample interviews transcripts;
- transcripts of classroom dialogues;
- photocopies of students' work;
- photographs or stills from digital video-recordings of students at work (subject to permission being available);
- photographs of displays or models put together by the students.

The purpose of both the outline and the checklist is to provide teacher-researchers with a framework for their report. While this is important, what perhaps is even more critical is that the format of a report encourages the teacher to stand back and to examine the process systematically by reflecting on or making a meta-analysis of the research.

Since originally writing this section for a previous edition, there have been a number of other books on action research published that treat this issue in some detail. Many of these are referred to in the further reading section at the end of this chapter. One of the most helpful is the chapter on 'Writing up your action research' in Valsa Koshy's (2010) *Action Research*. In it she not only provides advice on conventional formats such as research dissertations, but also describes more creative presentations, many of which are discussed later in the chapter. Her subsequent chapter on publishing action research is equally helpful.

Evaluating your research report

As most classroom research data will probably be presented in a written form, it is helpful to identify a set of questions that could provide the basis for evaluating them. Judith Bell, in her book *Doing Your Research Project* (2010: 251–2), provides us with an extensive and helpful list of such questions:

1   Is the meaning clear? Are there any obscure passages?
2   Is the report well written? Check tenses, grammar, spelling, overlapping passages, punctuations, jargon.
3   Is the referencing well done? Are there any omissions?
4   Does the abstract give the reader a clear idea of what is in the report?
5   Does the title indicate the nature of study?
6   Are the objectives of the study stated clearly?
7   Are the objectives fulfilled?
8   If hypotheses were postulated, are they proved or not proved?
9   Has a sufficient amount of literature relating to the topic been studied?
10 Does the literature review, if any, provide an indication of the state of knowledge in the subject? Is your topic placed in the context of the area of study as a whole?

11 Are all terms clearly defined?

12 Are the selected methods of data collection accurately described? Are they suitable for the task? Why were they appropriate for the task?

13 Are any limitations of the study clearly presented?

14 Have any statistical techniques been used? If so, are they appropriate for the task?

15 Are the data analysed and interpreted or merely described?

16 Are the results clearly presented? Are tables, diagrams and figures well drawn?

17 Are conclusions based on evidence? Have any claims been made that cannot be substantiated?

18 Is there any evidence of bias? Any emotive terms or intemperate language?

19 Are the data likely to be reliable? Could another researcher repeat the methods used and have a reasonable chance of getting the same or similar results?

20 Are recommendations (if any) feasible?

21 Are there any unnecessary items in the appendix?

22 Would you give the report a passing grade if you were the examiner? If not, perhaps an overhaul is necessary.

Colin Hook (1995: 291–2), in his book *Studying Classrooms*, provides a helpful checklist of questions that can be used to review one's research in any format you decide to present it:

- Did I collect the information as planned? Did it provide the information I needed?
- What problems did I have? What could I have done better? Should I employ other data-gathering methods?
- Did I gather all relevant available information? Should I have gathered pupils' opinions, parental views, and other teachers' feelings?
- In what ways can I use the information to make more effective teacher decisions? Is further information required?
- Can the information obtained be interpreted in other ways? Are my interpretations and conclusions valid?
- Have I presented the information in a clear way? Does the information indicate future teaching actions?
- Can I discuss the information with pupils, colleagues or parents?
- Who else could have been involved, how and when?
- What did I, the pupils, parents, colleagues, etc., get out of the investigation?
- What changes should I make in future investigations? Do my pupils, colleagues, etc., have suggestions?
- Can I interest colleagues in coordinating action research approaches, to collaborate in future studies?
- Do other teachers share my concerns? Do other teachers have skills which may help me in self-monitoring?

Making your classroom research report formative

Up to this point we have been concerned with the technical aspects of report writing. Now we need to turn to the heart of the matter – how to make our research inform action; how to make our research report formative.

Fiddy and Stronach (1987) were among the first to argue that we need to move from theories of transmission to theories of utilization of research data. Why is it, they ask, that we, as evaluators and researchers into educational practice, are so uninterested in the pedagogical relations between ourselves and our clients, especially since the evidence seems to be that our clients learn little for us, and value us still less? Their response is illuminating: they argue for the abandonment of external critique, the rejection of models for formative evaluation research, the end to writing reports, the development of pedagogy (rather than methodology), of new kinds of educational research, and for the reintegration of research and development.

Cousins and Leithwood (1993) also point out that researchers should take a knowledge utilization perspective. In their study, which linked information use and school improvement, they concluded that participants' perceptions of the sophistication, relevance and timeliness of information sources had a direct impact on information utilization for school improvement. In previous work on the utilization of evaluation results they identified a number of 'guidelines' on how to ensure that an evaluation leads to action (Cousins and Leithwood 1986). As this work is eminent and prolific and could be applied to all kinds of research, including action research, I have taken the liberty of adapting their conclusions by replacing the word 'evaluation' (used by the authors) with the word 'research'. So, they claim that research results are utilized most effectively when:

- research is appropriate in approach, methodological sophistication and intensity;
- the decisions to be made were significant to users and considered appropriate for the application of formally collected data;
- research findings were consistent with the beliefs and expectations of the users;
- users were involved in the research process and had a prior commitment to the benefits of the research;
- users considered the data reported in the research to be relevant to their problems;
- a minimum amount of information from other sources conflicted with the results of the research.

(Cousins and Leithwood 1986: 360)

I have also found Stake's (1967) 'countenance of educational evaluation' model (see Figure 10.1) helpful in thinking about organizing and reporting the outcomes of classroom research. It also provides a means for applying criteria and making judgements. Dissatisfied with the 'objective' (standardized tests) approaches in evaluation, Stake proposed a countenance approach more in keeping with the complex and

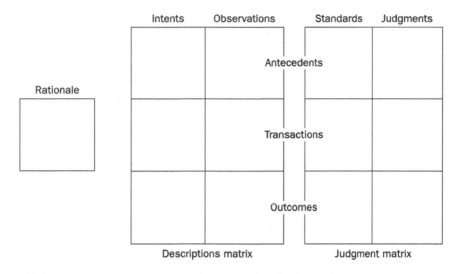

Figure 10.1   Stake's (1967) countenance of educational evaluation model.

dynamic nature of education. He distinguishes between *antecedents*, which are any prior condition which may relate to the outcomes; *transactions*, which are what actually occurred, 'the succession of engagements which comprise the process of education'; and *outcomes*, which are the impact of the change on those involved. In the model, he then contrasts the intentions at each phase with observations of what actually occurred. He assumed quite rightly that there should be a relationship between intentions and observations at each phase, and a logical flow through phases related to intentions, and an empirical flow through phases related to observations. The descriptive data so gathered and analysed illuminate the situation under review. What results from this methodological approach is a descriptive analysis of an educational programme that should be relatively uncontentious (given that it attempts to be objective) and illuminative (given that it relates intentions to observations of other forms of data gathering analysed in the conventional way).

Stake also proposes a judgement matrix in his model which allows the application of various criteria to the description of the educational programme. The classroom researcher, having completed the description of the educational programme and possibly negotiated it with the 'client', then proceeds to the more contentious area of the judgement matrix. The standards or criteria column may already have been agreed in advance and will obviously vary from case to case. National and/or local policy, educational theory or research, and commonly agreed good practice, can all provide standards against which to assess curricula in action. Once these standards have been articulated and set against the description matrix, the judgments become almost self-evident. At least the grounds for making judgements are clearly defined and open to scrutiny and debate.

A major advantage of Stake's matrix is that it clearly distinguishes between evidence and judgements. Because evaluation, and indeed classroom research, can be a highly politicized business, such an approach tends to reduce acrimony and defensiveness, particularly if the description and judgement matrices are completed independently and the description is negotiated before the standards are applied. From a developmental point of view it is also helpful if the standards or criteria applied in the judgement matrix are agreed with the 'client' and if the judgements based on the application of the matrices are arrived at collaboratively.

So let us take this train of thought a little further. Let us assume that a classroom researcher has generated some valid 'knowledge'. What key conditions must be present if someone is to take action congruent with the knowledge? Here, Louis and Miles (1992: 289) take a cut at what might be required:

- *Clarity*. The knowledge must be understood clearly – not be fuzzy, vague or confusing.
- *Relevance*. The knowledge is seen as meaningful, as connected to one's normal life and concerns – not irrelevant, inapplicable, impractical.
- *Action images*. The knowledge is or can become exemplified in specific actions, clearly visualized. Without such images, knowledge-based action is unlikely.
- *Will*. There must be motivation, interest, action orientation, and a will to do something with the knowledge.
- *Skill*. There must be actual behavioural ability to do the action envisioned. Without skill, the action will either be aborted or done incongruently with the knowledge undergirding it.

One can conclude from the foregoing discussions that a formative classroom research report:

- pays explicit attention to the change process;
- focuses on users' issues;
- involves users in the process;
- develops a pedagogy for learning from the research;
- utilizes a methodology consistent with its purpose;
- integrates research and development.

Action upon one's results should be the ultimate goal for all classroom researchers. Research, and in particular qualitative research, is less of a methodology and more a way of life! It is an approach that is applicable across a range of settings, describes and analyses phenomena on their own terms, and helps us to think constructively and to generate meaning out of complex and problematic situations. Consequently, it is also an approach that empowers individuals and increases feelings of efficacy. This sense of efficacy can only develop if we report our methodological procedures and establish a genuinely collaborative and critical research community that is committed to informed action.

Other formats for reporting research

Classroom researchers should not feel constrained by the traditional research report format when sharing the product of their research, as there are any number of approaches that can be used for reporting research. As Giroux (2005: 13) suggests, we need a 'politics and pedagogy developed around new languages capable of acknowledging the multiple, contradictory and complex subject positionings people occupy within different social, cultural and economic locations'. The important thing is for the information to be valid and to have been carefully analysed, and the fundamental point is that action should result from the research. Researchers in education have become increasingly interested in different forms of interpreting and representing data (Baumfield *et al.* 2013, Percelli 2005a, 2005b; Schratz 2001). Here are a few examples:

- *Cartoons or photography.* Often classroom researchers use the cartoon format or photographs to get a key finding from their research across in a powerful and accessible way (see, for example, Figure 10.2).
- *Video or film.* A visual representation using video or a digital camera provides concrete images that an audience can relate to their own situation.
- *Dance or theatre.* Once again a visual representation, a performance using students or professional dancers or actors has the potential to have a profound impact on the audience.
- *Fiction.* Using data or constructs from the research to tell a story often encourages reflection and discussion more effectively than the traditional report. As long as the quotations or events are 'real', a fictional setting may enhance the message.
- *Social media.* The use of web-based applications such as blogs and Twitter allows creation and exchange of ideas with an almost infinite audience and a permanence and accessibility that has yet to be duplicated. These elements create an effective platform for research sharing in a simple, quick and generally cost-effective format.
- *Diaries.* Using extracts from a diary to present insights from the research is valuable data.
- *Poetry.* This is another form of highlighting the learnings of one's research.
- *Data reduction and display.* Displaying reduced data is often a powerful way of stimulating discussion. This approach allows large amounts of data to be displayed economically and it could be accompanied by another page of questions, commentary or explanation that highlighted the main issues.
- *Posters.* In school or other education settings posters can be used to present much of the above material for a wider audience. This could also be in the form of a repeating PowerPoint presentation. The use of posters or presentations is also a good way of communicating your action research to pupils.
- A *patchwork approach.* Researchers could choose to use a comnination of approaches (film, poetry, reports, etc.) to communicate their findings. This 'patchwork' approach was pioneered by Winter (see, for example, Winter *et al.* 1999).

Figure 10.2   Reporting research using a cartoon format.
(Fiddy and Stronach 1987)

Finishing a research report could feel like sitting an exam without being quite sure what the question is, but in the knowledge that the world will read and mark your paper according to an unpredictable whim. The mental blocks, the mad desire to postpone writing for more research or for another coffee is normal, but one thing is certain: it is worth it.

Dissemination of results

At the beginning of this chapter I briefly discussed how powerful a classroom research report can be. I even claimed that reporting classroom research results has the potential to transform classroom practices around the world. This implies that the research will be disseminated. Classroom researchers should be aware that research is incomplete until it is in the public domain. Thus, decisions have to be made about who is going to disseminate the results and, coming back to our discussion earlier about the report's audience, to whom it will be disseminated and for what use.

There are a variety of ways in which you can disseminate the results of your research. The most immediate way of course is sharing the research within your own school. Teachers have the opportunity through staff meetings, presentations during the school's professional development days and informal discussions with colleagues not only to change practices across the school, but also to engage in professional dialogue about classroom research and promote a culture of inquiry within the school. Currently, many schools encourage their teachers to undertake small research projects and some of them require newly qualified teachers to conduct a classroom research project in their first term.

Another way of communicating research is through school networks. In England there are an increasing number of informal and formal school networks which allow the quick exchange of information between schools, which of course is a smart school improvement strategy. Formal networks such as those of the Specialist Schools and Academies Trust (SSAT) and the erstwhile National College for School Leadership (NCSL) networked learning communities project bring together practitioners at a local level and then connect local networks to the regional and national. Hence, the dissemination of such results is done on a bigger scale.

Baumfield *et al.* (2013: 160) note the following 'plus points' for teacher researchers sharing their learning in practitioner inquiry networks:

- developing a common educational identity through shared problems, shared solutions and a shared community;
- re-energizing enthusiasm for learning by seeing things from different perspectives;
- discovering new ways of doing things and picking up useful ideas;
- understanding the learner across the phases of their educational experience;
- crossing the boundaries between the different phases of education encourages more abstract thinking about educational issues;
- permission to think 'big thoughts'.

Publications can also make your work accessible to wider audiences and could include:

- chapters in books;
- papers in academic journals;
- articles in teacher magazines;
- presentations in education conferences.

There are an increasing number of books published by universities and organizations such as the SSAT and the NCSL (see Case Study 2.4 in Chapter 2 for two case studies published by the NCSL), presenting classroom research examples. There are also an increasing number of schools that publish research conducted by their own staff within the school but also externally.

However, the quickest, most powerful and nowadays possibly the most accessible approach to dissemination is the Internet – this is certainly true for developed countries and is becoming true for many developing ones. As mentioned earlier, technology has opened up opportunities for people to connect with others across the world and share information instantly. Classroom researchers are now publishing their results in their schools', networks' and their own personal websites. Imagine a colleague in China reading your research, identifying similarities between your school and theirs and deciding to adopt the practice suggested by your research in order to improve teaching and learning in their school!

Before concluding this section, it is worth reflecting more imaginatively on how classroom researchers can support their dissemination efforts. One particular example involves a rethink of the audience for classroom research and its intended purpose. Miles and Huberman's (1994: 305) 'matrix for objectives of dissemination strategy planning' (see Table 10.1) could effectively support classroom researchers' dissemination

Table 10.1   Matrix for objectives of dissemination strategy planning

	Size of audiences			
Level of Diffusion and Use	Innovators: those few with special interest, skill, motivation	Key persons: gatekeepers, leaders of opinion	Majority of potential audience	Everyone who might be affected
Awareness				
Reception of basic message				
Understanding				
Acceptance				
Adoption decision				
Utilization/ Implementation				
Integration				
Routinization				

Source: Miles and Huberman (1994: 305)

efforts. This is because it requires researchers to consider their audiences and sub-audiences and the effects it provides, which range from the simple awareness that the message exists to implementation and routinization.

Further reading

Sadly, teachers' research is still not acknowledged as being a vibrant vehicle for the production of theory for educational sustainability, and is often viewed as more of a professional development activity (see, for example, Furlong 2004). Classroom researchers have the responsibility for changing such perceptions and cultures by presenting their findings in the most appropriate manner and getting the dissemination process right.

The discussion of reporting research and dissemination in this chapter has been quite extensive and the main sources were cited. In addition, the various collections of case studies referred to elsewhere in the book provide examples of different ways and styles of reporting. Further advice is provided in Denscombe's (2007) *The Good Research Guide* (3rd edition), Bell's (2010) *Doing Your Research Project* (5th edition), McNiff and Whitehead's (2005) *Action Research for Teachers* and (2011) *All You Need to Know about Action Research*, Fox *et al.*'s (2007) *Doing Practitioner Research* and Taber's (2007) *Classroom-Based Research and Evidence-Based Practice*. The work of Baumfield *et al.* (2013) in *Action Research in Education* and Koshy (2010) in *Action Research for Improving Educational Practice*, already cited in this chapter, is particularly relevant. For specific advice on presenting data, Stephanie Evergreen's (2013) *Presenting Data Effectively: Communicating Your Findings for Maximum Impact* is useful. Lucinda Becker's (2014) *Presenting Your Research: Conferences, Symposiums, Poster Presentations and Beyond* is also helpful.

11 Teaching and learning as the heartland of classroom research

One of the themes that has become increasingly prominent in later editions of this book is the emphasis on moral purpose as the motivation for continuing professional development. This is no 'wishy-washy' idealism but a practical and strategic effort at designing learning experiences that enable every student to reach their potential irrespective of their background. It is this core idea that is at the basis of the current commitment to 'personalized learning'. It is an approach to schooling that I championed when I was the Chief Adviser on School Standards at the then Department for Education and Skills in the early to mid-2000s. A good example of a systemic approach to personalization is the *Excellence and Enjoyment: Learning and Teaching in the Primary Years* policy that we introduced during that time (DfES 2004).

Personalized learning is an idea that is capturing the imagination of teachers, parents and young people around the world. It has its roots in the best practices of the teaching profession, and it has the potential to make every young person's learning experience stretching, creative, fun and successful. This emphasis provides a bridge from prescribed forms of teaching, learning skills, curriculum and assessment to an approach that is predicated on tailoring schooling to individual need, interest and aptitude.

Charlie Leadbeater (2004: 16) clearly and sensitively identifies personalized learning as the key driver for the transformation of schooling:

> The foundation of a personalised education system would be to encourage children from an early age and across all backgrounds, to become more involved in making decisions about what they would like to learn and how. The more aware people are of what makes them learn, the more effective their learning is likely to be.

He continues:

> Personalised learning does not apply market thinking to education. It is not designed to turn children and parents into consumers of education. The aim is to promote personal development through self realisation, self enhancement and self development. The child/learner should be seen as active, responsible

and self motivated: a co-author of the script which determines how education is delivered.

And:

> The script of a system characterised by personalised learning . . . would start from the premise that the learner should be actively engaged in setting their own targets, devising their own learning plans and goals, choosing from a range of different ways to learn. . . . By making learning the guiding principle of the system, personalisation challenges some of the current divide and boundaries that exist – for example between formal and informal learning; between academic and vocational learning and between different ages and types of learners.

In one sense, personalized learning represents a logical progression from the standards and accountability reform strategies of the 1990s. These strategies marked an important first phase in a long-term large-scale reform effort. But in order to sustain system-wide improvement, societies are increasingly demanding strategies characterized by diversity, flexibility and choice.

In line with this, my view is that the genesis of personalization lies somewhere slightly different from the political emphasis with which it is currently associated. The foundations of personalization may be partly political, but mainly they reflect an ethical root. As I have already claimed, it is moral purpose that drives personalization. We see it most vividly in the concern of the committed, conscientious teacher to match what is taught, and how it is taught, to the individual learner as a person. That is not just a question of 'sufficient challenge' or aligning pedagogy to the point of progression that each learner has reached, even though that is vitally important. It is also part of the teacher's concern to touch hearts as well as minds, to nourish a hunger for learning and help equip the learner with a proficiency and confidence to pursue understanding for themselves.

The concrete expression of the phrase 'every child is special' – and the creation of an education system which treats them so – is what personalized learning is all about. That means overcoming the false dichotomies and the 'either/ors' which have bedevilled schooling for so long, so that for all pupils learning means 'both/and' – both excellence and enjoyment, both skills and enrichment, both support and challenge, both high standards and high equity, both present success and long-term participation, both deep engagement and broad horizons – and in so doing, breaking the link between socioeconomic disadvantage and attainment. That is the goal for personalized learning, and understanding how to reconcile these apparent dichotomies provides fertile ground for the contemporary teacher-researcher.

At the heart of personalized learning is its impact, not just on test scores and examination results, but on the student's learning capability. If the teacher can teach the student how to learn at the same time as assisting them to acquire curriculum content, then the twin goals of learning and achievement can be met at the same time. We made this point in *Models of Learning – Tools for Teaching* (Joyce *et al.* 2002: 7) when we argued that it is the teacher's task not simply to 'teach', but to create powerful contexts for learning. We expressed that idea and the essence of personalized learning as follows:

> Learning experiences are composed of content, process and social climate. As teachers we create for and with our children opportunities to explore and build important areas of knowledge, develop powerful tools for learning, and live in humanising social conditions.

It is the integration of curriculum content, teaching and learning strategies and the school cultures that enhance self-confidence that in my opinion provide the parameters for the work of teacher-researchers. But there is a significant barrier to progress in this area: despite the contemporary emphasis on the importance of classroom practice, the language or discourse about teaching remains in general at a restricted level. There is a need for a far more elaborate language with which to talk about teaching and more sophisticated frameworks against which to reflect on practice. Even in those instances where more precision of language is achieved, say in the debate on whole-class teaching, there are few operational definitions against which teachers can assess their own practice and thereby develop and expand their range of classroom practices. Quality teaching and learning must be underpinned by more elaborate and explicit frameworks for learning and teaching. It is here that the work of Good and Brophy (2007) in *Looking in Classrooms*, Hattie (2009) in *Visible Learning* and Hattie and Yates (2014) in *Visible Learning and the Science of How We Learn* is proving invaluable.

In this chapter I discuss some of the evidence on effective teaching and learning. This is for three reasons. The first is in order to provide a sharper focus for classroom research activities that relate to teaching and learning. The second is to offer specifications that can contribute to broader and richer discourse about the nature of teaching and learning. Third, it is principally through pedagogy that the teacher is best able to create increasingly personalized learning experiences for their students.

Although the evidence on effective teaching can help teachers become more imaginative in creating powerful learning environments for students, such research and strategies, however, should not be regarded as panaceas to be followed slavishly. Research knowledge and the various specifications of teaching can have many limitations, especially if they are adopted uncritically. Such knowledge only becomes useful when it is subjected to the discipline of practice through the exercise of the teacher's professional judgement. For, as Lawrence Stenhouse (1975: 142) said, such proposals are not to be regarded 'as an unqualified recommendation, but rather as a provisional specification claiming no more than to be worth putting to the test of practice. Such proposals claim to be intelligent rather than correct.'

As has been seen throughout this book, outstanding teachers take individual and collective responsibility to base their teaching on the best knowledge and practice available. But they then take those ideas and strategies and critically reflect on them through practice in their own and each other's classrooms. It is through reflection that the teacher harmonizes, integrates and transcends the necessary classroom management skills, the acquisition of a repertoire of models of teaching, and the personal aspects of their teaching into a strategy that has meaning for the students. This is the heartland of the synergy between teaching and learning and classroom research.

In developing the theme of this chapter I will discuss the nature of powerful learning; describe a framework for thinking about teaching; outline the concept of a model of teaching; give examples of three common teaching models; and reflect on the nature of teaching style and the integration of content and process in classroom practice.

Powerful learning

There is now an increasingly sophisticated literature on how learning occurs and on the ways in which the learning experience can be organized to make a positive difference to students. The impact is not just on test scores and examination results, but also on the student's learning capability. This is the heart of the matter: teachers teaching the students how to learn at the same time as assisting them to acquire curriculum content.

The purpose of teaching, therefore, is not only to help students to acquire curriculum knowledge but also to assist them in becoming powerful learners. The most effective curricular and teaching patterns induce students to construct knowledge – to inquire into subject areas intensively. The result is to increase student capacity to learn and work smarter. The trick of course is to find ways of raising levels of attainment while at the same time helping students become more powerful learners by expanding and making articulate their repertoire of learning strategies.

Powerful learning refers to the ability of learners to respond successfully to the tasks that they are set, as well as the tasks they set themselves – in particular to:

- integrate prior and new knowledge;
- acquire and use a range of learning skills;
- solve problems individually and in groups;
- think carefully about their successes and failures;
- evaluate conflicting evidence and think critically;
- accept that learning involves uncertainty and difficulty.

The deployment of such a range of learning strategies is commonly termed 'metacognition', which can be regarded as the learner's ability to take control over their own learning processes. The key point is that within whatever context learning takes place, it involves an 'active construction of meaning'. This carries implications for the management of learning opportunities. As learning is interactional, it occurs only when the learner makes sense of particular experiences in particular contexts. This 'making sense' involves connecting with an individual's prior knowledge and experience. Thus, new learning has to relate to, and ultimately 'fit with', what individuals already understand. Learning should therefore be seen as a process as much as producing end results.

This interactive view of learning is mirrored later in the chapter by a discussion of how a teaching strategy can also be a model of learning. But here I am getting ahead of myself. Having briefly discussed the process of learning, we now need to give some attention to the skills of learning that need to be taught and acquired.

If we are serious about personalized learning then we need to be clear as to the typology of the skills students should gain in order to develop their personal effectiveness and employability. These skills fall into three categories:

- functional skills;
- thinking and learning skills;
- personal skills.

The argument so far has led us to a position where it is clear that skills are a vital part of what it means to be educated. Having identified the three skills sets in which students should gain mastery it is worth looking in a little more detail at what such a framework entails.

Functional skills are literacy, numeracy and ICT. In most countries these are regarded as key priorities and therefore tend to be taught and assessed in the core subjects of mother tongue, maths and ICT.

Thinking and learning skills are those young people need to acquire in order to become effective learners. Gaining mastery of these skills equips students to raise their achievement by developing their ability to:

- improve their achievement by applying a wide range of learning approaches in different subjects;
- learn how to learn, with the capability to monitor, evaluate, and change the ways in which they think and learn;
- become independent learners, knowing how to generate their own ideas, acquire knowledge and transfer their learning to different contexts.

The specific thinking and learning skills identified in the *Excellence and Enjoyment* (DfES 2004) mentioned earlier were superseded by the personal, learning and thinking skills (PLTS) a framework developed by the then Qualifications and Curriculum Agency. The PLTS materials have subsequently been archived but can still be found in the National Archive (dated 15 February 2011). They describe the qualities and skills needed for success in learning and life. The PLTS framework has been developed and refined over a number of years in consultation with employers, parents, schools, students and the wider public.

The framework comprises six groups of skills:

- independent inquirers;
- creative thinkers;
- reflective learners;
- team workers;
- self-managers;
- effective participants.

For each group of skills, a focus statement sums up the range of skills and qualities involved. In the materials they are accompanied by a set of outcome statements that describe the relevant skills, behaviours and personal qualities.

Table 11.1   ELLI dimensions

Dimension	Description
Changing and learning	A sense of myself as someone who learns and changes over time
Critical curiosity	An orientation to want to 'get beneath the surface'
Meaning making	Making connections and seeing that learning 'matters to me'
Creativity	Risk-taking, playfulness, imagination and intuition.
Interdependence	Learning with and from others and also being able to manage without them
Strategic awareness	Being aware of my thoughts, feelings and actions as a learner, and able to use that awareness to manage learning processes
Resilience	The readiness to persevere in the development of my own learning power

The PLTS are only illustrative of one approach to classifying learning and thinking skills and there are many others. One of the most popular is the Effective Lifelong Learning Inventory (ELLI), particulary as it gives a visual presentation of a student's learning profile and compares that with national norms (Deakin Crick *et al.* 2004). The seven ELLI dimensions are shown in Table 11.1.

Personal skills are those that young people need to acquire in order to develop their personal effectiveness, and there is some obvious overlap here with the PLTS. Gaining mastery of these skills equips students to manage themselves and to develop effective social and working relations. The specific skills that I suggest should comprise personal skills are as follows:

Communication (and personal presentation)
- speak effectively for different audiences;
- listen, understand and respond appropriately to others;
- participate effectively in group discussions;
- read fluently a range of literary and non-fiction texts and reflect critically;
- write fluently for a range of purposes and audiences, including critical analysis of own and others' writing.

Diligence, reliability, and capability to improve
- plan, organize and timetable effectively;
- initiative and self-motivation;
- willingness to learn and progress;
- reflect on own work and identifying ways to improve;
- understand how decisions taken now can affect the future.

Working with others (social skills and team work)
- contribute to small-group and whole-class discussion and tasks;
- work with others to meet a challenge – negotiate, resolve differences and support others;

- social skills and awareness and understanding of others' needs;
- leadership skills.

Moral and ethical awareness
- (spiritual) understand sense of self, strengths and weaknesses, unique potential, and will to achieve;
- (moral) understand difference between right and wrong, concern for others, consequences of actions and forgiveness;
- (social) understand responsibilities and rights of being a family and community members (local, national and global), how to relate to others and work for common good;
- (cultural) understand and respect own and other cultural traditions, appreciate and respond to a variety of experiences.

This framework provides clarity on the skills students should gain. But to ensure students gain mastery of these skills there needs to be agreement on how the skills should be:

- embedded in teaching and learning;
- developed coherently across the curriculum.

This is important because in most systems these skills are not specified or developed in a systematic way and progression is assumed rather than explicit.

In terms of functional skills it would seem sensible that in most systems, as in England, literacy, numeracy and ICT should be (a) taught and assessed in the core subjects of English, maths and ICT; and (b) have clear levels of progression written into National Curriculum attainment targets and tests. Having said that, functional skills are increasingly being mapped against GCSEs and particularly for vocational qualifications and apprenticeship programmes where there is plenty of advice on how to teach them.

This leaves thinking and learning skills and personal skills to accommodate. As these are cross-curricular (i.e. they transcend subject boundaries) they are best acquired and developed through teaching and learning across the curriculum. In line with the argument at the end of this chapter, the most appropriate way of embedding these skills is through improved guidance and training in teaching and learning across the curriculum.

This skills framework is consistent with trends in other countries. For example, the OECD's (2005) Definition and Selection of Competencies Project classified individuals' key competencies for a successful life into three broad categories:

1 *Use tools interactively* (both physical and socio-cultural ones)
   a. Use language, symbols and texts interactively
   b. Use knowledge and information interactively
   c. Use technology interactively.
2 *Interacting in heterogeneous groups and specifically to:*
   a. Relate well to others
   b. Co-operate, work in teams
   c. Manage and resolve conflicts.

3   *Acting autonomously*
    a.   Act within the big picture
    b.   Form and conduct life plans and personal projects
    c.   Defend and assert rights, interests, limits and needs.

So in summary, the clarity provided by a single skills framework, allied with better guidance and training in pedagogy, will itself create greater coherence across any national curriculum. This is the necessary foundation for ensuring that the essence of personalization is available for every student. As has been argued at length, the central characteristic of effective teachers is their ability to create powerful learners as well as knowledgeable students. The purpose of the framework for teaching, proposed below, is to suggest a way in which all teachers can do just that.

A framework for thinking about teaching

In *School Improvement for Real* (Hopkins 2001) I introduced a framework for thinking about teaching and learning. I briefly refer to it again here as it still seems to me to provide a useful starting point in the quest to develop a language and practice for teaching. Figure 11.1 illustrates the four elements of the framework that interestingly are often regarded as being contradictory rather than complementary. Let us look at each of them in turn.

I start with *teaching skills* because these are the basic building blocks of teacher competence. These are the everyday classroom management skills that most teachers became familiar with during their initial training and that they continue to refine as part of

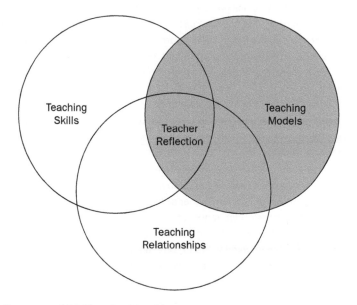

Figure 11.1   Four ways of thinking about teaching.

their reflection on professional practice. These are behaviours such as: content coverage, engaged time (i.e. students learn more when they are on task for a high proportion of class time), active teaching, structuring information, wait time and effective questioning.

There is an extensive research literature on teaching effects that are replete with cues and tactics necessary for effective teaching. Consistently high correlations are achieved between student achievement scores and classroom processes (Brophy 1983; Brophy and Good 1986). The research evidence on those teaching behaviours most closely associated with student achievement gains is now very sophisticated. An excellent summary is provided by Bert Creemers (1994: 88) in his book *The Effective Classroom*. They are taken from his 'basic model of educational effectiveness' that sees the quality of instruction as having three main components: curriculum, grouping procedures and teacher behaviour. These are all of course essential aspects of the skill sets teachers need to personalize learning. The characteristics of teacher behaviour seen in Box 11.1 all have strong empirical support in the research literature. Other excellent summaries are found in Daniel Muijs and Dave Reynolds's (2011) *Effective Teaching: Evidence and Practice* and Chris Kyriacou's (2009) *Effective Teaching in Schools*.

Box 11.1   Characteristics of teacher behaviour associated with student achievement gains

- *Management of the classroom* to create a situation where learning can take place. This implies an orderly and quiet atmosphere in the classroom, although learning itself requires more than a well-organized class. Moreover, effective teaching itself contributes to the management of the class.
- *Provision of homework.* If properly organized, homework contributes to effectiveness. This implies a clear structure of assignments, and provision and evaluation of homework.
- *Expectations.* Teachers (and schools) can influence their students' outcomes. We can expect those expectations to become apparent in the actual teacher behaviours.
- *Clear goal setting.* This includes a restricted set of goals, and an emphasis on basic skills and on cognitive learning and transfer. The content should be chosen in line with these goals.
- *Structuring the content.* This includes the ordering of the content according to the hierarchy ordered goals. The use of advanced organizers can also structure the content for students. The use of prior knowledge can increase students' own contributions and responsiveness for learning.
- *Clarity of presentation*, which implies the elements mentioned above but also refers to the transfer process itself (avoiding vagueness and incomplete sentences).
- *Questioning* (by means of low- and higher-order questions) keeps students at work and can be used to check their understanding.
- *Immediate exercise after presentation.* Like questioning, exercises provide a check for understanding and can be used to clarify problems.
- *Evaluating* whether the goals are obtained, by means of testing, providing feedback and corrective instruction.

The second component is what I have called *teaching relationships*. These are less technical and are more related to the teacher's commitment to their students and belief in the power of high expectations. A supportive, rigorous and optimistic learning environment is fundamental for high levels of student achievement. For me, a key aspect of teaching is the teacher's ability to generate and sustain an authentic relationship with their students. For example, the teacher 'who made a difference' is a common topic of conversation following an admission that 'I am a teacher'. To many educators a prime indicator of the 'effective' school is one in which a high proportion of pupils 'have a good or "vital" relationship with one or more teachers'.

The influence of expectations is often a subtle one, and is felt within a myriad of classroom interactions. The ways in which the teacher sets tasks, arranges groups, locates the responsibility for learning and provides feedback are all illustrations of how teachers can give messages of high expectations and support that condition and enhance student behaviour. It implies establishing the classroom as a safe and secure learning environment in which pupils can expect acceptance, respect and even warmth from their teachers, without having to earn these – they are intrinsic rights that are extended to all pupils, without prejudice, simply because they are there.

I had a somewhat paradoxical example of this a few years ago when I was in a school in Antofagasta, a mining town in the North of Chile. The school was new, built by the local mining company and situated right next to a *favela*. It was one of the most deprived shanty towns I have ever seen. During the visit the headteacher took me aside and said animatedly: 'Do you know, David, that the best tool we have for helping these children is not our brain but our heart?' He was a kind man and I knew what he meant. But I only half agreed with him. Of course those children needed love and support and acceptance, but they also needed the knowledge and skills to enable them to escape from the *favela*, to transcend their context and not to be imprisoned within it. A teaching relationship in the way I am describing here embodies both and is at the heart of personalized learning.

These two perspectives on high-quality teaching are not discrete. It is the practice of fine teachers to combine these elements through a process of *reflection* to create an individual style. This is the third element of the framework. The concept of 'teaching style' has been well documented in the literature (see, for example, the series of studies by Bennett 1976, 1988; Galton *et al.* 1980; Galton 1999). Instead of focusing on discrete teacher behaviour, as does the 'process–product' research associated with specific teacher effects, this research explores the relative effectiveness of different teaching styles or collections of teacher behaviours. Consequently, it may be that critical systematic reflection is a necessary condition for quality teaching. This is not reflection for reflection's sake, but in order to continue to develop a mastery of one's chosen craft. It is through reflection that the teacher harmonizes, integrates and transcends the necessary classroom management skills and the personal aspects of their teaching into a strategy that has meaning for their students.

In my experience it is these three elements, well integrated into a distinctive individual approach, that most people would regard as being the definition of a good, indeed very good, teacher. In England, for example, such a teacher would be highly regarded both by external inspectors and by their peers. But for me this is a necessary but not a sufficient condition for the quality of teaching required to personalize learning.

As we saw earlier in the chapter, personalized learning is about developing learning capability and involving students in creating their own meaning and learning pathways. In some ways – and perhaps this is a little unfair – the approach to teaching I have just described could be regarded as just a refinement, albeit a sophisticated one, of the traditional 'transmission' or 'recitation' approach to teaching. This method is in stark contrast to the approach to teaching envisioned by advocates of personalized learning, where the teacher is cast in an entirely different role – that of a creator of increasingly powerful learning experiences. It is this approach to teaching that provides the fourth element in the framework – *teaching models*.

Earlier in the chapter I made the point, as I have just done above, that it is the teacher's task not simply to 'teach', but to create powerful contexts for learning. I then quoted from our book *Models of Learning – Tools for Teaching* (Joyce *et al.* 2002). Let me now complete the quotation (Joyce *et al.* 2002: 7) in support of the argument that a good teaching strategy can also be a powerful learning strategy:

> Our toolbox is the models of teaching, actually models for learning that simultaneously define the nature of the content, the learning strategies, and the arrangements for social interaction that create the learning environments of our students.
>
> Through the selection of appropriate models, content can become conceptual rather than particular, the process can become constructive inquiry instead of passive reception, and the social climate can become expansive not restrictive. Our choices depend on the range of our active teaching repertoire and our efforts to expand it by developing new models and studying those developed by others.

It is the integration of 'content, process and social climate' that explains how the learning experience can be organized and personalized to make a positive difference to students. The impact is not just on test scores and examination results, but also on the students' capacity to learn. As I have already said, if the teacher can teach the student how to learn at the same time as assisting them to acquire curriculum content, then the twin goals of learning and achievement can be met at the same time.

Thus, imagine a classroom where the learning environment contains a variety of models of teaching that are not only intended to accomplish a range of curriculum goals, but also designed to help students increase their competence as learners. At the risk of gilding the lily, allow me a final quote from Joyce *et al.* (2002):

> In such classrooms the students learn models for memorising information, how to attain concepts and how to invent them. They practise building hypotheses and theories and use the tools of science to test them. They learn how to extract information and ideas from lectures and presentations, how to study social issues and how to analyse their own social values. These students also know how to profit from training and how to train themselves in athletics, performing arts, mathematics and social skills. They know how to make their writing and problem solving more lucid and creative. Perhaps most

importantly, they know how to take initiative in planning personal study, and they know how to work with others to initiate and carry out co-operative tasks. As students' master information and skills, the result of each learning experience is not only the content they learn but also the greater ability they acquire to approach future learning tasks with confidence and to create increasingly effective learning environments for themselves.

Bruce Joyce developed this approach in his pioneering work *Models of Teaching* (Joyce and Weil 2009) which was first published in 1972 and is now in its eighth edition. Joyce describes and analyses over 30 different models of teaching – each with its own 'syntax', phases and guidelines – that are designed to bring about particular kinds of learning and to help students become more effective learners. It is in this way that the use of teaching models forms part of an overall strategy for enhancing teacher professionalism and the key tool for personalizing learning.

Models of learning – tools for teaching

Models of teaching simultaneously define the nature of the content, the learning strategies, and the arrangements for social interaction that create the learning environments of students. Models of teaching are also models of learning. How teaching is conducted has a large impact on students' abilities to educate themselves. Each model has its own core purpose that relates not only to how to organize teaching, but also to ways of learning. So, for example, if in whole-class teaching the teacher uses the advance organizer model to structure a presentation, the student can use the same method as a means of extracting information and ideas from lectures and presentations. Some examples of the relationship between teaching and learning strategy are given in Table 11.2.

It is important to be clear about what is meant by a 'model of teaching'. As the idea is exotic to the repertoires of many teachers, one needs to be quite concrete in

Table 11.2 Examples of the relationship between model of teaching and learning skills

Model of teaching	Learning skill
Advanced organizer (or whole-class teaching model)	Extracting information and ideas from lectures and presentations
Group work	Working effectively with others to initiate and carry out cooperative tasks
Inductive teaching	Building hypotheses and theories through classification
Mnemonics	Memorizing information
Concept attainment	Attaining concepts and how to invent them
Synectics	Using metaphors to think creatively

explaining the concept. This is what I will attempt to do in the following section. An initial distinction would be to regard the evidence on teaching skills as providing the teacher with tactical knowledge, whereas the research on 'models of teaching' gives teachers strategic knowledge about how to create whole-classroom settings to facilitate learning.

In *Models of Learning – Tools for Teaching* (Joyce *et al.* 2002) and the *Creating the Conditions for Teaching and Learning* (Hopkins and Harris 2000) handbook based on experiences in IQEA schools, a range of contrasting and complementary teaching strategies are described. These are drawn from Joyce's original four families of teaching models, namely the information processing, the social, the personal, and the behavioural families. Here are brief descriptions of three of the models of teaching and learning, followed by a more curriculum-focused example.

Seeing that we have now become familiar with the concept of effect size, it may be helpful to give an indication of the range of effect sizes associated with the various families of models of teaching. Bruce Joyce was an early adopter of effect size as a means of measuring the impact of models of teaching on student learning (Joyce *et al.* 2009). This is a summary of the effect sizes of the four families of the models of teaching:

- *information processing* – a mean effect size over 1.0 for higher-order outcomes;
- *cooperative learning* – a mean effect size between 0.3 and 0.7;
- *personal models* – a mean effect size of 0.3 or more for cognitive, affective and behavioural outcomes;
- *behavioural models* – a mean effect between 0.5 and 1.0; best representatives are for short-term treatments looking at behavioural or knowledge of content outcomes.

The whole-class teaching model

In active whole-class teaching the teacher controls pupils' learning and seeks to improve performance through direct instruction, whole-class questioning, discussion and learning activities (Hopkins and Harris 2000).

CASE STUDY 11.1

A class of Year 7 pupils is being introduced to rhythm in poetry as part of a unit on sound effects in language. The objectives of the lesson are to refine pupils' listening powers, in particular their sense of volume, beat and pace; to appreciate the force of repetition and variation of tempo; to understand the relationship between meaning and beat; to appreciate how writers use these elements to create dramatic effects in their writing. The teacher has chosen Vachel Lindsay's ballad, 'The Daniel Jazz', as an example.

The lesson begins with the title of the poem. The class is asked to work out what it means. Who was Daniel? What has jazz got to do with him? There is a whole-class discussion to ascertain prior knowledge of the class using a range of questioning techniques. Taking the medley of ideas, the teacher builds up a complete version of the story for the class.

The teacher then develops the jazz/story connection and challenges the class to say what they understand by 'jazz writing'. Students are asked to write down at least two ideas on the relationship between music and words. Students share their ideas with the person next to them and together they produce two or three more ideas.

After a few minutes the teacher asks for responses to the questions and elicits terms which might include: DRUM BEAT, RHYTHM, NOISE, LOUD, FAST, SLOW, BASS, TIMING, REPETITION and so on. Some of these concepts are written on the board and stay as reference points for the rest of the lesson.

The teacher then displays the first ten lines of 'The Daniel Jazz'. The teacher reads the first four lines and asks if any of the words on the board apply to this section of the poem. The class recites the lines together emphasizing the beat. A *Sun* newspaper report of the Daniel incident at a local zoo is introduced to the class. The class tries to recite it but fails. The difference between the two pieces of writing is posed as a question to the class.

In pairs, the class is asked to identify any differences in pace and rhythm in the first 20 lines of the poem. After a few minutes pairs report back with examples. At this point the teacher can assess the degree to which the concepts are being understood and adjust teaching accordingly. More demonstration may be needed to reinforce the concepts of rhythm and pace.

A provided worksheet asks pupils to identify the slow and fast lines in the 20 lines they are now getting familiar with and explain in the writing space provided what makes them slow and why the writer has varied the pace. Partners discuss their results and then the teacher asks for some examples, praising and refining pupil contributions as is appropriate.

The conclusion to the lesson is an accretive recital. Two pupils say the first line, then two more join in for the second and so on until the whole class are jazzing their way through the lines, feeling the beat.

This model of teaching enables pupils to order, absorb, understand and relate different areas of knowledge efficiently. It is not a matter of instruction alone. As well as enabling students to process information, the model also allows for pupil interaction so that they learn from each other as well as the teacher and extend their repertoire of social skills. Whole-class teaching is about talking with pupils, listening to them and guiding their learning activities.

Whole-class active teaching is essentially composed of three components or phases:

1   Pupils are formally presented with a problem, issue, area of knowledge or set of skills through lecture or demonstration.
2   Pupils develop understanding through systematic questioning and disciplined inquiry.
3   Pupils apply understanding through a series of set tasks.

The model presupposes a coherent instructional programme based on a clear set of overarching goals. The instructional model works as part of an integrative teaching and learning plan that may include cooperative group work and independent study. Employing a range of teaching activities influences pupil motivation and is likely to engage them in learning. Non-stop teacher presentation or instruction involving taking notes, answering questions from textbooks and recycling information in homework is tedious and repetitive. Mixing the palette of teaching approaches is more likely to engage pupils in learning, as will mixing modes of delivery and format.

It is important to emphasize that whole-class teaching is a strategic approach to teaching that focuses not only on basic skills and cognitive processes, but also on promoting learning strategies, problem-solving and social support. Teachers using the whole-class model address these more complex instructional goals by using a range of techniques to structure strategic learning. Some of these key strategies are as follows:

> *Understanding.* This is a prerequisite to clarity and involves matching the new information to the learners' present knowledge. Does the teacher:
> - determine students' existing familiarity with the information presented?
> - use terms that are unambiguous and within the students' experience?
>
> *Structuring.* This involves organizing the material to promote a clear presentation; stating the purpose, reviewing main ideas, and providing transitions between sections. Does the teacher:
> - establish the purpose of the lesson?
> - preview the organization of the lesson?
> - include internal summaries of the lesson?
>
> *Sequencing.* This involves arranging the information in an order conducive to learning, typically by gradually increasing its difficulty or complexity. Does the teacher:
> - order the lesson in a logical way, appropriate to the content and the learners?
>
> *Explaining.* When explaining principles and relating them to facts through examples, illustrations or analogies, does the teacher:
> - define major concepts?
> - give examples to illustrate these concepts?
> - use examples that are accurate and concrete as well as abstract?
>
> *Presenting.* This refers to volume, pacing, articulation and other speech mechanics. Does the teacher:
> - articulate words clearly and project speech loudly enough?
> - pace the sections of the presentation at rates conducive to understanding?
> - support the verbal content with appropriate non-verbal communication and visual aids?
>
> (adapted from Good and Brophy 2007)

In summary, the whole-class model of teaching includes the following five phases:

1   *Review*
   - Review the concepts and skills from the previous lesson (and if appropriate the homework).
2   *Presenting information*
   - Lecture or talk:
     - Preview the outline and scope of the lecture.
     - Introduce key terms or concepts.
     - Lecture proceeds in small steps, starting with what is familiar and using lively explanations and illustrations.
   - Demonstration:
     - Preliminaries – a guide as to what to observe and expect.
     - Preview – purpose is outlined.
     - Rehearsal – teachers go through each step.
     - Reprise – procedures are repeated.
3   *Involving pupils in discussion*
   - Focus on meaning and promoting student understanding through fast-paced discussion.
   - Assess student comprehension through high-quality questioning.
4   *Engaging pupils in learning activities*
   - Design activities to focus on content.
   - Implementation of learning activities.
5   *Summary and review*
   - Pupils ask follow-up questions, share findings and conclusions.
   - Teacher reinforces key points, emphasizes central ideas and sums up achievements.

The cooperative group work teaching model

As a model of teaching, cooperative group work has a powerful effect in raising pupil achievement because it harnesses the synergy of collective action. It combines the dynamics of democratic processes with the processes of academic inquiry. It encourages active participation in learning and collaborative behaviour by developing social as well as 'academic' skills. Thus the model requires pupils to practise and refine their negotiating, organizing and communication skills, define issues and problems, develop ways of solving them including collecting and interpreting evidence, hypothesizing, testing and re-evaluating.

The model is highly flexible and draws on a wide range of methods – individual research, collaborative inquiry and plenary activities – and allows the integration of them all into a powerful teaching tool. The teacher is able to conduct a more subtle and complex learning strategy that achieves a number of learning goals simultaneously. Thus, styles can vary from didactic to 'light touch' teaching where the teacher is more an adviser and guide than a director. Two popular approaches to cooperative group learning are 'numbered heads' and the 'jigsaw'. Here are examples of these approaches.

CASE STUDY 11.2

Numbered heads

In an English lesson the teacher is focusing on the punctuation of direct and indirect speech. First, the class is divided into named groups of four and each pupil is allocated a number. From a displayed passage of unpunctuated dialogue and description each group is asked to identify the direct speech. Everyone knows that after 2 minutes of discussion there will be silence signalled by a bell ringing and that one of them will have their number called and will have to respond. This motivates groups to share information and make sure everyone knows the answer. It gives every pupil a chance to shine and, because they have the group behind them, no one is made anxious about answering. Successful responses bolster both individual and collective confidence, which can be boosted further by some form of team award system.

Jigsaw

In food technology a teacher sets up a question or problem for inquiry and divides pupils into equal-sized groups called 'home groups'. Typical topics might include food hygiene in the home, safe practice in the kitchen, processed versus organic foodstuffs, dangerous additives and so on. Each group is given an identical task and suggested list of roles/jobs. For 5 minutes groups discuss the 'problem' and allocate roles/jobs. The home groups then divide, and those with identical jobs form new expert groups whose function is to collect relevant information. After a period of research the original home groups are reformed and expert knowledge pooled to solve the problem or map the issue.

There are many other examples of cooperative learning strategies (Hopkins and Harris 2000):

Twos to fours or snowballing. Children work together in pairs, perhaps on a mathematical problem or science experiment. They then join with another pair to explain what they have achieved, and to compare this with the work of the other pair. This provides a valuable opportunity to express understanding, and to respond to the views of others in a supportive context.

Rainbow groups. A way of ensuring that children experience working alongside a range of others is to give each child in a group a number, or a colour. When the group has worked together, all the children of the same number or colour form new groups to compare what they have done.

Envoys. Often, in group work, the teacher is concerned that they will be under pressure from many different directions. Envoying helps children to find help and support without necessarily having recourse to the teacher. If a group needs to check something, or to obtain information, one of the group can be sent as an 'envoy' to the library, or book corner, or another group, and then will report back. Another use is to ask groups to send an envoy to a different group to

explain what they have done, obtain responses and suggestions, and bring
them back to the group.

Listening triads. This strategy encourages children, in groups of three, to take on
the roles of talker, questioner or recorder. The talker explains or comments on
an issue or activity. The questioner prompts and seeks clarification. The
recorder makes notes, and at the end of the (brief) time, gives a report of the
conversation. Next time the roles are changed.

Critical friends. A group member is responsible for observing the ways in which
the group works together. Using a simple guide list (which children can devise),
the observer watches and listens as the children work. The group then
discusses this information. This helps children to develop their own evaluative
strategies.

Effective group work involves an agreed set of ground rules that are based on
self-respect for individuals and directed at creating efficient working patterns.
These ground rules are negotiated as part of an introductory all-class session
and refined by each group afterwards to suit their particular concerted needs. Framed
as negatives or positives, these 'commandments' should establish norms of civilized
and democratic behaviour and, if developed collaboratively, will be accepted and
followed more readily. The rules should be simple, reasonable and just. They include,
for example:

- No one should interrupt another.
- No one should abuse another.
- No one should ignore another.
- Criticism must be justified and evidenced.
- Different opinions should be respected.
- Praise should be given.
- All members should offer help and share knowledge.

For cooperative methods of learning to be effective, they have to be planned,
implemented and monitored very carefully. An ideological commitment to the idea is
not enough and, indeed, can result in poorly conceived group activities that may quickly
become a shambles. While cooperative methods have an enormous potential for
encouraging success in the classroom, this is unlikely to be the outcome unless they are
introduced in a systematic and coordinated way. Facilitating effective small-group
learning means helping group members perceive the importance of working together
and interacting in helpful ways.

The inductive teaching model

Inductive teaching is a model from the information-processing family. Its main purpose
is to encourage pupils to build, test and to use categories to organize their thinking
about a particular topic or subject area. We use the inductive model as a basis of our

curriculum frameworks for cross-curricular inquiry projects as well as developing our student's problem-solving skills (Bright Tribe 2014b).

CASE STUDY 11.3

A Year 10 class is being introduced to different styles of portrait painting as part of their GCSE course. Initially the teacher gives each individual an A4 handout containing numbered photographs of different kinds of portraits. The portraits represent a range of styles and are from different centuries. For 5 minutes the teacher gets the class to look at the photographs individually. The class is then divided into pairs and the teacher instructs each pair to categorize the portraits by grouping certain photographs together using the numbers to group the categories. The pairs set about this task, placing the portraits into groups and giving each category a name. The teacher makes it clear that some portraits could be placed in several categories. She also reassures the pupils by telling them that any categories that can be named and justified are acceptable.

After 15 minutes or so, the teacher pauses this activity and asks several of the pairs to share their classification with the whole class and their reasons for classifying the portraits in this way. The pairs offer a series of numbers that are written up by the teacher for the whole class to view. While this is happening, other pupils look at their own classifications to ascertain whether they have reached similar conclusions or not. Having provided a set of numbers, the other pupils are then asked by the teacher to guess the rationale behind the classification. One pair offers 'seventeenth century' as one category while another offers 'Cubism' as a category. Eventually the initiators of the classification are asked to tell the class why they grouped the data together and the teacher helps the whole class look for links between the data chosen.

After several pairs have provided their categories and the class has worked out their reasons for grouping the data together, the teacher then hands each pair some additional photographs of portraits. The pairs are then asked to reconsider their categories with respect to the new data. The pupils are given time to allocate the new data within existing categories, or to recategorize the whole data set. Once they have done this task, the teacher once again asks selected pairs to share their classification and the labels they have given each category.

The teacher lists the different categories and asks the pupils to add any categories not represented by the list. The teacher then asks the pupils to choose one category and to paint a portrait in this style.

The inductive teaching model is a powerful way of helping pupils to learn how to construct knowledge. The model focuses directly on intellectual capability and is intended to assist pupils in the process of mastering large amounts of information. Within teaching there are numerous occasions when pupils are required to sort and classify data. However, in many cases the sorting process is viewed as an end in itself. Pupils are usually required to understand the 'one correct way of classifying'. Teachers know that there are usually many ways of classifying, but they choose one for simplicity.

The inductive method allows pupils to understand a variety of classifications in a structured way that includes a variety of teaching techniques within one method. Without opportunity for reclassification or hypothesizing, learning potential is limited and the development of high-order thinking is restricted. The inductive model of teaching consists of a number of discrete phases that cannot be rushed or omitted. Inductive inquiries are rarely brief because the very nature of the inquiry requires pupils to think deeply. The key activity in the inductive model is the collecting and sifting of information in order to construct categories or labels. This process requires pupils to engage with the data and seek to produce categories in which to allocate the data. It requires them to generate hypotheses based upon this allocation and to test out these hypotheses by using them to guide subsequent work.

The flow of the inductive model involves:

- identifying the information relevant to a topic or a problem;
- grouping individual items into categories that have common attributes;
- classifying the information and developing labels for the categories (this also involves identifying and exploring critical relationships and making inferences);
- creating hypotheses and predicting consequences.

The inductive teaching model follows a sequence of different phases. In the first phase pupils are presented with information or data sets and are required to sort the data into categories. The data sets are derived from a subject area and are intended to facilitate learning about a particular topic or theme. The data sets can be assembled by the teacher in advance of the lesson or collected by the pupils with guidance from the teacher. If assembled by the teacher, the data sets will be prepared with certain concepts in mind. To engage pupils in this model, teachers need to begin by presenting data sets to them and in subsequent lessons to encourage pupils to create and generate their own data sets. It is important that pupils have experience of the inductive model in all its phases and have success in learning with this model before embarking upon more sophisticated and complicated data sets.

To be really effective, data classification needs to occur several times. The initial phase of the classification is particularly important because this is where concepts are generated and applied. Following this initial phase, additional data or new information that requires some reclassification or refinement of the categories may be added. Adding new data means that concepts are challenged, requiring pupils to think again about their initial classification. Through this iterative process pupils obtain control over the data and can understand related concepts more readily.

Inductive teaching increases pupils' ability to form concepts and to create linkages between different concepts. It also enables pupils to have a wider perspective on the topic in question and to think more broadly about the subject matter. Another, important aspect of the inductive model is the collective nature of the inquiry and the group responsibility to contribute to the compilation of categories. By allowing individuals to share their ideas with the whole class, different perspectives on the same data and challenges to thinking are inevitable.

There are many other advantages to the use of the model:

- It engages pupils in higher-order thinking.
- It involves variety in that the stages are taught in different ways so it supports a variety of learning styles.
- Once the data set has been prepared, it can be easily kept from one year to another and its tangibility means that it is likely to get incorporated into schemes of work.
- Once the data set has been prepared, it is easy to share among members of staff and across different schools.
- Providing teachers keep to the stages of the model, it provides a varied and stimulating way to learn.

In summary, the inductive model of teaching involves the following six phases (Joyce and Calhoun 1998):

Phase One: Identify the domain
- Establish the focus and boundaries of the initial inquiry.
- Clarify the long-term objectives.

Phase Two: Collect, present, and enumerate data
- Assemble and present the initial data set.
- Enumerate and label the items of data.

Phase Three: Examine data
- Thoroughly study the items in the data set and identify their attributes.

Phase Four: Form concepts by classifying
- Classify the items in the data set and share the results
- Add data to the set.
- Reclassification occurs, possibly many times.

Phase Five: Generate and test hypotheses
- Examine the implications of differences between categories.
- Classify categories, as appropriate.
- Reclassify in two-way matrices, as well as by correlations, as appropriate.

Phase Six: Consolidate and transfer
- Search for additional items of data in resource material.
- Synthesize by writing about the domain, using the categories.
- Convert categories into skills.
- Test and consolidate skills through practice and application.

A brief note on the nature of teaching style and the integration of content and process

In this chapter I have argued that teaching and learning should provide the central focus for the work of the teacher-researcher – it is their heartland. The position I have taken is that the teacher-researcher needs to become increasingly specific about those teaching strategies that promote more effective learning. This is for two reasons. First, this is the best way to communicate professional knowledge to other teachers. Second, in the belief that a good teaching strategy is also a good learning strategy, it is by the same token the best way to communicate learning skills to our students.

We need clarity on the concepts and precision on principles such as this if we are to put professional knowledge, as Lawrence Stenhouse once said, to the test of practice. 'Putting to the test of practice', however, requires a capacity to integrate, unite and transcend functionalist approaches. I hope that is clear by now. If not, let me, in concluding this chapter, cite two further examples of the ways in which the teacher-researcher stands at the fulcrum of establishing a professional practice for education.

First, it is ultimately my belief that effective teaching and learning must be seen within a holistic framework. The comparative study of policies aimed at improving teacher quality we conducted for the OECD identified six characteristics of high-quality teachers (Hopkins and Stern 1996: 510):

- commitment;
- love of children;
- mastery of subject didactics;
- a repertoire of multiple models of teaching;
- the ability to collaborate with other teachers;
- a capacity for reflection.

Although it is convenient to group teachers' desired capacities and behaviours into categories, these attributes all interact in practice. For example, one French teacher elegantly defined teacher quality as 'savoirs, savoir-faire, et savoir-être', this is trans-latable perhaps as 'knowledge, knowing how to do, and knowing how to be' (Hopkins and Stern 1996: 503).

Second, and in the same way, it is at the school level that there needs to be a powerful integrative force. As Lawrence Downey (1967) once evocatively put it: 'A school teaches in three ways, by what it teaches, by how it teaches and by the kind of place it is.' It is a consideration of the context and conditions that support effective teaching and learning that provides a focus for the following chapter and I hope for much of the book.

Let me illustrate this thought by extending the earlier discussion of the importance of 'learning to learn' and ways of achieving this within a whole-school context. The recent emphasis in schools on 'learning to learn' has the great advantage that successful teachers become better skilled themselves in integrating the teaching and learning of skills into subject content. There are a variety of strategies that are being employed, and these include:

- subject-specific programmes that contribute to pupils' understanding, think-ing and learning of key skills in a subject context;
- discrete skills programmes (learning to learn lessons) that enable an explicit focus on skills with reference to a broad range of subject content and contexts;

- cross-curricular programmes that ally clarity on learning skills with a focus on subject content to help students transfer their learning between lessons.

It is difficult to say which approach is better than the other. In our experience, however, it depends on what fits best into the schools context, and on how well the programme is being implemented. Above all, however, it is how well these programmes link together curriculum, teaching strategies and the school's whole approach to learning. Our view is that any of these programmes should be systematically embedded in the curriculum and have strong links between teaching and learning. Figure 11.2 shows how the integration of such a programme into the curriculum could take place. There are three elements of the figure that, when linked together, serve to summarize the key issues in this chapter.

First, the school as in A must have adopted a clear model of learning that is consistently applied. Many models are suitable as long as they are developmental, i.e. move from low to high learning skills. In the figure I have used Gagné's (1965) classification. Frameworks developed by Bloom (1956) – revised as Anderson and Krathwohl (2000) – or Claxton (1999) would also be appropriate.

The second element at B is the judicious and strategic application of the models of learning – the 'tools for teaching' approach described earlier. The key point of course is that any model of learning has the potential to develop specific learning skills. So, the curriculum planning task becomes ensuring that there is clarity on the specific learning skill that needs to be developed, and that this is then matched to an appropriate model of teaching.

When this approach is applied to the whole school, as in C, there will be a methodology for progressively developing learning skills across the curriculum. This occurs horizontally – in any term or year a student is consistently being exposed to a range of learning strategies – and vertically – these learning strategies are progressively developed at a more sophisticated level with more demanding curriculum content as the student progresses through school.

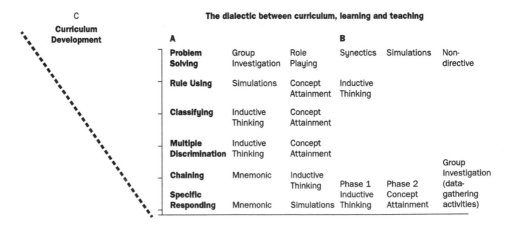

Figure 11.2   The dialectic between curriculum, learning and teaching.

Finally, a comment on the debate around whether whole-class or group activity should dominate, or what should be the balance between whole-class, small-group, and individual activities. Settling that question leads to the broader question of what will work best for children, because it is the models of learning and teaching chosen, rather than the grouping arrangements adopted, that will directly affect student achievement. In these classes, students are taught directly models for learning that they use when working as members of the class community, in small collaborative groups, and as individuals. The more efficient models of teaching assume that the whole class will be organized to pursue common learning objectives within which individual differences in achievement are comfortably accommodated. Thus, their creators have a vision of the whole class and a vision of small-group work and individual work as part of the overall educational scheme (Joyce and Calhoun 1997: 16). Or as Bruce Joyce elegantly phrased it, the operational repertoire of the teacher is the critical element in the calculus of effects.

Further reading

Much of this chapter has been based on previous writing on teaching and learning. The key text here is *Models of Teaching* (Joyce and Weil 2009). In *Models of Learning – Tools for Teaching* (Joyce *et al.* 2002), we adapted the original manuscript for a trans-American audience, and *Creating the Conditions for Teaching and Learning* (Hopkins and Harris 2000) reports on the use of these materials in IQEA schools (see also Hopkins *et al.* 1997). In terms of the different models of teaching described in this chapter, further information on whole-class teaching can be found in Good and Brophy (2007); on cooperative group work, Robert Slavin (1994) is an accessible source; and on inductive teaching, Joyce and Calhoun's (1997) *Learning to Teach Inductively* is excellent. The literature on how children learn (Wood 1998), the different types or 'multiple intelligences' (Gardner 1993, 2011) and the descriptions of a range of learning styles (Kolb 1984) are helpful in designing increasingly effective learning experiences within authentic school improvement contexts. James *et al.*'s (2006a) research paper 'Learning How to Learn, in Classrooms, Schools and Networks' as well as James *et al.* (2006b) *Learning How to Learn: Tools for Schools* are an essential read on learning to learn. Useful sources for the research on teaching also include Kyriacou (2009), Anderson and Krathwohl (2000), Claxton (1999) and Muijs and Reynolds (2011), together with the other studies reported earlier in this chapter.

12 Teacher research, school improvement and system reform

In the first edition of this book I was clear that teacher research should embody a 'classroom exceeding' perspective and argued for enhanced collaborative action amongst teacher-researchers. Subsequent editions have expanded on that theme as I began to emphasize the importance of the role of the teacher-researcher in both school improvement and system reform. Somewhat self-indulgently in successive editions of the book, I have taken the opportunity to use the final chapter to reflect on this theme and to give examples of how in my most recent educational work, teacher research, in its broadest sense, provides the essential link between professional development, school improvement and system reform. I continue that tradition here with a reflection on the system reform efforts we have recently been involved with in Victoria, Australia.

This chapter provides an exemplification of two of the key insights emerging from the last decade of research on school and system reform (Hopkins 2013). The first is Sir Michael Barber's (2009) observation that it was the school effectiveness research in the 1980s that gave us increasingly well-defined portraits of the effective school and led in the 1990s to increasing knowledge of more reliable school improvement strategies. In the same way, we have in the last decade begun to learn more about the features of an effective educational system, but are only beginning to understand the dynamics of improvement working simultaneously at the various system levels. The second insight also belongs to Michael Barber, and is from the McKinsey report *How the World's Best Performing School Systems Come Out on Top* (Barber and Mourshed 2007): that 'the quality of an educational system cannot exceed the quality of its teachers'. These two truisms provide the context for this chapter which focuses on the improvement of student achievement through the development of professional practice within a systemic context.

The purpose here is to deepen the analysis of strategies for improvement at the classroom, school and local level by using the 'powerful learning' framework developed in the Northern Metropolitan Region (NMR) of Melbourne, Victoria, Australia as an example. In the first section of the chapter, the context of school reform in Melbourne is described together with an outline of the school improvement strategy designed to deliver on both moral purpose and the student achievement goals of enhanced literacy, numeracy and curiosity. In the following section, the 'theories of action' and the subsequent *Curiosity* booklet derived from the instructional rounds strategy that proved critical in deepening the culture of teaching and learning in the NMR are described in some detail. Finally, the leadership strategies adopted to ensure that implementation occurs at a level sufficient to impact on student learning and achievement are presented. The chapter concludes with a set of theories of action for classroom, school and system improvement.

School Reform in Melbourne's Northern Region

Melbourne is Australia's second largest city and has a population of just over 4 million. The NMR, which covers the city's northern suburbs, includes more than 200 government primary, secondary and special schools, 80,000 students and 7500 principals and teachers. It is culturally and socio-economically diverse and is home to some very affluent communities as well as some of Australia's poorest urban communities.

The school system has three sectors – a government system that caters for around 70% of students, a Catholic system that has around 20% of all enrolments and a range of independent or private schools that are often faith-based and that account for the remaining students. The government school sector – the focus of this chapter – is highly devolved with more than 90% of all funding going directly to schools. Representatives of the school and the Education Department appoint principals, and principals determine the staff composition of the school staff and appoint teachers.

The approach adopted in the NMR in utilizing the powerful learning framework as a strategy for successful school reform at the local level is described in some detail here, in the belief that it can provide a transferable model for other settings (Hopkins *et al.* 2011).

Successful school systems around the world – those that have high levels of equity in student achievement and success – are characterized by moral purpose and clarity of goals that have direct implications not just for schooling, but also for the way society develops (Mourshed *et al.* 2010). This is also the case in the NMR, which continues to strive to become a world-class educational system. The moral purpose for school reform in the NMR is to:

> Provide a high quality education for all students regardless of background. This is to ensure that the conditions are in place to enable every student in the region to reach their potential. This moral purpose is reflected in a small number of tangible, but ambitious objectives, for student learning and achievement that are being vigorously pursued. These goals are also in line with the reform areas [in the 'National Partnership Agreements' that were agreed] with the Federal Government.
>
> The goal is for all students in [the region] to be literate, numerate and curious, with schools continuing to provide a broad-based 21st century curriculum.
>
> (Hopkins 2011: 8)

Through setting such a goal and establishing the process of school reform to achieve it, the ambition is that in a relatively short space of time students, their parents, carers, teachers and other stakeholders, will notice a real difference. For example, the NMR defines the following goals for 2013 (Northern Metropolitan Region 2009: 9):

- A student finishing primary school will demonstrate individual performance at or above national standards in literacy and numeracy and a sharp curiosity for learning. Thus literate, numerate and curious became the rallying call for school improvement across the region.
- A student finishing secondary school will have a clear well-defined pathway to further training and education.
- Parents and carers will have a substantive and meaningful engagement with their child's school and teachers and a clear understanding of their child's progress against national standards.
- Teachers will have world-class professional skills, be highly regarded in their school communities and have continuing access to quality professional learning opportunities.
- The community will have confidence that individual student performance meets national standards and that graduates of NMR schools are capable of making valuable contributions as citizens and employees.

If these are the goals, then the approach to school improvement adopted by the NMR is the means of achieving them. The model shown in Figure 12.1 identifies the crucial elements of an effective school, demonstrates their interdependence and provides a guide to strategic action. This is an action framework designed to help both those working directly in schools and those working at district or regional level, to more effectively manage the realignment of top-down and bottom-up change over time. This approach not only illustrates how a region such as the NMR is balancing top-down and bottom-up change in practical ways, but also introduces a new concept, for Australia at least, of successful change by moving from the inside out rather than the outside in.

The main features of the approach are as follows.

1   In the centre is powerful learning, which represents the school's goal that every student will reach their potential, together with a definition of achievement that embraces standards of literacy, numeracy and learning capability (curiosity). Such a learning focus will not only raise standards, but also reduce the range of performance in a school, thus simultaneously 'raising the bar and narrowing the gap'.
2   Effective schools are not simply an amalgam of disparate elements. There are some essential features that need to be in place that lay the basis for greatness – these are the preconditions for effectiveness, upon which all else is built. Without these, a school will be unable to achieve or sustain excellence. These three features, represented in the second ring of Figure 12.1, are:
    - the importance of instructional leadership;
    - the quality of teaching;
    - a culture of orderliness and high expectations.

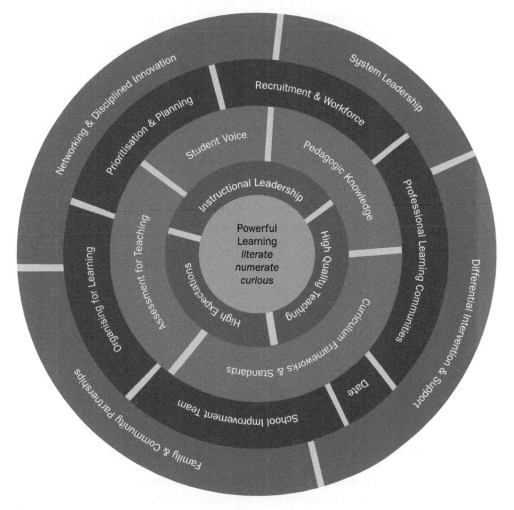

Figure 12.1 The powerful learning regional school improvement strategy framework.
(reproduced from Northern Metropolitan Region 2009: 13).

3 The next ring is comprised of those essential ingredients of effective class-room practice necessary for powerful learning:
- the teacher's repertoire of teaching and learning strategies, commonly known as pedagogical knowledge;
- the organization of curriculum in terms of frameworks and standards;
- the way that learning is assessed in order to inform teaching;
- the ways in which students are involved in their learning and the organization of the school.
4 The organizational conditions supportive of high levels of teaching and learning are detailed as the key elements found in the next ring:
- collaborative planning that focuses on student outcomes;

- professional learning that is committed to improvement of classroom practice;
- regular use of data, inquiry and self-evaluation to improve teaching;
- the recruitment of teaching staff and the deployment of the whole school workforce;
- the identification of a school improvement team to provide the research and development capacity for the school;
- the way in which the school is organized to most effectively promote learning.

5　The broader systemic context of the school is represented in the outer ring of the diagram by reference to four obligations and opportunities enjoyed by all schools in the NMR:
- the opportunity to network with other schools in order to share good practice and engage in disciplined innovation;
- the way in which schools embrace and respond to the needs and opportunities provided in their locality from parents, carers and communities;
- the new opportunities for principals to engage in broader forms of 'system leadership' where they take on a range of roles in supporting other principals and schools;
- the opportunity to engage in more purposeful reflection on the effectiveness of the school's provision provided by the region's regular reviews of schools and the subsequent planning and differential intervention and support determined by the school's current performance.

A further perspective needs to be added that is critical to an understanding of the NMR approach and its general applicability. Most school reform assumes that change comes from the outside in. The logic, in Australia, goes something like this:

> A high quality policy or program is developed and then implemented, with the assumption that it will impact upon the school and be internalised through the school's planning processes. In turn, it is assumed this will impact on classroom practices and will therefore positively affect the learning and achievement of students.
>
> (Hopkins 2011: 11)

It is as if the drive comes from the outer circle of the diagram and permeates the various layers, hopefully reaching the powerful learning of students in the centre.

However, in our experience, in those schools that have made the jump 'from good to great' the linear logic of policy implementation has been inverted. Instead of doing better, or more efficiently, from the outside in, they start from the centre of the circle and move outwards; these schools begin at the other end of the sequence, with student learning. It is as if they ask: 'What changes in student learning and performance do we wish to see this year?' Having decided these, they then discuss what teaching strategies will be most effective in bringing them about, and reflect on what modifications are required to the organization of the school to support these developments. Finally, they embed within their school improvement plans those policy initiatives that provide the best fit with the school's vision, values and goals for enhancing student achievement. It is these schools that appear to be the most effective at interpreting the national, state and regional reform agenda. The underlying purpose of the powerful learning framework described above is to generate this degree of confidence and agency in schools. In so doing, it exposes the paucity of simple autonomy as a recipe for systemic educational reform. It is this framework that provides the scaffolding for 'inside-out' working.

After several years, it was clear that significant progress had been made in terms of literacy and numeracy. Taken as a whole, all of the performance measures available – National Program for Assessment – Literacy and Numeracy (NAPLAN) data, Year 12 Achievement achievement data, Year 12 or equivalent completion data, student, teacher and parent opinion data – were tracking in a strongly positive direction. Literacy and numeracy data for years Years 3, 5, 7 and 9 showed that the region had in broad terms gone from being one of the poorest performing to one of the better performing of the state's nine regions, with all data sets either above or very close to state means. Year 12 performance data had grown significantly particularly in terms of a dramatic reduction in the number of very poorly performing schools. Growth in Year 12 attainment by age 19 showed the greatest increase of any of the regions in the period 2001–10. Student, teacher and parent opinion data, gathered annually, also showed ongoing and significant growth (Hopkins 2011).

Instructional rounds and the whole-school theories of action

Although commendable, the progress on student gains in literacy and numeracy made in NMR has parallels with a number of other regions and districts (Hopkins 2013). Short-term increases on these measures are often achieved through the use of top-down and instrumental strategies. The real challenge is to sustain these improvements into the medium and long term and *at the same time* enhance the learning skills, the spirit of inquiry or curiosity of our students. This is where the focus on implementation and inside-out working becomes so important. It is in this respect that our work is perhaps unique, so we need to set the scene in a little more detail.

The use of instructional rounds (described in Chapter 6) was the key strategy in generating a common language of instructional practice within the NMR. To do this we refined the generic instructional rounds leadership strategy, associated with the work of Richard Elmore and his colleagues, that was being adopted across the state (City *et al.* 2009). Our approach worked iteratively, but systematically, from the existing knowledge base of individual teachers to develop theories of action that discipline and deepen the culture of teaching and learning of all teachers in the school and the NMR. Critical to the success of the instructional rounds approach has been the development of *theories of action*. A theory of action is a link between cause and effect: *if* we take a particular action, *then* we expect that action to have specific effects. A theory of action connects the actions of teachers with the consequences of their actions – the learning and achievement of their students.

As our experience with instructional rounds has continued to deepen in Wales (Caerphilly County Borough Council 2012), in Australia (Northern Metropolitan Region 2011) and in London and elsewhere, five important lessons have been learned:

1   Despite the phase or context of schooling, the theories of action were in most cases very similar.
2   This is not a 'pick and mix' approach – all the theories of action have to be integrated into the teacher's professional repertoire if they are to impact in a sustained way on student learning.
3   Most importantly, all the theories of action are characterized by an approach to teaching that has inquiry at its centre.
4   Some of the theories of action relate to the school and some to the practice of individual teachers.
5   All of the theories of action have a high level of empirical support in the educational research literature (Hattie 2009).

So, to summarize, through the instructional rounds process an approach to teaching has been developed from the practice of teachers – across the NMR – that if consistently applied will enhance not just the achievement, but also the spirit of inquiry of all students. The four whole-school theories of action emerging from the instructional rounds process are as follows:

1   When schools and teachers set high expectations and develop authentic relationships, students' confidence and commitment to education increase and the school's ethos and culture deepen.
2   When teacher-directed instruction becomes more enquiry focused, then the level of student achievement and curiosity increases.
3   By consistently adopting protocols for teaching, student behaviour, engagement and learning are enhanced.
4   By consistently adopting protocols for learning, student capacity to learn, skill levels and confidence are enhanced.

The implications of these whole-school theories of action are discussed in more detail later. Meanwhile, it is to the theories of action for teachers that we now turn.

The six theories of action for teachers

Below are the six theories of action for teachers and teaching that emerged from our work with schools in the NMR and elsewhere. Together with the four whole-school theories of action noted in the previous section, they comprise the content of the *Curiosity* booklet that we recently published (Northern Metropolitan Region 2011). This handbook that has a two-page spread devoted to each theory of action: the left-hand page contains a description of the individual theory of action, much as above; the right-hand page showcases an educational artefact or tool that teachers can use to implement the theory of action in behavioural terms that increase their level of professional skill to a point that it impacts on the learning of their students.

Harnessing learning intentions, narrative and pace

When teachers set learning intentions, use appropriate pace and have a clear and strong narrative about their teaching and curriculum, students are more secure about their learning, and achievement and understanding are increased.

It has become very clear from the instructional rounds that when teachers are clear about their learning intentions, the students become more engaged and feel more secure in their learning. But it is about more than just setting a learning intention or goal; importantly, it is also about linking the intention to the learning outcome and success criteria for the lesson, as well as ensuring curriculum progression. This becomes the basis for the narrative of the lesson. Teachers with a strong sense of narrative are able to engage with deviation, knowing how to bring the discussion back on track. Pace is also necessary to keep the lesson lively and, through increasing tempo, deal with potential low-level disruption. A learning intention for a lesson or series of lessons is a statement that describes clearly what the teacher wants the student to know, understand and be able to do as a result of the learning and teaching activity. In formulating the learning intention it is essential to consider three components:

- an action word that identifies the performance to be demonstrated;
- a learning statement that specifies what learning will be demonstrated;
- a broad statement of the criterion or minimum standard for acceptable performance (e.g. 'By the end of the lesson you will be able to describe foundation concepts and questions in . . .').

Setting challenging learning tasks

When learning tasks are purposeful, clearly defined, differentiated and challenging, the more powerful, progressive and precise the learning for all students.

In many of the instructional rounds conducted, we found that, by and large, most students did not find the tasks they were set very challenging. Yet it is the tasks that students do that predict their performance. This requires setting tasks that are within the student's 'zone of proximal development', if their learning is to progress. Usually, this involves having three or four 'graded tasks' available for each group with scaffolding around the task to ensure success. In *Looking in Classrooms*, Good and Brophy (2007) identified the six components listed below as central to scaffolding support for pupils carrying out tasks:

1   Develop student interest in accomplishing the intended goal of the task.
2   Demonstrate an idealized version of the actions to be performed.

3 Simplify the task by reducing the steps.
4 Control frustration and risk.
5 Provide feedback that identifies the critical features of discrepancies between what has been produced and what is required.
6 Motivate and direct the student's activity to maintain continuous pursuit of the goal.

Closely associated with scaffolding is the gradual transfer of responsibility for managing learning. As students develop expertise they begin to assume responsibility for regulating their own learning, by asking questions and by working on increasingly complex tasks with a concomitant increase in learner autonomy.

Framing higher-order questions

When teachers systematically use higher-order questioning, the level of student understanding is deepened and their achievement is increased.

John Hattie reports in *Visible Learning* (2009: 182) that questioning is the second most prevalent teaching method, after teacher talk. Most teachers spend between 35% and 50% of their time in questioning. Questioning has a positive impact on student learning – but this effect is associated more with higher-order questioning which promotes more conceptual thinking and curiosity. The evidence suggests that most teachers ask low-level questions, related more to knowledge acquisition and comprehension. Research studies suggest that 60% of teachers' questions recall facts and 20% are procedural in nature. Bloom's taxonomy (Anderson and Krathwohl 2000) of learning objectives is widely used as a basis for structuring questions, particularly higher-order questions:

- *Knowledge* – recall previous material learned.
- *Comprehension* – demonstrate understanding of facts and ideas.
- *Application* – solve problems by applying knowledge, facts and skills learnt in different ways and situations.
- *Analysis* – examine information and break into parts, make connections and support ideas and arguments.
- *Evaluation* – present judgements, recommendations and opinions.
- *Synthesis* – compile information in different, more creative ways; choose other solutions.

The following sequence works well, as this approach makes everyone responsible for generating an answer, particularly when combined with some of the simple cooperative techniques:

- Frame a question to the whole class.
- Allow students time to think – 'wait time'.
- Only then call on someone to respond.

Connecting feedback and data

When teachers consistently use feedback and data on student actions and perform-ance, behaviour becomes more positive and progress accelerates.

Feedback is one of the most powerful influences on student achievement. That is clear from both psychological theory and research. Hattie (2009: 173) provides a powerful insight, as he describes his attempts to understand feedback:

> It was only when I discovered that feedback was most powerful when it is from the student to the teacher that I started to understand it better. When teachers seek, or are at least open to, feedback from students as to what students know, what they understand, where they make errors, when they have misconceptions, when they are not engaged – then teaching and learning can be synchronized and powerful. Feedback to teachers helps make learning visible.

In considering data and feedback that moves beyond the purely academic, Hattie suggests that a behavioural focus on student performance helps students to recognize the linkage between effort and outcome. In addressing this behavioural dimension of student performance and achievement, it is recommended that the teacher should:

- model beliefs;
- focus on mastery;
- portray skill development as incremental and domain-specific;
- provide socialization with feedback;
- portray effort as investment rather than risk.

Committing to assessment for learning

When peer assessment and assessment for learning are consistently utilized, student engagement, learning and achievement accelerate.

The generally accepted definition of assessment for learning is: 'The process of seeking and interpreting evidence for use by learners and their teachers to decide where the learners are in their learning, where they need to go and how best to get there' (Assessment Reform Group 2002).

This may be organised differently in different schools, but the rationale is always the same:

1   Clear evidence about how to drive up individual attainment.
2   Clear feedback for and from pupils, so there is clarity on what they need to improve and how best they can do so.
3   Clarity for students on what levels they are working at, with transparent criteria to enable peer coaching.
4   A clear link between student learning and lesson planning (Hopkins 2007a).

The OECD (2005) project on formative assessment concluded that it is one of the most useful strategies in improving student performance. The following practices most consistently emerged during their research:

- Establishment of classroom cultures that encourage interaction and the use of assessment. tools, establishment of learning goals and tracking individual student progress.
- Use of varied instruction methods to meet diverse student needs.
- Use of varied approaches to assess student understanding.
- Feedback on student performance.
- Adapting instruction to meet learner needs requires active involvement of students in the learning process.

Teachers need to continue to develop their understanding of how students learn so they can help them to: reflect on how they learn; develop learning strategies and apply them in different circumstances; and engage in high-quality dialogue with teachers, peers and others.

Implementing cooperative group structures

If teachers use cooperative group structures/techniques to mediate between whole-class instruction and students carrying out tasks, then the academic performance of the whole class will increase as well as the spirit of collaboration and mutual responsibility.

As we saw in the previous chapter, cooperative group work has a powerful effect in raising pupil achievement because it encourages active participation in learning and collaborative behaviour by developing social as well as academic skills. It is most commonly used as part of the direct instruction model, both as part of teacher instruction and the structuring of group activities, although at times the teacher will use the approach to structure a whole lesson or series of lessons.

There is a wide range of strategies that comprise cooperative group work. They are all underpinned by the following five principles (Johnson and Johnson 1994):

1   Positive interdependence, where all members of a group feel connected to each other in the accomplishment of a common goal – all individuals must succeed for the group to succeed.
2   Individual accountability, where every member of the group is held responsible for demonstrating the accomplishment of their learning.
3   Face-to-face interaction, where group members are close in proximity to each other and enter into a dialogue with each other in ways that promote continued progress.
4   Social skills: human interaction skills that enable groups to function effectively (e.g. taking turns, encouraging, listening, clarifying, checking, understanding, probing). Such skills enhance communication, trust, leadership, decision-making and conflict management.

5   Processing, where group members assess their collaborative efforts and target improvements.

The *Curiosity* booklet

As teachers and principals quickly embraced the theories of action it became apparent that, while the 'different' style and language of the *Curiosity* booklet was highly engaging, it was the strong research base that stood behind the various theories that made the propositions so compelling. Our colleague John Hattie generously encouraged us to use his work to illustrate the likely effect size associated with each of the theories of action (Hattie 2009). This reinforced the view among principals and teachers that although significant progress had already been made, the possibilities were boundless if the theories of action were applied with precision.

The almost fervent adoption of the *Curiosity* booklet was reinforced by our emerging understanding of neuroscience that was being disseminated across the region at the same time. Work from a range of cognitive scientists (including Willingham 2009; Medina 2008; Hardiman 2012; Jensen 2005) further encouraged practitioners. For example, Daniel Willingham's (2009) notion that 'People are naturally curious but we are not naturally good thinkers; unless the cognitive conditions are right, we will avoid thinking' served to emphasize the importance of a whole-school focus on inquiry. His notion that 'People are naturally curious, but curiosity is fragile' reinforced the need not only to set challenging tasks but also set to tasks that are just right – that is, tasks that are neither too easy nor too hard but right in the zone of proximal development.

We have been both surprised as well as gratified by the enthusiasm that the *Curiosity* booklet has generated among teachers and principals. Although we say it ourselves, in a short time it has assumed an iconic status, representing as it does the teachers' commitment to their own professional learning and the principals' engagement with school improvement and student learning. What became rapidly apparent, however, is that despite this enthusiasm and almost universal adoption, some schools were far better able to implement the theories of action in authentic ways. This is the conundrum we seek to reflect on in the next section.

Confronting the 'killer' theory of action

As part of the ongoing inquiry into classroom, school and system improvement described in this chapter, we have identified ten theories of action that, when taken together, enhance not only the learning outcomes of students but also their learning capability – in a word, their 'curiosity'. As we have seen, these ten theories of action fall into two groups: those that pertain to the whole-school level, that enable teachers to do their work; and those that relate to the teacher level, that enable them to create more effective and enquiring learning environments for their students.

As our inquiry developed, it soon became clear the second of the school level theories of action was not only the most powerful, but also the most difficult to implement. In a slightly expanded form, it is:

> When teacher directed instruction is infused by a 'spirit of inquiry', then the level of student engagement and achievement increases. This is the foundation stone for not only high-quality teaching, but also the development of curiosity.

Although most of the schools we were working with had identified a set of theories of action related to teacher behaviours to focus on and had introduced professional learning opportunities for teachers to develop them, this did not mean that the 'spirit of inquiry' also became realized. We began worrying about why this was so difficult to achieve, and in trying to resolve the conundrum identified five interlinking and sequential conditions that seem to be in place when schools realize this desideratum. Although most schools were implementing some of the theories of action (condition 2) through professional learning approaches (condition 3), in many cases this only resulted in superficial and variable impact. It was only when there was narrative (condition 1) and consistency (condition 4), that the change in culture (condition 5), that embraced the spirit of inquiry, was reliably achieved.

When working at scale we found it necessary to develop frameworks that not only assist schools through this process, but also allow them to more precisely monitor the impact of implementation. In this brief description of the five conditions, there is also reference to the monitoring frameworks that schools can use to confront and overcome the killer theory of action!

Each of the five conditions contributes strategically to the emerging story or narrative of the school's own journey of school improvement. The narrative is critical. It serves as the means of uniting the work of the system, the school and the classroom. Stories are treated differently and better by the brain than any other memories. Stories also act as the currency of our thoughts, storing value and enabling exchange. In the school improvement context, stories enable us to purposefully share the core elements of our work and serve to unite – around a common rallying point, better outcomes for students – the district or region, the school and the classroom. Finally, stories act as the brain's flight simulators and allow us to effectively rehearse our work before we do it. In the school context, telling the school improvement stories acts almost exactly as a 'dress rehearsal' for doing the work. In a classroom, telling the story of the lesson or a sequence of instructions not only gives students a chance to mentally practice what they will do, it also provides a clear path for the teacher to follow.

The story of the curiosity journey is introduced

A clear reform narrative for student learning is developed and consistently applied over time, with an urgency that translates the vision of curiosity into clear principles for action. This narrative is the task of leadership to develop. It is based on detailed and strategic planning, but is couched in a language that is understandable by staff, students and the community and that links moral purpose to action in practical and concrete ways. Above all, it highlights the connection between curiosity, inquiry, problem-solving and collaboration as the necessary ingredients of a teaching and learning culture that results not just in high standards but also student empowerment.

Table 12.1 The monitoring framework

School →
Journey
    Improvement
    ↓ Dimension
	Awful to Adequate	Adequate to Good	Good to Great

Environment	Orderly	Learning	Self directed
Teaching Practice	Consistency	Share best practice	Models of learning, tools for teaching
Curriculum	Literacy and numeracy basics	Literacy and numeracy across curriculum	Cross curricular enquiry projects
Assessment	Ownership for progress of students	Assessment of learning	Students set own targets and monitor progress
Data	Establish systems for data use	Monitor student progress through data	Formative and student use of data
Leadership	Developing leadership capacity	Distributed leadership	System leadership

Monitoring framework. The schools position on the 'performance cycle' from awful to adequate, from adequate to good and from good to great (Table 12.1) is used as a basis for developing the narrative.

Key pedagogic strategies are selected

High-leverage theories of action related to student learning are selected and implemented strategically and operationally. 'High-leverage' relates to the ability of the theory of action not only to have virtually immediate impact on the teaching and learning practices of the school, but also to lay the foundation for future action. So, for example, many schools at the start of their journey will select 'learning intentions' as these will, when even only partially implemented, impact on student expectations and engagement and lay the basis for differentiated task setting and peer assessment, which have increased power to enhance student achievement and learning. Over time this will also influence the ways in which the narrative of the curriculum within the school evolves, from simply covering content, to a series of sequential and integrated problem-solving activities.

Monitoring framework. The three-year planning framework, which is essentially a Gantt chart detailing what activity will be taken and when, provides a means of not only building the narrative, but also ensuring that priorities are selected that will not only produce short-term gains, but also lay the foundation for the next phase of the work. The framework prioritizes the teaching strategies to be developed and deployed, the length of the proposed cycles of inquiry associated with each strategy and the timing of success checks for each strategy.

Professional learning is placed at the heart of the process

In schools where staff development implies going on a course, and classroom observation is both hierarchical and evaluative, putting professional learning at the heart of the process marks a distinctive and necessary break with tradition. However, it is only forms of professional learning that emphasize non-judgemental peer observation, support through triads, disciplined by clear definitions and protocols that will develop professional practices that have a predictable impact of student learning and achievement. Going even further, replacing normative approaches to performance management with teacher portfolios of examples of such work is not only characteristic of high-achieving schools, but also the hallmark on 'inside-out' working.

Monitoring framework. The Joyce and Showers (2002) coaching model is used to ensure that the appropriate phases and sequencing of professional learning activities are in place. For example, if a school was implementing Theory of Action 1, 'Harnessing learning intentions, pace', the first phase would be based on the theory and explain and justify the new approach. The second, demonstration, phase shows or models how the work is done in practice. The next phase is the practice phase where teachers practice in non-threatening situations. From here, the next phase sees teachers receiving feedback. The final and critical phase is where teachers in triads (groups of three) or other groupings coach each other. Unless the coaching phase is reached the professional development process (and the teaching strategy) will have no impact on student learning. Teachers will have developed their knowledge about the strategy but will not have the requisite skills to implement it.

Consistency across the whole school is seen as paramount

Leadership works self-consciously to ensure that over time the vision of curiosity and spirit of inquiry is pervasive – carefully monitored and supported by robust and highly reliable school structures. The 'loose coupling' so characteristic of 'underperforming' and 'coasting' schools is incrementally tightened. Although this is essential in reducing within-school variation a word of caution needs to be entered here. Although top-down approaches are useful in schools that are dysfunctional and badly underperforming, autocratic or charismatic forms of leadership need to be used judiciously with schools on the 'inside-out' journey. Putting into place structures to ensure consistency needs to be done in a way that leads to forms of lateral and professional accountability and does not prejudice the emerging and often fragile episodes of professional learning.

Monitoring framework. The Hall and Hord (1987) 'levels of use' framework is used to identify and progress the levels of implementation required to impact directly on student learning. Unless teacher practice reaches level 4a – Routine, then it is unlikely that there will be any significant impact on student performance. The levels in the model are as follows:

- *Level 0: Non-use.* No interest shown in the innovation and no action taken.
- *Level 1: Orientation.* Begins to gather information about the innovation.
- *Level 2: Preparation.* Begins to plan ways to implement the innovation.
- *Level 3: Mechanical.* Concerned about mechanics of implementation.
- *Level 4a: Routine.* Comfortable with innovation and implements it as taught.
- *Level 4b: Refinement.* Begins to explore ways for continuous improvement.
- *Level 5: Integration.* Integrates innovation with other initiatives; does not view it as an add-on; collaborates with others.
- *Level 6: Renewal.* Explores new and different ways to implement innovation.

Cultures are changed and developed

A culture of disciplined action and a professional ethos that values curiosity and inquiry is embedded and deepened over time as a consequence of the impact of the work structures implied by the previous four conditions. As Andy Hargreaves (1994) once wrote:

> it is not possible to establish productive school cultures without prior changes being effected in school structures that increase the opportunities for meaningful working relationships and collegial support between teachers. The importance of the structural option of restructuring, therefore, may be less in terms of its direct impact on curriculum, assessment, ability grouping and the like, than in terms of how it creates improved opportunities for teachers to work together on a continuing basis.

Monitoring framework. An adapted and electronic version of David Hargreaves and colleagues' 'culture game' (see Hargreaves 1999) is used to monitor the development and cohesiveness of the school's culture over time, as seen in Figure 12.2.

So it is the interaction of the first four conditions that results in the fifth – a culture of teaching and learning in the school that prizes the 'spirit of inquiry' that results in high standards and deeper levels of learning. It should be increasingly clear that the mechanistic and instrumental approaches to school improvement associated with charismatic leadership and management are totally unable to deliver the high standards, the adaptive learning and the sustainability that are the hallmarks of outstanding schools and systems. It is the skill of leadership that develops and nurtures the narrative, embraces and sequences the theory of actions, creates the professional learning opportunities and allows the tightening of the loose coupling that ensures consistency. It is the interaction of these conditions that together produces the cultural change that sustains the inquiry and keeps on giving.

Coda: Theories of action for classroom, school and system reform

One of the consequences of our work in Melbourne and the state of Victoria is an increasing awareness of the myth that 'one size fits all' in school and system reform. Three points need to be reiterated. The first is that this analysis applies equally to

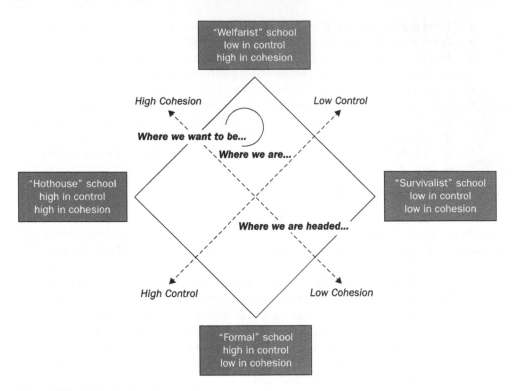

Figure 12.2   Grid showing school cultures.

individual schools or groups of schools, as it does to national or local governments and systems. The second point is that, unfortunately, most of the time single strategies or policy initiatives tend to be worked on discretely, rather than as a set of complementary and mutually supportive policies as proposed here. Third, and critically, the set of strategies that have been selected need to be precisely aligned to the growth state or performance phase of the school or system.

The work described in this chapter has given us the opportunity to develop the following set of theories of action for classroom, school and system improvement:

1   When schools and systems are driven by moral purpose then all students are more likely to fulfil their potential.
2   When the focus of policy is on the quality of teaching rather than structural change then student achievement will increase.
3   When schools and teachers are of high quality then poverty is no longer a determinant of educational success.
4   When the focus is on powerful learning then students will both attain more and develop their cognitive and social skills.
5   When teachers acquire a richer repertoire of pedagogic practice then students' learning will deepen.

6　When data are used to monitor, feedback and enhance student performance then students' progress will more quickly accelerate.

7　When teachers and schools consistently search for ways to improve what they are already doing (rather than adopting fads) then the student learning experience also deepens and outcomes improve,

8　When leadership is instructionally focused and widely distributed then both teachers and students are able to fully capitalize on their capacity to learn and achieve.

9　When teachers and leaders employ more precise strategies for teaching, learning and improvement then the whole system benefits.

10　When the system as a whole takes learning rather than teaching seriously then moral purpose is achieved.

The overarching or meta-theory of action is something like this: when all the distinct but interrelated parts of what we know about classroom, school and system improvement are aligned and working together, all students, schools. as well as the system as a whole will realize their individual and collective potential. The purpose of this case study of school and system improvement in Melbourne is to illustrate how we have attempted to realize this theory of action in practice and to demonstrate how deeply the principles of classroom research by teachers are enmeshed within it.

Further reading

This chapter has touched on a broad range of issues related to classroom, school and system improvement that has generated a vast supporting literature in the recent past. Much of this has been reviewed in my school improvement trilogy – *School Improvement for Real* (2001), *Every School a Great School* (2007a) and *Exploding the Myths of School Reform* (2013). The work of Michael Fullan continues to be highly influential; see, for example, his *The New Meaning of Educational Change* (2007), *Change Leader* (2011a), his 'Wrong Drivers' paper (2011b) and *Professional Capital* (Hargreaves and Fullan 2012). There is also the growing literature on system reform such as Fenton Whelan's (2009) *Lessons Learned: How Good Policies Produce Better Schools*, the McKinsey group's *How the World's Best Performing School Systems Come Out on Top* (Barber and Mourshed 2007) and *How the World's Most Improved School Systems Keep Getting Better* (Mourshed *et al.* 2010). A number of other multinational effectiveness studies have contributed to this field, such as *World Class Schools: International Perspectives on School Effectiveness* (Reynolds *et al.* 2002) and *School Effectiveness and Improvement Research, Policy and Practice* (Chapman *et al.* 2012). Finally, for those interested, there are the insights from symposia such as the *International Education Leaders' Dialogues* (Barber *et al.* 2009), the G100 *Transformation and Innovation – System Leaders in the Global Age* workshop (Hopkins 2007b); research compendiums such as the *International Handbook of Educational Change* (Hargreaves *et al.* 2009); and international reviews such as our recent 'School and System Improvement: A Narrative State of the Art Review' (Hopkins *et al.* 2014).

References

Acheson, K. and Gall, M. (1997) *Techniques in the Clinical Supervision of Teachers*, 4th edn. New York: Longman.

Adelman, C. (1981) *Uttering, Muttering*. London: Grant McIntyre.

Ainscow, M., Hargreaves, D.H. and Hopkins, D. (1995) Mapping the process of change in schools, *Evaluation and Research in Education*, 9(2): 75–90.

Anderson L.W. and Krathwohl, D.R. (eds) (2000) *A Taxonomy for Learning, Teaching, and Assessing: A Revision of Bloom's Taxonomy of Educational Objectives*. New York: Longman.

Armstrong, M. (1980) *Closely Observed Children*. London: Writers and Readers.

Armstrong, M. (1982) The story of five stories: an enquiry into children's narrative thought. Unpublished mimeo.

Assessment Reform Group (2002) *Assessment for Learning: 10 Principles. Research-Based Principles to Guide Classroom Practice*. London: AGR.

Atweh, B., Kemmis, S. and Weeks, P. (eds) (1998) *Action Research in Practice: Partnership for Social Justice in Education*. London: Routledge.

Auerbach, C.F. and Silverstein, L.B. (2003) *Qualitative Data: An Introduction to Coding and Analysis*. New York: New York University Press.

Barber, M. (2009). From system effectiveness to system improvement, in A. Hargreaves and M. Fullan (eds) *Change Wars*. Bloomington, IN: Solution Tree.

Barber, M. and Mourshed, M. (2007) *How the World's Best Performing School Systems Come Out on Top*. London: McKinsey.

Barber, M., Fullan, M., Mackay, A. and Zbar, V. (2009) Building excellent education systems: From conception to implementation at scale. Seminar Series Paper No. 189, Centre for Strategic Education, Melbourne.

Barrow, R. (1986) Empirical research into teaching, the conceptual factors, *Educational Research*, 28(3): 220–30.

Baumfield, V., Hall, E. and Wall, K. (2013) *Action Research in Education*, 2nd edn. London: Sage.

Bazeley, P. and Jackson, K. (2013) *Qualitative Data Analysis with NVivo*. London: Sage.

Becker, H. (1958) Problems of inference and proof in participant observation, *American Sociological Review*, 28: 652–60 (reprinted in R. McCormick (ed.) (1982) *Calling Education to Account*. London: Heinemann).

Becker, L. (2014) *Presenting Your Research: Conferences, Symposiums, Poster Presentations and Beyond*. London: Sage.

Bell, J. (2010) *Doing Your Research Project*, 5th edn. Buckingham: Open University Press.

Bennett, N. (1976) *Teaching Styles and Pupil Progress*. London: Pergamon Press.

Bennett, N. (1988) The effective primary school teacher; the search for a theory of pedagogy, *Teaching and Teacher Education*, 4(1): 19–30.

Beresford, J. (1998) *Collecting Information for School Improvement.* London: David Fulton.

Beresford, J. (1999) Matching teaching to learning. *Curriculum Journal,* 10(3): 321–44.

Beresford, J. (2003) *Creating the Conditions to Involve Pupils in their Learning.* London: David Fulton.

Bloom, B.S. (1956) *Taxonomy of Educational Objectives. Handbook I: The Cognitive Domain.* New York: David McKay.

Bollington, R. and Bradley, H. (1990) *Training for Appraisal: A Set of Distance Learning Materials.* Cambridge: University of Cambridge Institute of Education.

Bolster, A. (1983) Towards a more effective model of research on teaching, *Harvard Educational Review,* 53(3): 294–308.

Borman, G., Slavin, R., Cheung, A., Chamberlain, A., Madden, N. and Chambers, B. (2007) Final reading outcomes of the National Randomized Field Trial of Success for All, *American Educational Research Journal,* 44(3): 701–31.

Bowen, B., Forsyth, K., Green, J. *et al.* (n.d.) *Ways of Doing Research in One's Own Classroom.* Cambridge: University of Cambridge Institute of Education, Ford Teaching Project.

Bradbury, H. and Reason, P. (2001) Conclusion: Broadening the bandwidth of validity: issues and choice-points for improving the quality of action research, in P. Reason and H. Bradbury (eds) *Handbook of Action Research: Participative Inquiry and Practice.* London: Sage.

Briggs, A.R.J. and Coleman, M. (eds) (2007) *Research Methods in Educational Leadership and Management,* 2nd edn. London: Paul Chapman.

Bright Tribe (2014a) *Designing for Powerful Progress.* Stockport: Bright Tribe.

Bright Tribe (2014b) *High Quality Teaching for Powerful Progress.* Stockport: Bright Tribe.

British Educational Research Association (2000) *Good Practice in Educational Research Writing.* http://www.bera.ac.uk/researchers-resources/publications/good-practice-in-educational-research-writing-2000 (accessed 25 April 2014).

Brooker, R. and MacPherson, I. (1999) Communicating the processes and outcomes of practitioner research: an opportunity for self indulgence or a serious professional responsibility? *Educational Action Research,* 7(2): 207–21.

Brophy, J. (1981) Teacher praise: a functional analysis, *Review of Educational Research,* 51(1): 5–52.

Brophy, J. (1983) Classroom organisation and management, *Elementary School Journal,* 83(4): 266–85.

Brophy, J. and Good, T. (1986) Teacher behaviour and student achievement, in M. Wittrock (ed.) *Handbook of Research on Teaching,* 3rd edn. New York: Macmillan.

Bryman, A. (2004) *Social Research Methods,* 2nd edn. Oxford: Oxford University Press.

Burnaford, G., Fischer, J. and Hobson, D. (2001) *Teachers Doing Research: The Power of Action through Inquiry,* 2nd edn. Mahwah, NJ: Lawrence Erlbaum Associates.

Burton, D. and Bartlett, S. (2005) *Practitioner Research for Teachers.* London: Paul Chapman.

Caerphilly County Borough Council (2012) *Caerphilly Skills Strategy: Theories of Action for Leading Learning.* Caerphilly: CCBC.

Cambridge University (1994) *Mapping Change in Schools: The Cambridge Manual of Research Techniques.* Cambridge: University of Cambridge Institute of Education.

Campbell, D. and Russo, J. (1999) *Social Experimentation.* Thousand Oaks, CA: Sage.

Campbell, D. and Stanley, J. (1963) Experimental and quasi-experimental designs for research on teaching, in N. Gage (ed.) *Handbook of Research on Teaching*. Chicago Rand McNally.

Carr, W. (ed.) (1989) *Quality in Teaching*. Lewes: Falmer Press.

Carr, W. (1995) *For Education*. Buckingham: Open University Press.

Carr, W. and Kemmis, S. (1986) *Becoming Critical*. Lewes: Falmer Press.

Carr, W. and Kemmis, S. (2005) Staying critical. *Educational Action Research*, 13(3): 347–58.

Chapman, C., Armstrong, P., Harris, A., Muijs, D., Reynolds, D. and Sammons. P. (eds) (2012) *School Effectiveness and Improvement Research, Policy and Practice*. Abingdon: Routledge.

City, E.A., Elmore, R.F., Fiarman, S.E. and Titel, L. (2009) *Instructional Rounds in Education: A Network Approach to Improving Teaching and Learning*. Cambridge, MA: Harvard Education Press.

Claxton, G. (1999) *Wise Up: The Challenge of Lifelong Learning*. London: Bloomsbury.

Coalition for Evidence-Based Policy, (2007) *When Is It Possible to Conduct a Randomized Controlled Trial in Education at Reduced Cost, Using Existing Data Sources? A Brief Overview*. Washington, DC: Coalition for Evidence-Based Policy.

Cogan, M. (1973) *Clinical Supervision*. Boston: Houghton Mifflin.

Cohen, L., Manion, L. and Morrison, K. (2011) *Research Methods in Education*, 7th edn. London: Routledge.

Congdon, P. (1978) Basic principles of sociometry, *Association of Education Psychologists Journal*, 4(8): 5–9.

Cook, T.D. and Campbell, D.T. (1979) *Quasi-Experimentation: Design and Analysis for Field Settings*. Chicago: Rand McNally.

Cooperrider, D., Whitney, D. and Stavros, J. (2003) *Appreciative Inquiry Handbook*. Bedford Heights, OH: Lakeshore.

Corey, S. (1953) *Action Research to Improve School Practice*. New York: Teachers College Press.

Counsell, C. (2011) Disciplinary knowledge for all, the secondary history curriculum and history teachers' achievement, *Curriculum Journal*, 22(2): 201–25.

Cousins, J.B. and Leithwood, K.A. (1986) Current empirical research on evaluation utilization, *Review of Educational Research*, 56(3): 331–64.

Cousins, J.B. and Leithwood, K.A. (1993) Enhancing knowledge utilization as a strategy for school improvement, *Knowledge: Creation, Diffusion, Utilization*, 14(3): 305–33.

Creemers, B. (1994) *The Effective Classroom*. London: Cassell.

Creswell, J.W. (2014) *Research Design: Qualitative, Quantitative, and Mixed Methods Approaches*, 4th edn. Thousand Oaks, CA: Sage.

Croll, P. (2000) *Systematic Classroom Observation*, 2nd edn. Lewes: Falmer Press.

Cronbach, L.J. (1975) Beyond the two disciplines of scientific psychology, *American Psychologist*, 30: 116–27.

Daniels, D.H., Beaumont, L.J. and Doolin, C.A. (2001) *Understanding Children: Interview and Observation Guide for Educators*. Maidenhead: McGraw-Hill/Open University Press.

Deakin Crick, R., Broadfoot P. and Claxton G. (2004) Developing an effective lifelong learning inventory: The ELLI Project, *Assessment in Education*, 11(3): 247–72.

Deakin University (1998) *The Action Research Reader.* Geelong, Vic.: Deakin University Press.

Delamont, S. (1983) *Interaction in the Classroom.* London: Methuen.

Delamont, S. (1984) *Readings on Interaction in the Classroom.* London: Methuen.

Delamont, S. (1992) *Fieldwork in Educational Settings.* Lewes: Falmer Press.

Denscombe, M. (2007) *The Good Research Guide,* 3rd edn. Buckingham: Open University Press.

Denzin, K.N. and Lincoln, Y.S. (eds) (2003) *Collecting and Interpreting Qualitative Methods Volume 3.* London: Sage.

Denzin, N. and Lincoln, Y. (2011) *The Sage Handbook of Qualitative Research,* 4th edn. London: Sage.

DES (Department of Education and Science) (1989) *Planning for School Development.* London: HMSO.

DfES (Department for Education and Skills) (2004) *Excellence and Enjoyment: Learning and Teaching in the Primary Years.* London: DfES.

DfES (Department for Education and Skills) (2007) *Leading Improvement Using the Primary Framework: Guidance for Headteachers and Senior Leaders.* London: DfES.

Dillon, J. (1983) Problem finding and solving, *Journal of Creative Behaviour,* 16(2): 97–111.

Downey, L. (1967) *The Secondary Phase of Education.* Boston: Ginn.

Doyle, W. (1987) Research on teaching effects as a resource for improving instruction, in M. Wideen and I. Andrews (eds) *Staff Development for School Improvement.* Lewes: Falmer Press.

Duggan, W. (2007) *Strategic Intuition: The Creative Spark in Human Achievement.* New York: Columbia University Press.

Dunn, W. and Swierczek, F. (1977) Planned organizational change: toward grounded theory, *Journal of Applied Behavioural Science,* 13(2): 135–57.

Ebbutt, D. (1985) Educational action research: some general concerns and specific quibbles, in R. Burgess (ed.) *Issues in Educational Research.* Lewes: Falmer Press.

Ebbutt, D. and Elliott, J. (eds) (1985) *Issues in Teaching for Understanding.* York: Longman.

Economic and Social Research Council (2012) *ESRC Framework for Research Ethics.* http://www.esrc.ac.uk/_images/framework-for-research-ethics-09-12_tcm8-4586.pdf (accessed 6 May 2014).

Elbaz, F. (1983) *Teacher Thinking – A Study of Practical Knowledge.* London: Croom Helm.

Elliott, J. (1976) *Developing Hypotheses about Classrooms from Teachers' Practical Constructs.* Cambridge: University of Cambridge Institute of Education, Ford Teaching Project.

Elliott, J. (1991) *Action Research for Educational Change.* Buckingham: Open University Press.

Elliott, J. (2005) Becoming critical: the failure to connect, *Educational Action Research,* 13(3): 359–74.

Elliott, J. and Adelman, C. (1976) *Innovation at the Classroom Level: A Case Study of the Ford Teaching Project,* Unit 28, Open University Course E203: Curriculum Design and Development. Milton Keynes: Open University Educational Enterprises.

Elliott, J. and Ebbutt, D. (1985a) *Facilitating Educational Action Research in Schools.* York: Longman.

Elliott, J. and Ebbutt, D. (eds) (1985b) *Case Studies in Teaching for Understanding.* Cambridge: Cambridge Institute of Education.

Elliott, J. and Norris, N. (2012) *Curriculum, Pedagogy and Educational Research: The Work of Lawrence Stenhouse,* London & New York: Routledge.

Evergreen, S.D.H. (2013) *Presenting Data Effectively: Communicating Your Findings for Maximum Impact.* Thousand Oaks, CA: Sage.

Fiddy, R. and Stronach, I. (1987) How can evaluation become formative? Norwich: CARE, University of East Anglia (mimeo).

Fielding, M. (1994) Valuing difference in teachers and learners: building on Kolb's learning styles to develop a language of teaching and learning, *Curriculum Journal,* 5(3): 393–417.

Fielding, M. (2001) Students as radical agents of change, *Journal of Educational Change,* 2(2): 123–41.

Fielding, M. (2004) Transformative approaches to student voice: theoretical underpinnings, recalcitrant realities, *British Educational Research Journal,* 30(2): 295–311.

Fisher, R. (1966) *The Design of Experiments,* 8th edn. Edinburgh: Oliver and Boyd.

Flanders, N. (1970) *Analysing Teaching Behaviour.* Reading, MA: Addison-Wesley.

Flint, K. (2014) *Practice, Research, and Education: A Philosophical Inquiry.* London: Continuum.

Flint, K. and Peim, N. (2012) *Rethinking the Education Improvement Agenda.* London: Continuum.

Fox, M., Martin, P. and Green, G. (2007) *Doing Practitioner Research.* London: Sage.

Frost, D., Durrant, J., Head, M. and Holden, G. (2000) *Teacher-Led School Improvement.* London: Falmer Press.

Fullan, M. (2007) *The New Meaning of Educational Change,* 4th edn. London: Cassell.

Fullan, M. (2011a). *Change Leader.* San Francisco: Jossey-Bass.

Fullan, M. (2011b) Choosing the wrong drivers for whole system reform. CSE Seminar Series paper no. 204. Centre for Strategic Education, East Melbourne.

Furlong, J. (2004) BERA at 30. Have we come of age? *British Educational Research Journal,* 30(3): 343–58. www.bera.ac.uk/publications (accessed 13 August 2007).

Gage, N. (1978) *The Scientific Basis of the Art of Teaching.* New York: Teachers College Press.

Gagné, R.M. (1965) *The Conditions of Learning.* New York: Holt, Rinehart, and Winston.

Galton, M. (1978) *British Mirrors.* Leicester: University of Leicester School of Education.

Galton, M. (1999) *Inside the Primary Classroom: Twenty Years On.* London: Routledge.

Galton, M., Simon, B. and Croll, P. (1980) *Inside the Primary Classroom.* London: Routledge & Kegan Paul.

Gardner, H. (1993) *Frames of Mind: The Theory of Multiple Intelligences,* 2nd edn. London: Fontana Press.

Gardner, H. (2011) *The Unschooled Mind: How Children Think and How Schools Should Teach,* 25th edn. New York: Basic Books.

Gibson, R. (1986) *Critical Theory and Education.* London: Hodder and Stoughton.

Giroux, H. (2005) *Border Crossings: Cultural Workers and the Politics of Education,* 2nd edn. New York: Routledge.

Glaser, B. and Strauss, A. (1967) *The Discovery of Grounded Theory.* New York: Aldine.

Glass, G., McGaw, B., and Smith, M. (1981) *Meta Analysis in Social Research*. Newbury Park, CA: Sage.

Goldhammer, R., Anderson, R. and Krajewski, R. (1993) *Clinical Supervision: Special Methods for the Supervision of Teachers*, 3rd edn. Fort Worth, TX: Harcourt Brace Jovanovich.

Good, T. and Brophy, J. (2007) *Looking in Classrooms*, 10th edn. Boston: Pearson Education.

Hall, G.E. and Hord, S.M. (1987) *Change in Schools: Facilitating the Process*. Albany: State University of New York Press.

Halsall, R. (ed.) (1998) *Teacher Research and School Improvement: Opening Doors from the Inside*. Buckingham: Open University Press.

Hamilton, D., Macdonald, B., King, C. *et al.* (eds) (1977) *Beyond the Numbers Game*. Berkeley, CA: McCutchan.

Hammersley, M. (1987) Some notes on the terms of 'validity' and 'reliability', *British Educational Research Journal*, 13(1): 73–81.

Hammersley, M. (ed.) (1993) *Controversies in Classroom Research*, 2nd edn. Buckingham: Open University Press.

Hammersley, M. and Atkinson, P. (2007) *Ethnography: Principles in Practice*, 3rd edn. London: Routledge.

Hardiman, M. (2012) *The Brain-Targeted Teaching Model for 21st-Century Schools*. Thousand Oaks, CA: Corwin.

Hargreaves, A. (1994) *Changing Teachers, Changing Times*. Toronto: OISE Press.

Hargreaves, A. and Fullan, M. (1998) *What's Worth Fighting For Out There?* New York: Teachers College Press.

Hargreaves, A. and Fullan, M. (2012) *Professional Capital: Transforming Teaching in Every School*. New York: Teachers College Press.

Hargreaves, A., Lieberman, A., Fullan, M. and Hopkins, D. (eds) (1998) *International Encyclopaedia of Educational Change*. Dordrecht: Kluwer.

Hargreaves, A., Lieberman, A., Fullan, M. and Hopkins, D. (2009) *Second International Handbook of Educational Change*, Volumes 1 and 2. Dordecht: Springer.

Hargreaves, D.H. (1995) School culture, school effectiveness and school improvement, *School Effectiveness and School Improvement*, 6(1): 23–46.

Hargreaves, D.H. (1999) Helping practitioners explore their school's culture, in J. Prosser (ed.), *School Culture*. London: Paul Chapman.

Hargreaves, D.H. (2004) *Personalising Learning – 2: Student Voice and Assessment for Learning*. London: SSAT.

Hargreaves, D.H. and Hopkins, D. (1991) *The Empowered School*. London: Cassell.

Hattie, J. (2009) *Visible Learning: A Synthesis of over 800 Meta-analyses Relating to Achievement*. Abingdon: Routledge.

Hattie, J. (2012) *Visible Learning for Teachers*. London: Routledge.

Hattie, J. and Yates, G. (2014) *Visible Learning and the Science of How We Learn*, Abingdon: Routledge.

Hitchcock, G. and Hughes, D. (1995) *Research and the Teacher*, 2nd edn. London: Routledge.

Hook, C. (1995) *Studying Classrooms*, 2nd edn. New York: Hyperior Books.

Hopkins, D. (1982) Doing research in your own classroom, *Phi Delta Kappan*, 64(4): 274–5.

Hopkins, D. (1984a) Teacher research: back to the basics, *Classroom Action Research Network Bulletin*, 6: 94–9.

Hopkins, D. (1984b) Towards a methodology for teacher based classroom research, *School Organization*, 4(3): 197–204.

Hopkins, D. (1989) *Evaluation for School Development*. Milton Keynes: Open University Press.

Hopkins, D. (2000) Powerful learning, powerful teaching and powerful schools, *Journal of Educational Change*, 1(2): 135–54.

Hopkins, D. (2001) *School Improvement for Real*. London: Routledge/Falmer.

Hopkins, D. (2002) *Improving the Quality of Education for All*, 2nd edn. London: David Fulton.

Hopkins, D. (2007a) *Every School a Great School*. Maidenhead: McGrawHill/Open University Press.

Hopkins, D. (ed.) (2007b) *Transformation and Innovation: System Leaders in the Global Age*. London: Specialist Schools and Academies Trust.

Hopkins, D. (2011) *Powerful Learning: Taking Educational Reform to Scale*, paper no. 20. Melbourne: Education Policy and Research Division, Office for Policy, Research and Innovation, Department of Education and Early Childhood Development.

Hopkins, D. (2012) *The Adventure Learning Schools Handbook*. Carlisle: Adventure Learning Schools.

Hopkins, D. (2013) *Exploding the Myths of School Reform*. Camberwell, Vic.: ACER Press, and Maidenhead: Open University Press.

Hopkins, D. and Harris, A., with Singleton, C. and Watts, R. (2000) *Creating the Conditions for Teaching and Learning. A Handbook of Staff Development Activities*. London: David Fulton.

Hopkins, D. and Stern, D. (1996) Quality teachers, quality schools, *Teaching and Teacher Education*, 12(5): 501–17.

Hopkins, D., Bollington, R. and Hewett, D. (1989) Growing up with qualitative research and evaluation, *Evaluation and Research in Education*, 3(2): 61–80.

Hopkins, D., Munro, J. and Craig, W. (2011) *Powerful Learning: A Strategy for Systemic Educational Improvement*. Camberwell, Vic.: ACER Press.

Hopkins, D., Stringfield, S., Harris, A., Stoll, L. and Mackay, T. (2014) School and system improvement: a narrative state-of-the-art review, *School Effectiveness and School Improvement: An International Journal of Research, Policy and Practice*, 25(2): 257–81.

Hopkins, D., West, M., Ainscow, M., Harris, A. and Beresford, J. (1997) *Creating the Conditions for Classroom Improvement*. London: David Fulton.

Hull, C., Rudduck, J. and Sigsworth, A. (1985) *A Room Full of Children Thinking*. York: Longman.

Hustler, D., Cassidy, T. and Cuff, T. (eds) (1986) *Action Research in Classrooms and Schools*. London: Allen & Unwin.

James, M., Black, P., McCormick, R., Pedder, D. and Wiliam, D. (2006a) Learning how to learn, in classrooms, schools and networks: aims, design and analysis, *Research Papers in Education*, 21(2): 101–18.

James, M., Black, P., Carmichael, P., Conner, C., Dudley, P., Fox, A., Frost, D., Honour, L., MacBeath, J., McCormick, R., Marshall, B., Pedder, D., Procter, R., Swaffield, S., and Wiliam, D. (2006b) *Learning How to Learn: Tools for Schools*. London: Routledge.

Jensen, E. (2005) *Teaching with the Brain in Mind*, 2nd edn. Alexandria, VA: Association for Supervision and Curriculum Development.

Johnson, R.T. and Johnson, D.W. (1994) An overview of co-operative learning, in J. Thousand, A. Villa and A. Nevin (eds) *Creativity and Collaborative Learning*. Baltimore, MD: Brookes Press.

Joyce, B. and Calhoun, E. (1997) Learning to teach inductively. Mimeo, Pauma Valley, CA.

Joyce, B. and Calhoun, E. (1998) *Learning to Teach Inductively*. Needham Heights, MA: Allyn & Bacon.

Joyce, B. and Showers, B. (1984) Transfer of training: The contribution of coaching, in D. Hopkins and M. Wideen (eds) *Alternative Perspectives on School Improvement*. Lewes: Falmer Press.

Joyce, B. and Showers, B. (2002) *Student Achievement Through Staff Development*, 3rd edition, Alexandria VA: Association for Supervision and Curriculum Development.

Joyce, B. and Weil, M. (2009) *Models of Teaching*, 8th edn. Upper Saddle River, NJ: Pearson.

Joyce, B., Calhoun, E. and Hopkins, D. (1999) *The New Structure of School Improvement: Inquiring Schools and Achieving Students*. Buckingham: Open University Press.

Joyce, B., Calhoun, E. and Hopkins, D. (2002) *Models of Learning – Tools for Teaching*, 2nd edn. Buckingham: Open University Press.

Joyce, B., Calhoun, E. and Hopkins, D. (2009) *Models of Learning – Tools for Teaching*, 3rd edn. Maidenhead Open University Press.

Kelle, U (2000) Computer-assisted analysis: coding and indexing, in M.W. Bauer and G. Gaskell (eds) *Qualitative Researching with Text, Image and Sound*. London: Sage.

Kemmis, S. (1983) Action research, in T. Husen and T. Postlethwaite (eds) *International Encyclopaedia of Education: Research and Studies*. Oxford: Pergamon.

Kemmis, S. (1988) Action research in retrospect and prospect, in Deakin University, *The Action Research Reader*. Geelong, Vic.: Deakin University Press.

Kemmis, S. (2005) Knowing practice: searching for saliences, *Pedagogy, Culture and Society*, 13: 391–426.

Kemmis, S. (2006) Participatory action research and the public sphere, *Educational Action Research*, 14(4): 459–76.

Kemmis, S. and McTaggart, R. (1988) *The Action Research Planner*, 3rd edn. Geelong, Vic.: Deakin University.

Kincheloe, J. (2004) Redefining and interpreting the object of study, in J. Kincheloe and K. Berry, *Rigour and Complexity in Educational Research: Conceptualising the Bricolage*. Maidenhead: Open University Press.

Knight, O and Benson, D. (2013) *Creating Outstanding Classrooms: A Whole-School Approach*. Abingdon: Routledge.

Kolb, D.A. (1984) *Experiential Learning*. Englewood Cliffs, NJ: Prentice Hall.

Koshy, V. (2010) *Action Research for Improving Educational Practice*. London: Sage.

Kyriacou, C. (2009) *Effective Teaching in Schools*, 3rd rev. edn. Cheltenham: Nelson Thornes.

Lankshear, C. and Knobel, M. (2004) *A Handbook for Teacher Research: From Design to Implementation*. Maidenhead: Opern University Press.

Lawton, D. (1989) *Education, Culture and the National Curriculum*. London: Hodder and Stoughton.

Leadbeater, C. (2004) *Learning about Personalisation: How Can We Put the Learner at the Heart of the Education System?* Nottingham: Department for Education and Skills.

Lewin, K. (1946) Action research and minority problems, *Journal of Social Issues*, 2(4): 34–46.

Lincoln, Y. and Guba, E. (1985) *Naturalistic Inquiry*. Beverly Hills, CA: Sage.

Lortie, D. (2002) *School Teacher*, 2nd edn. Chicago: University of Chicago Press.

Louis, K.S. and Miles, M. (1992) *Improving the Urban High School*. London: Cassell.

MacDonald, B. and Walker, R. (eds) (1974) *Innovation, Evaluation Research and the Problem of Control*. Norwich: CARE, University of East Anglia Press.

Magee, B. (1973) *Popper*. London: Fontana/Collins.

May, N. and Rudduck, J. (1983) *Sex Stereotyping and the Early Years of Schooling*. Norwich: University of East Anglia Press.

McCormick, R. and James, M. (1989) *Curriculum Evaluation in Schools*, 2nd edn. London: Routledge.

McIntyre, D., Pedder, D. and Rudduck, J. (2005) Pupil voice: comfortable and uncomfortable learnings for teachers, *Research Papers in Education*, 20(2): 149–68.

McKernan, J. (1996) *Curriculum Action Research*, 2nd edn. London: Routledge.

McNiff, J. (2013) *Action Research: Principles and Practice*, 3rd edn. London: Routledge.

McNiff, J. and Whitehead, J. (2005) *Action Research for Teachers: A Practical Guide*. London: David Fulton.

McNiff, J. and Whitehead, J. (2011) *All You Need to Know about Action Research*. London: Sage.

Medina J. (2008) *Brain Rules*. Brunswick, Vic.: Scribe.

Mertler, C. (2009) *Action Research: Teachers as Researchers in the Classroom*, 2nd edn. Los Angeles: Sage.

Miles, M. and Huberman, M. (1984) Drawing valid meaning from qualitative data: toward a shared craft, *Educational Researcher*, 13(5): 20–30.

Miles, M. and Huberman, M. (1994) *Qualitative Data Analysis: An Expanded Sourcebook*, 2nd edn. Beverly Hills, CA: Sage.

Mills, G.E. (2009) *Action Research: A Guide for the Teacher Researcher*, 4th edn. Upper Saddle River, NJ: Pearson.

Mourshed, M., Chijioke, C. and Barber, M. (2010) *How the World's Most Improved School Systems Keep Getting Better*. London: McKinsey.

Muijs, D. and Reynolds, D. (2011) *Effective Teaching: Evidence and Practice*, 3rd edition. London: Sage.

Munro, J (1999) Learning more about learning to improve teacher effectiveness, *School Effectiveness and School Improvement*, 10(2): 151–71.

National College for School Leadership (2004) *Establishing a Network of Schools*, Networked Learning Communities Think Piece No. 2. Nottingham: NCSL.

Nixon, J. (ed.) (1981) *A Teacher's Guide to Action Research*. London: Grant and McIntyre.

Northern Metropolitan Region (2009) *Powerful Learning: Northern Metropolitan Region School Improvement Strategy*. East Melbourne: Department of Education and Early Childhood Development.

Northern Metropolitan Region (2011) *Curiosity and Powerful Learning: Northern Metropolitan Region School Improvement Strategy*. East Melbourne: Department of Education and Early Childhood Development.

O'Leary, M. (2013) *Classroom Observation: A Guide to the Effective Observation of Teaching and Learning*. London: Routledge.

OECD (2005) *The Definition and Selection of Key Competencies*. www.oecd.org (accessed 1 February 2014).

Oja, S.N. and Smulyan, L. (1989) *Collaborative Action Research*. Lewes: Falmer Press.

Open University (1976) *Personality and Learning*, Course E201. Milton Keynes: Open University Educational Enterprises.

Patton, M.Q. (2002) *Qualitative Evaluation Methods*. Beverly Hills, CA: Sage.

Percelli, V. (2005a) Heavy fuel, in C. Mitchell, O'Reilly Scanlon and S. Weber (eds) *Just Who Do We Think We Are? Methodologies for Self Study in Teacher Education*. Abingdon: RoutledgeFalmer.

Percelli, V. (2005b) Re-imagining research, re-presenting the self: putting arts media to work in the analysis and synthesis of data on 'difference' and 'disability', *International Journal of Qualitative Studies in Education*, 18(1): 63–83.

Polanyi, M. (1973) *Personal Knowledge*, corrected edn. Chicago: University of Chicago Press.

Pring, R. (2012) Teacher as researcher, in D. Lawton, P. Gordon, M. Ing *et al.* (eds) *Theory and Practice of Curriculum Studies*. Abingdon: Routledge .

Rapoport, R. (1970) Three dilemmas in action research, *Human Relations*, 23(6): 499–513.

Reason, P. and Bradbury, H. (2001) *Handbook of Action Research: Participative Enquiry and Practice*. London: Sage

Reed, A. and Bergemann, V. (2004) *Guide to Observation, Participation and Reflection in the Classroom with Forms for Field Use CD-ROM*. Maidenhead: McGraw-Hill/Open University Press.

Reynolds, D., Creemers, B., Stringfield, S., Teddlie, C. and Shaffer, G. (eds) (2002) *World Class Schools: International Perspectives on School Effectiveness*. London: RoutledgeFalmer.

Riley, K. and Rustique-Forrester, E. with Fuller, M. *et al.* (2002) *Working with Disaffected Students: Why Students Lost Interest in School and What We Can Do About it*. London: Paul Chapman.

Robson, C. (2011) *Real World Research*, 3rd edn. Chichester: John Wiley and Sons.

Rowland, S. (2012) *The Enquiring Classroom: An Introduction to Children's Learning*. Abingdon: Routledge.

Rudduck, J. (1981) *Making the Most of the Short Inservice Course*. London: Methuen.

Rudduck, J. (ed.) (1982) *Teachers in Partnership: Four Studies of Inservice Collaboration*. York: Longman.

Rudduck, J. (1991) *Innovation and Change*. Buckingham: Open University Press.

Rudduck, J. and Flutter, J. (2004) *How to Improve Your School: Giving Pupils a Voice*. London: Continuum.

Rudduck, J. and Hopkins, D. (eds) (1985) *Research as a Basis for Teaching*. London: Heinemann.

Rudduck, J. and Sigsworth, A. (1985) Partnership supervision, in D. Hopkins and K. Reid (eds) *Rethinking Teacher Education*. London: Croom Helm.

Rudduck, J., Berry, M., Brown, N. and Frost, D. (2000) Schools learning from schools, *Research Papers in Education*, 15(3): 259–74.

Sachs, J. (2003) *The Activist Teaching Profession (Professional Learning)*. Buckingham: Open University Press.

Sagor, R. (2000) *Guiding School Improvement with Action Research*. Alexandria, VA: Association for Supervision and Curriculum Development.

Sagor, R. (2011) *The Action Research Guidebook*, 2nd edn. Thousand Oaks, CA: Corwin Press.

Sandford, N. (1970) Whatever happened to action research? *Journal of Social Issues*, 26(4): 3–23.

Schön, D.A. (1991) *The Reflective Practitioner*. New York: Basic Books.

Schön, D.A. (1996) *Educating the Reflective Practitioner: Toward a New Design for Teaching and Learning in the Professions*. San Francisco: Jossey-Bass.

Schratz, M. (2001) A visual approach to evaluation in schools. Paper presented at the Second Visual Conference of the Centre for Applied Research in Education, University of East Anglia.

Schwandt, T. and Halpern, E. (1988) *Linking Auditing and MetaEvaluation*. Beverly Hills, CA: Sage.

Simon, A. and Boyer, E. (1975) *Mirrors for Behaviour: An Anthology of Classroom Observation Instruments*. Philadelphia: Research for Better Schools.

Simons, H. (1982) Suggestions for a school self evaluation based on democratic principles, in R. McCormick (ed.) *Calling Education to Account*. London: Heinemann.

Simons, H. (1987) *Getting to Know Schools in a Democracy*. Abingdon: Routledge.

Slavin, R.E. (1986) Best-evidence synthesis: An alternative to meta-analytic and traditional reviews, *Educational Researcher*, 15(9): 5–11.

Slavin, R.E. (1994) *Cooperative Learning: Theory, Research, and Practice*, 2nd edn. Boston: Pearson.

Slavin, R.E. and Madden, N. (2009). *Two Million Children: Success for All*. Thousand Oaks: Sage.

Smith, L. and Geoffrey, W. (1968) *The Complexities of an Urban Classroom*. New York: Holt, Rinehart and Wilson.

Smyth, M. and Williamson, E. (eds) (2004) *Researchers and their 'Subjects': Ethics, Power, Knowledge and Consent*. Bristol: Policy Press.

Stake, R.E. (1967) The countenance of educational evaluation, *Teachers College Record*, 68: 523–40.

Stake, R.E. (1995) *The Art of Case Study Research*. Thousand Oaks, CA: Sage.

Stenhouse, L. (1970) *The Humanities Project*. London: Heinemann. (Revised edition by Rudduck, J. (1983) Norwich: University of East Anglia Press.)

Stenhouse, L. (1975) *An Introduction to Curriculum Research and Development*. London: Heinemann.

Stenhouse, L. (1979) Using research means doing research, in H. Dahl, A. Lysne and P. Rand (eds) *Spotlight on Educational Research*. Oslo: Universitetsforlaget.

Stenhouse, L. (1980) Product or process: a response to Brian Crittenden, *New Education*, 2(1): 137–40.

Stenhouse, L. (1983) *Authority, Education and Emancipation*. London: Heinemann.

Stenhouse, L. (1984) Artistry and teaching: the teacher as focus of research and development, in D. Hopkins and M. Wideen (eds) *Alternative Perspectives on School Improvement*. Lewes: Falmer Press.

Strauss, A. (1987) *Qualitative Analysis for Social Scientists*. Cambridge: Cambridge University Press.

Strauss, A. and Corbin, J. (1998) *Basics of Qualitative Research*, 2nd edn. London: Sage.

Street, H. and Temperley, J. (eds) (2005) *Improving Schools through Collaborative Enquiry*. London: Continuum Press.

Taber, K.S. (2007) *Classroom-Based Research and Evidence-Based Practice. A Guide for Teachers*. London: Sage.

Walker, R. (1989) *Doing Research*. London: Routlege.

Walker, R. and Adelman, C. (1990) *A Guide to Classroom Observation*. London: Routledge.

Webb, R. (ed.) (1990) *Practitioner Research in the Primary School*. Lewes: Falmer Press.

Weinberg, D. (2002) *Qualitative Research Methods*. Oxford: Blackwell Publishers.

Whelan, F. (2009) *Lessons Learned: How Good Policies Produce Better Schools*. Fenton Whelan.

Whitman, W. (1855/1959) *Leaves of Grass*. New York: Viking.

Willingham, D. (2009) *Why Don't Students Like School? A Cognitive Scientist Answers Questions about How the Mind Works and What It Means for the Classroom*. San Francisco: Jossey-Bass.

Winter, R. (1989) *Learning from Experience*. Lewes: Falmer Press.

Winter, R., Buck, A. and Sobiechowska, P. (1999) *Professional Experience and the Creative Imagination*. London: Routledge.

Wood, D. (1998) *How Children Think and Learn*. Oxford: Basil Blackwell.

Wragg, E.C. (2011) *An Introduction to Classroom Observation*, classic edn. London: Routledge.

Yin, R. (2013) *Case Study Research: Design and Methods*, 5th edn. London: Sage.

Yoder, P. and Symons, F. (2010) *Observational Measurement of Behavior*. New York: Springer.

Young, R. (1989) *A Critical Theory of Education: Habermas and our Children's Future*. New York: Harvester Wheatsheaf.

Zeichner, K.M. and Noffke, S.E. (2001) Practitioner research, in V. Richardson (ed.) *Handbook of Research on Teaching*, 4th edn. Washington, DC: American Educational Research Association.

Index

EVERY SCHOOL A GREAT SCHOOL

David Hopkins

978-0-33522-099-I (Paperback)
2007

eBook also available

The book argues that, for 'every school a great school' to become a reality, requires a move from individual school improvement efforts and short term objectives to a sustainable system-wide response that seeks to re-establish a balance between national prescription and schools leading reform.

Achieving this goal requires strategies that not only continue to raise standards, but also build capacity within the system. David Hopkins identifies four key educational 'drivers' that, if pursued, have the potential to deliver 'every school a great school':

- Personalized learning
- Professionalized teaching
- Networking and innovation
- Intelligent accountability

www.openup.co.uk

OPEN UNIVERSITY PRESS
McGraw · Hill Education

EXPLODING THE MYTHS OF SCHOOL REFORM

David Hopkins

9780335263141 (Paperback)
2013

eBook also available

In this new book, David Hopkins looks at the failure of educational reform efforts to impact on the learning and performance of students, due to misguided action based on a number of myths associated with school reform which remain prevalent in education. The purpose of this book is to present a comprehensive, accessible and strategic overview of what is currently known about school and system reform in the 21st century.

Key features:

- Challenges and perspectives from research, policy and practice
- Draws on international benchmarking studies to support its objectives and claims
- Each of ten chapters addresses a perceptible fallacy, such as the myths that poverty determines performance

www.openup.co.uk

OPEN UNIVERSITY PRESS
McGraw · Hill Education